ROWING
TO NIAGARA
FALLS

ROWING TO NIAGARA FALLS

First published in 2021 in Lithuania by BALTO Publishing House

"Irklais iki Niagaros Krioklių"

A Biographical Novel.

Translated from Lithuanian by Laima Vincė Sruoginis

ISBN 9798745703690

RIMA KARALIENE

ROWING
TO NIAGARA
FALLS

A novel based on true events

2021

FOREWORD

I met Sofija Grucova in June 1978 when I was thirteen years old. That was when I first came to row at the Vilnius Žalgiris Boathouse located on the confluence of the Rivers Neris and Vilnelė. To be honest, I did not actually meet with Coach Grucova then, but rather with her influence and reputation at the Club. From my very first days of training, my new teammates did their best to "introduce" me to life at the Žalgiris Club by explaining the significance of the people associated with the team. "See those girls over there," they pointed on my first day, "they are *Grucova's girls.*" The emphasis on the words, *Grucova's girls,* made it clear to me that these girls belonged to a special elite club. Those words were spoken with the deepest reverence and respect. At the same time, I detected a hint of envy in their voice. At least, that was my interpretation at the time. From that moment on, whenever I saw them, I would gaze at *Grucova's girls* with secret admiration. Whenever I spotted Coach Grucova herself, I'd pull my shoulders back and try my hardest to impress her. I must admit, I was also a little afraid of her. Coach Grucova was reserved and did not talk a lot. For this reason, I thought she was strict. However, I rarely crossed paths with *Grucova's girls* because they were a few years older than me, and we never raced together. Our summer camps also took place separately.

I admire Grucova's girls even today. I admire how they maintain a warm relationship with their former coach, although they are already in their sixties. She is always eagerly awaited at masters races. They eagerly listen to her advice, and then, with youthful pride, show off their medals to her, pose together for photographs, and, just as when they were all young, compete with each other as to who has earned the honour of sitting beside her to watch a race or take hold of her hand. To this day, *Grucova's girls* all refer to her as their second mother. They reminisce about how she was demanding, but very attentive at the same time. They are all grateful to her for forming a masters rowing club, for getting them back into their boats. When she returned from Germany, where she trained a club team, she inspired them to get back into their boats, write training plans, seek results.

I had the good fortune of working with Sofija Grucova as my coach in 1983, five years after we first met. The Lithuanian Soviet Socialist Republic Rowing Team was preparing for the Soviet Championship, the *Spartakiad*.[1] The competition was a Soviet version of their Olympics – something like an internal Olympics. Teams from all fifteen Soviet Republics and the Soviet team competed in the Soviet Olympics and every sport was represented. After the long training season and trial races ended, I was placed on the quad crew. Then, I participated in the Trakai Žalgiris Club summer rowing training camp. Three girls from different crews, who all had different coaches, were assigned to the crew together with me. For some reason, one of them refused to row unless she could be coached by her own coach. We lost a few days of training "on the shore" trying to convince her to get back into the boat. However, being stubborn, she refused to give in. The leaders of the Lithuanian Rowing Federation called a meeting to resolve the issue. At the time, I was the

---

1   The *Spartakiad* of the Peoples of the USSR was a mass multi-sport event in the Soviet Union which lasted from 1956–1991. Athletes from the fifteen Soviet Republics and the Eastern Bloc competed against each other in the *Spartakiad*.

stroke on the quad. I was invited into the meeting and asked a question: Would the team be strong enough to compete if they threw the stubborn girl off the team? As much as I wanted to teach that troublemaker a lesson, I answered "no" because the crew truly was good, and I did not want to weaken the team just to make a point. The Federation had already come to a decision – they appointed Coach Sofija Grucova to our crew because she had not coached any of the girls before and could therefore remain impartial. I nodded in agreement, but inside I was frightened. The image that I had made of Coach Grucova over the past five years boded a difficult and trying time for me.

Perhaps I was the only one who had those feelings of foreboding. The work we did with our new coach evened out the stress between us and the team came together as friends. I remember those few weeks of training camp with enormous nostalgia now. We formed a crew that was athletically strong, but also very friendly. Our Lithuanian rowing team bonded with a strong sense of unity and belonging, respect for each other, and the shared goal of becoming the best team in the Soviet Union. Although this is not the topic of this book, seven families of rowers formed out of that team.

Coach Grucova turned out to be completely different than I'd imagined her. We never heard a single strict or mean word come out of her mouth. She chose her every word carefully. She never erupted into emotional outbursts or anger. We never heard her raise her voice. Of course, we also behaved respectfully and were dedicated to the team. When you reach that level in sports (although were still all very young, around 18 – 20 years old, and I was just 18) you are conscious of the fact that every action your take will have an effect of your team's racing results. There was no time or desire to party all night long, as was the usual in the junior summer camps. We didn't even take the time to go for a swim in the lake on a hot July day (the summer was very hot) because we knew that swimming would use up our energy that we needed to save for racing. Coach Grucova was always precise and never late. She was always prepared before we were, and so we did our best never to be late as well. Coach would film our training sessions from a motorboat and then the next day, or the day after that (the time it took for her to travel to Vilnius to develop the film) we would sit together with the curtains closed, watching images of ourselves rowing on the wall to the sound of the humming projector. Then we would all together analyse our every move and strategize how we could correct our mistakes. In the eyes of the Federation leadership, we were not considered among the most promising crews, so they didn't even assign us a masseuse. We "didn't have a chance to win a medal" in their eyes. Coach Grucova took over the job of a masseuse. After the evening training session, she would massage each of us for half an hour on the table in her room. If we needed to return to Vilnius from Trakai for any reason, she would drive us. She felt that it would be too much of a waste of our time or energy to walk to the Trakai train station from the boathouse, then walk back, and waste an hour in both directions on the train. We could better use that time for sleep or rest. She saved us our money on train tickets, and it never even occurred to us how much of her own money she was spending on gasoline.

The Soviet Championship ended with a spectacular team win for the Soviet Lithuanian rowing team. In total, thirty-nine of our rowers won gold, silver, and bronze medals. Our quadruple scull (me, Rima Liutkaitytė, Asta Pažereckaitė (mother of Olympic prize winner, Mindaugas Griškonis), Valda Paulauskaitė, Sandra Brazauskaitė, and cox, Aušra Gudeliūnaitė) won a bronze medal. The only two teams that got ahead of us were the Russian team and the pan-Soviet team. We took the Lithuanian Rowing Federation leaders by complete surprise. The only person who'd had faith in us was our coach, Sofija Grucova.

Since the day of our victory at the Soviet Olympics, I've carried a strong sense of guilt around with me. After our unexpected win and spectacular performance, the four of us girls, together with our boyfriends from the team (me with my future husband, Aivaras) and other team friends took off for the Moscow city centre to celebrate our glorious victory. We did not even consider, or realize, or even care, that Coach Grucova was waiting for us all with a bottle of "Soviet Champagne" that she had managed to purchase precisely in anticipation of this occasion. I cannot imagine how our coach must have felt after our win when not a single one of us thought to thank her or to include her in our celebration. After all, she was the one who had trained us and had led us to the starting pontoon and to our victory.

When lay beneath Sofija's exterior of calm, reservedness, and on occasion, coldness, I learned only in 2016 when I was researching my first book, *Rowing Through the Barbed Wire Fence*. Pretending that I was collecting material for the Rowing Museum, but in reality conducting research in order to better understand the atmosphere of rowing in the early years, I visited as many older rowers as I could manage to find. I asked questions, bossed them around, showed them photographs, leafed through their photo albums, bought every single video clip of rowers from the Central Archives, and did everything I could to revive their memories, and force them to tell me more. I recorded our conversations, listened intently, visited them twice, or in some cases three or four times. When I listened to Sofija Grucova's story, which she had hidden away inside of her and kept silent for decades, I was moved to the point of tears.

I hadn't even completed my first book yet and I already started making plans to write a second book, this time about Sofija Grucova. The image that I had constructed around the persona of Coach Grucova collapsed. It took some time before she agreed to give me permission to write her story. That is understandable. What she had suffered is so painful, and so intense, that at first, she was afraid of reliving all that hurt that she had pushed deep inside. I gifted Sofija Grucova a copy of this manuscript on her 80th birthday, May 1, 2019.

At the end of October 2019, inspired by Sofija's story, my husband I travelled to Canada. On All Saints Day we visited the grave of Ignacy Gruca, Sofija's father. Then we visited his home in Niagara Falls. The house had been sold to new occupants years ago. We drove around Ontario and Quebec. We visited Toronto, Quebec City, Wilna, Montreal, and the Olympic rowing venue and Olympic village.

At the end of that year, Sofija called me and told me that she had decided to give me permission to publish her book. She admitted that she hadn't even gotten to the end of the book and tried to blame it on a lack of time.

"Rima, I trust you," she said. "Publish the book as it is. I'll probably never read it."

At first, I found it difficult to believe that Sofija Grucova would not find the time to read my book, my carefully written one hundred and fifty pages all about her. Then, realization dawned on me.

"Coach," I said, "you're probably afraid to read it?"

"Yes, Rima, you caught me out... I'm afraid..."

Rima Karaliene

CHAPTER ONE

AUGUST 21, 1967, JELGAVA, LATVIA

"Sofija! Sofija! Are you home?"

The woman's voice called out to her in Russian.

Six-year-old Sofija leapt off the sofa, yanked open the window, poked her head out, and looked down onto the street below.

Galina Aleksandrovna! Did you bring me soup? Sofija wondered.

"Sofija, my child, come out into the courtyard! And bring your bowl," the woman called out.

With her fingers frozen from the cold, Sofija grabbed an old enamel bowl from the table. She slipped her cold feet into her shoes and quietly opened the door that led to the building's hallway. On her tippy toes she slipped out of her flat and ran down the stairs. The cold grey hallway reeked of mould. At the bottom of the stairs a tiger-striped kitten was mewing in the corner. Yesterday it had shown up with its mother.

"Are you lost?" Sofija asked, crouching down to pet the kitten.

The trembling kitten backed off fearfully. It was still too small to manage the stairs.

Mama had not been home for a few days already. There had been no word since they took her away on Monday. As usual. Those horrible men in military uniforms and blue caps showed up and took Mama away.

Lately, they showed up more and more often. They would shout and harass her. Sofija could not understand their language. She did not know why they behaved the way they did. She did not understand why they hated Mama. What had Mama done to them? It was terrifying to be home alone. No one ever came to see her.

"Where is your coat? Your hat?" Galina asked.

Galina was wearing a floral headscarf and a fur jacket that kept slipping down her shoulders. She unwrapped her bundle, pulling away the towel, revealing a small cooking pot filled with thick potato soup. She carefully poured a portion of soup into Sofija's bowl.

"Hold your bowl straight, so the soup doesn't spill," Galina warned. "Has your Mama come back?"

Sofija shook her head, no. She pressed her cold palms to the warm bowl and felt warmth spreading throughout her body. The soup smelled just the way Mama made it. She fought back her tears.

I miss my Mama, Sofija thought.

"Thank you," she said politely.

Her lips were blue from the cold and it was hard to get them to obey and speak words.

Galina buttoned Sofija's sweater. She looked her over from head to foot. She shook her head and sighed.

"Run on home now," she said, stroking Sofija's hair. She glanced around to make sure she had not been seen, and then hurried off up the hill towards the last doorway in the row of two-story houses. When she reached her door, she turned to check if Sofija had gone home. "Poor thing," she said quietly to herself.

By the time little Sofija had carefully carried her bowl of soup upstairs to her flat, it had cooled. But her freezing palms held the soup's warmth. She didn't care. The soup would still taste good, even if it were cold. She ate slowly, only half a spoonful at a time, so that she could fully enjoy her one meal for the day. She would save the very last bit of potato for the kitten downstairs. If it wasn't for Galina Aleksandrovna, all she would have for sustenance would be the freezing cold water from the tap. On the opposite side of the street, the bells of the Church of Saint Peter and Paul began to toll. Beyond her window the sky grew dark and thick snowflakes began to slide from the sky.

* * *

"Sofija! Are you coming?" an impatient voice called from the court-yard. That voice had probably been calling her for a while, only she hadn't noticed. "Are you still in your room? Take your umbrella!"

"I'm coming! Just a minute!" Sofija responded.

Usually, she was the first one ready, but today she had lost track of time as her thoughts drifted back to her childhood. She didn't even notice when the rest of the team left the hotel room.

Why did I suddenly remember that episode with the soup? And Galina Aleksandrovna? It's not cold out, and it's just a little after lunch... What a compassionate woman she was. Maybe because she was Jewish? She had a hundred times more humanity than her Lithuanian husband. Or maybe, it was because she was a woman? And a mother. Galina Aleksandrovna... If it hadn't been for her, I never would have survived.

Galina Aleksandrovna was the wife of the editor of *Soviet Lithuania*. She was a Jew from Leningrad,[1] but every day she secretly brought Sofija a bowl of soup. That was the only food she ever ate when Mama was not at home. Galina was afraid of her own husband, a typical Lithuanian turncoat KGB agent. He had the power to throw his own wife out as an "enemy of the State" for feeding that little "criminal". When she would hear Galina under her window, calling out softly in Russian: "Come out

---

1   Present day Saint Petersburg.

into the courtyard and bring your bowl", her hands would tremble with joy. That meant she had one more day to live. But it also meant that on that day Mama would not come home.

The morning was damp, and now it was raining. After a beautiful sunny week, that summer warmth was clouded over with signs of the approaching autumn.

The trials were scheduled for tomorrow afternoon. Therefore, they would not have a second training session today. They could take a break and rest.

They could ease up on those time-trials, Sofija thought to herself as she prepared to go out. *What's the point? We're not going to get anymore rowing in. It's just a waste of our energy. It would be better let us take a rest. We won't have enough time to rest up before the competition.*

Once they were granted the afternoon off, the girls decided to forgo their usual nap after lunch to get out to the shops to buy necessary items for their trip: film for their cameras, toothpaste, and other small items.

Since the middle of August, the Soviet[2] women's rowing team had been training in Jelgava, a small town on the shores of the River Lielupė, 40 kilometres from Riga, the capital of Latvia. For years, the most important USSR rowing team training camps took place here. Both the men's and women's' teams trained here. Just as soon as the women's teams departed, the men's teams arrived. At times, both male and female teams trained together.

Their large hotel was located a five-minute walk away from the boat-house. It was strange that the coaches had decided that during the last

---

2   The Union of Soviet Socialist Republics (Russian: *Sojuz Sovetskich Socialis-ticheskich Respublik),* commonly referred to as the USSR. This state existed from December 30, 1933 to December 8, 1991.

training session the team would row in the river, and not in still water. Perhaps that was because they were eating too well in the hotel? They received special ration coupons for athletes that granted them the privilege to eat large portions of pork chops. There were even enough coupons left over to indulge in quality dairy products.

The trip to the European rowing championship was only five days away. *Not much could change at this point*, Sofija thought to herself. *The boat is sliding beautifully and the girls feel strong. They are in a good mood. Most important now is not to overtrain and ruin everything we have accomplished to this point. Hope we would not face a head wind, like last year in Amsterdam. God forbid, we'll get carried away like feathers just as we did then. We can't compete against those German girls. The German girls are tall and stocky. A head wind is nothing to them. But for us, it's a disaster, like rowing into a wall.*

Sofija shook off the unpleasant memory. After they passed the finish line, she simply could not get out of the boat. It was as though her legs ceased to obey her. Her legs were covered in red and blue bruises. *I can't imagine getting through that a second time,* she mused to herself.

Her first performance on the USSR team had not been a success. At least, that was the judgement of the team's coaches. Placing second was the same as losing the race to them. Although for her, as the new stroke[3] on the team, the silver medal felt like an enormous accomplishment. All the girls on their crew were petite. The tallest member of their quad was only one metre seventy-two centimetres tall. She, as stroke, was only one meter sixty-eight centimetres in height. But they were quick. They always fared better when they rowed with a tailwind. However, you cannot go

---

3   The rower closest to the stern of the boat, responsible for the stroke rate and rhythm.

against Mother Nature. That was especially true in the Bosbaan Canal[4]
where the wind direction changed every fifteen minutes and a wind tun-
nel in the canal could develop into a whirlwind. If the wind changes its
direction even just slightly, the entire race turns into the luck of the draw.

After her unsuccessful race in Amsterdam, Sofija constantly worried
that she would be replaced with a girl who was heavier and stronger than
she was. It only made matters worse that she was from Lithuania. Every
training session turned into a challenge where she had to prove herself or
be replaced with a girl from Moscow or Leningrad. At any moment, they
could come and simply say to her: "We must strengthen the team." Then
she would be replaced. They saw it happen all the time, and not just on
the women's crew, but on the men's as well.

Finally, the composition of the USSR quad had been established. Sofija, just like last year, was chosen as stroke. That position was almost the
same as the captain's position; however, she always reminded the crew
that her position was not the same as a captain's because she only set the
tempo for the rowers but was not their leader. The coxswain held that
seat and was loud, but that was because it was the nature of her position.
She had to call out the commands, so that all four women would hear
them. If the wind were strong, she had to shout especially loud, so that
her voice would be heard over the wind. Of course, she was also responsible for keeping the boat on a straight course.

*It would be fun if Genovaitė could be here with us, but she didn't work
out for the quadruple sculls. She's really good as a single. She's not fast enough
for a quad. Her stroke[5] is long. Her stroke rate is low. On the quad you've got*

---

4   A rowing canal in Amsterdam, Holland.

5   The propulsive portion of the stroke from the time the oar blade enters the
     water ('catch') until it is removed from the water ('release').

to move fast. It's awesome that she won for singles. She's worthy of the championship, Sofija reflected.

Genovaitė Šidagytė made it onto the team on her first try. She and Sofija became friends from the very first day they met at the Institute of Physical Education dorm. It was Sofija, who after taking in Genovaitė's build, convinced her to switch from bicycling to rowing.

Sofija hurriedly grabbed her sweater and umbrella, paused in front of the mirror to push her short curly brunette hair away from her face, and headed for the door. The most important competition of the season was only a week away. Her sense of pride and anticipation was on the rise, overpowering the anxiety that she always felt before the start of a race.

She was reaching for the door handle when she heard someone knocking on her door. The sound was completely unexpected and caused her to jump back. She felt as though she'd been struck by lightning. She would never get used to the sound of a knock on the door. That sound always brought her back to her painful childhood memories.

Usually those who knocked on their door back then didn't wait for anyone on the inside to open it. They'd kick open the door, and so hard that it knocked against the wardrobe standing beside it. Whatever was placed on the top shelf would fall to the bottom. Mama would whisper, "hide," and Sofija would crawl behind the curtain and hold her breath, so that the curtain would not move. Then, the KGB agents, who stank with a putrid smell, wearing their blue hats, would burst inside the room and grab her mother and drag her away. How old was she? Six? Seven? Was it 1945? Or 1946? She was too frightened even to cry. She would crouch in the corner, behind the curtain, covering her face with her hands until it was all over. Then she would wait... Wait for Mama to come home. And eventually Mama would come home, exhausted, with black eyes, sunken cheeks, and her clothing filthy. Without saying a word, Mama would pull her into her arms and hold her tight.

When they took Mama away, she would wait in hiding for a day, two days, three days, a week or longer. Or maybe that's how long it seemed? Maybe it was only three days? The time passed very slowly when she waited for Mama to come home. She would wait all alone in the cold, in the dark, without food, without any people around. It was better in summer. Then it would not get dark so early and she fell asleep while it was still light outside. In the winter she was more frightened. It seemed as though the sun had barely risen when only a few hours later it set again. In winter she would curl up in Mama's scarf on the old sofa, tucking her feet beneath her, trembling from cold and from fear.

It's true that there were people on the other side of the wall, but the thought of those people only caused Sofija to tremble more. They were horrible. In 1945, when the Russians occupied Vilnius, those people walked into her family's flat without so much as knocking. A terrible man from Moscow, with the surname Golosov, and his local Lithuanian wife, Aldona, announced that they were moving in. They threw away all Mama's possessions, everything they had in the living room, kitchen, and bathroom, while keeping the best things for themselves. Sofija and her mother had to huddle in the one remaining small room that was left after the strangers moved in. They could only enter the kitchen on the rare occasions when the new occupants were not at home. The quiet life they had lived up until that point transformed into a living hell. On the other side of their flat's wall, they heard screams, curses, the sounds of prostitutes entertaining Golosov, Russian songs being sung. God forbid you accidentally ran into one of them in the doorway. Sofija would hear them shout in Russian at Mama, "Shut up you disgusting Polack!" She heard other words shouted at her mother as well, but she did not understand those words yet. Ten years have passed since those horrible people moved out, but Sofija still lived with the fear of the sound of someone knocking on the door. She probably would never recover from that fear.

She remembered the times when through her window she saw a truck filled with armed Russian soldiers heading down the street. Then, one of the neighbours shouted: *"Oblava!"* They would be surrounded and then the attack began. They would all quickly hide wherever they could. The soldiers never knocked either. They'd storm in, turning out the drawers, grabbing whatever they could get their hands on. They took everything they could carry – clothing, food, dishes, tablecloths. They arrested people from the other flats, giving them barely enough time to grab a few things wrapped in a bundle. Those people never returned. She could hear their screams and cries ringing in her ears for a long time afterwards. The fear never left her until the next *Oblava*.

Afterwards, strangers would move into those peoples' empty flats. Most of the time they were Russian families. They were mean and rough. After the Russians came, there would be more trash and noise in the courtyard. It was frightening to so much as step outside.

"Sofija, are you there?" a voice asked in Russian.

It was Boris Schirtladze, the head coach.

Sofija opened the door. She was shocked and surprised to see the team's head coach standing there in the doorway. He was completely altered. His face was pale, his eyes were full of anxiety, his lips were trembling, and his cheeks were twitching. Noticing that she was on her way out, he filled the doorframe with his body, preventing her from stepping past him.

"Wait a moment, we need to talk," he said in an anxious voice.

"Yes, I am listening Boris Mikhailovich. Did something happen?"

The moments before he finally spoke seemed to last an eternity. It was extremely rare for the head coach to come and pay a visit. Something serious had to have happened for him to come to Sofija's room. Usually, if there was an issue, the coach asked everyone from the team to meet him in the hotel lobby. Or he invited each of them individually downstairs into the lobby for a meeting.

Did something happen to Mama, Sofija thought. *Maybe Mama died? Or there was an accident? A fire? What?* Her thoughts raced and she grew anxious. *What could have happened to make Boris Mikhailovich look so frightened? Why was he silent?*

"Sofija, the KGB want to speak with you. Tomorrow you must meet with them at the KGB headquarters in Vilnius."

"Me?" Sofija gasped. "Why me?"

"I don't know, Sofija. I can only guess that something is amiss with your documents."

"But they granted me a foreign travel passport."[6]

"I don't know any more than what I told you. I'm shocked myself. They called me today from the Sports Committee."

"How can this have happened? Last year when I travelled to the Netherlands, they had no problem with me. And then we travelled to Grünau."

"Did something happen in Grünau that I don't know about? You understand that you can't do anything while you are abroad that won't be noticed and notated."

"Nothing happened! Really, nothing! Oh, Boris Mikhailovich, if you

6   In the former Soviet Union, Soviet citizens had an internal passport that was used inside the USSR, and an external passport for foreign travel. Only Soviet citizens who met special KGB requirements were granted an external passport and were allowed to travel outside the borders of the USSR.

know something more, please tell me."

"I don't know anything, really I don't. They called and said you should hurry."

A loud ringing sounded in Sofija's ears. Her entire body went weak. She felt as though there weren't a single muscle in her body that she could move.

"There's a train leaving for Vilnius at three. Here's money for your ticket," Boris Mikhailovich said, handing her three roubles. "You must report to the KGB at nine o'clock sharp. There's a train back here that departs at twelve noon. You ought to be able to make it. If you don't, the next train leaves at five thirty. The trials are tomorrow at five. It would be good if you made it back on time. But if you don't make it back, please don't worry about it."

"Does Natalia Sergeyevna know?" Sofija asked in a frightened voice. Natalia Sergeevna Sanina was the coach for their women's quad.

"I will explain everything to her."

Sofija stood frozen in place and could not move. *Why?* she thought to herself. *What did I do? What happened? Is this about Mama?*

"Sofija, do you hear me?" the head coach said nervously.

He clearly was concerned about how this news affected one of the most important members of the team just days before their trip abroad to the European Rowing Championship. If the KGB ordered Sofija to stay home, their position in the championship was lost.

"Hey, Sofija!" he repeated.

"Yes, I hear you," Sofija said, pulling herself together. Only, there was a lump caught in her throat. She wanted to say something, but the words in her head were scrambled and she found it difficult to concentrate.

"The train leaves at three. Did you hear me?"

The lump in her throat had taken away her voice. She nodded her head to show that she understood, but her legs refused to obey her. She wanted to run away, but she couldn't. Her heart was beating against her chest. Weakness washed over her body.

The head coach was also at a loss for words. It was the first time he had ever received a phone call from the KGB. There had been times when the paperwork was slow. There were times when a team member was not issued permission to travel abroad. But never before had one of his athletes been invited to meet personally with the KGB. Therefore, he could not advise Sofija on what she should do, how she should talk to them, how she ought to behave.

Sofija's hands trembled as she nervously clutched her room key. Her face grew pale, and she grew feverish. She struggled to put it all together in her head: "I am invited to meet with the KGB? Why? The train leaves at three. I must return to Vilnius. What will I tell the other girls? It takes ten minutes to reach the station. To the KGB… They are horrible people. Beyond horrible, they are vicious animals. They will shout at me and I will cry. Maybe not? Maybe they are different now? Nothing good can come out of any conversation with the KGB. What could I do to avoid having to go see them? Maybe someone else could go instead of me? Maybe I should just go see them right away and not wait for tomorrow? No, that's not even possible. It must be tomorrow."

"Did you understand everything I said," Boris Mikhailovich asked, checking in with her again.

"Yes, I understood. I'm going to go tell the girls now," Sofija said.

She stepped out of her room and tried to lock her door. However, her hands were shaking so badly the key slipped out of her hands and fell to the floor. Sofija picked the key up and tried to lock the door again, but her hands were trembling so badly she could not position the key in the lock.

"Don't say anything to the girls just yet."

Sofija stopped what she was doing and stared at Boris Mikhailovich.

"There's no need to frighten them. Tell them you have an emergency and need to go home. Tell them I gave you permission. Think of something."

"Oh," Sofija whispered, at a loss for words.

"Don't tell them anything right now. Everything will take care of itself," the head coach said unconvincingly.

"Okay," Sofija nodded. She turned and walked down the long red carpeted hallway towards the stairwell.

She walked as though in a dream, not noticing a mop and bucket of water standing in the middle of the hallway. Normally she would have no problem stepping around the bucket, but today her foot caught on its edge, almost tipping the dirty water over onto the rug.

"What's wrong with you? Are you blind?" the cleaning woman growled at her.

"I'm sorry," Sofija said. She paused, took two deep breaths to steady her nerves, and then walked down the stairs and exited onto the street.

She felt as though she'd just been told she was going to jail.

She looked up at the overcast sky, shrugged, then spotted the silhouettes of her teammates walking towards the city centre.

Her feet tangled together as she stumbled, then began to run towards them. She felt as though she were running in a dream, when your feet seem to move but you remain in place. A lump pressed down on her throat. She forgot to open her umbrella. The rain grew stronger and soon water was dripping off her curls, down her cheeks, running into her eyes. Her heart was beating rapidly, like it did before starting a race, when it seemed as though everyone around her could hear the sound of her pounding heart, and even her deep breaths could not help contain her fear.

Sofija ran, stumbling as she went. Raindrops plopped down the collar of her raincoat, sliding down her sweaty back. As she ran, thoughts raced through her mind: "Maybe someone is playing a mean joke on me? Maybe they want to throw me off the team? There are only a few days left until our trip. They couldn't issue another person exit documents fast enough if they threw me off the team. Would our standby teammates do this to me? What does the KGB have to do with any of this?" Then she thought, "Oh, what should I tell the girls? Should I tell them the truth? Or not? I can't hide anything from them? I must tell them I'm leaving. The trials are tomorrow. But no one is changing the seating of the crew."

A week ago, all the teams were formed. Galina Konstantinova lost her place in the singles and ended up seated in the quad behind her. They rowed fast together, perfectly. There was no reason to dismantle the crew.

"What took you so long?" Aleksandra Bochiarova, whom everyone called Sasha, asked her, not hiding her annoyance. She was in seat two.[7]

"I was talking with Boris Mikhailovich," Sofija said and then sighed

---

7   The places in a racing boat are numbered. The first place or bow seat, at the front of the boat, is where the first rower sits, the first to cross the finish line. He sees the entire team in front of him. After him come the second rower, the third, and so on. The stroke is seated last. In a double scull and a pair he is second, in a quad and a four fourth, in an eight, the eighth. The entire team sits behind the back of the stroke.

deeply.

"About what?"

"Oh, nothing... I need to return to Vilnius."

"Did something happen?" Tatiana Markvo asked. She was in the bow in the quad.

"It's about my paperwork," Sofija said evasively. Her trembling lips, however, betrayed her anxiety.

"Is something wrong?"

"No, it's nothing, but they want me to be in Vilnius tomorrow to take care of it."

It was apparent that her teammates were as surprised as she was. Sofija realized then that they couldn't have betrayed her or set her up. But still, why the KGB?

The girls saw that Sofija could not focus or string together a coherent sentence. Her movements were jerky and sudden. She took a step and tripped and almost fell flat on her face.

"Are you really okay?" Sasha asked, looking Sofija up and down.

"Why do you ask?"

"You don't seem yourself."

"Really? Nonsense! I'm perfectly fine!" Sofija forced herself to smile warmly. She even began to hum a tune cheerfully to completely disguise her unease.

"Sofija, wait!"

It was Sofija's Lithuanian friend, Genovaitė calling out to her. They usually passed their free time together.

"Šidagytė? You're coming too?" Sofija asked, surprised to see her friend.

The girls liked to address each other by their surnames as a joke.

"Yes, I'm coming. I also need to buy a few things."

"It's raining."

Genovaitė gazed at her girlfriend in surprise.

"What?" Sofija asked.

"Nothing… Do you have time off after lunch?"

"And?"

"They gave me Konstantinova's boat. I can't seem to get through to her. I thought maybe you could help me with rigging?"

A week ago, during the trial races Genovaitė had won against Galina Konstantinova by eleven seconds. She became the best single scull rower in her country. Konstantinova had won the European champion title four years in a row. Before that, she won the bronze medal. It seemed as though she were unbeatable. But here came this Lithuanian girl out of nowhere who beat her.

"I heard," Sofija said and smiled.

"What's wrong? Why do you look so anxious?"

"Me?"

"You, you," Genovaitė said, gazing at her friend with concern. She had never seen Sofija of the steel nerves this scattered before.

"Nothing."

"Hey, do you hear me, Sofija?"

"I hear you. Stop shouting."

"Can you help me rig the boat? I really don't have a clue how to do it right."

"Okay, I can take a look tomorrow evening."

"Could you do it today? Tomorrow are trials, and I'd like to give it a go."

"I can't. I won't be around after lunch."

"What?"

"I have to go to Vilnius."

"What happened?"

"Oh, nothing serious."

"Tell me and hurry up about it!" Genovaitė said defiantly. "I can see that something's wrong."

Sofija glanced around her to check if anyone could hear them. Satisfied that there wasn't anyone else around who could understand Lithuanian, she said to her friend in a whisper, "They told me to report to the KGB."

"Why?"

"I don't know."

"Did someone inform on you?"

"I can't imagine what they would have on me to inform about?"

"You didn't say anything foolish to anyone, did you?"

"I don't think I did…"

"Then don't worry about it. Everything should be alright. This isn't your first time abroad, is it?"

Immediately Sofija regretted having told her friend. Not because she thought Genovaitė would tell anyone, but because she did not want to appear weak. Besides, Boris Mikhailovich had asked her not to tell anyone, and what did she do the very first time someone asked? She was overcome with fear, weakness. She felt so vulnerable. In that moment, she felt as though she needed to talk with someone, find comfort, support.

"Of course, it'll all be fine," Sofija agreed in a voice that did not sound in the least convincing.

"Just don't worry about it. Everything will be fine."

"You know, I think I won't walk downtown after all. I've got to leave for Vilnius."

"What time is the train?"

"Three."

"It's only one."

"I'll go get ready to leave," Sofija said. Switching to Russian, she called out to her teammates up ahead, "Girls, I'm not going to town with you!"

It was hard for her to concentrate or even think. She could scarcely tell what was happening around her. *I'd better go lie down*, she thought to herself. *Maybe that will calm me.*

CHAPTER TWO

AUGUST 21, 1967, JELGAVA – VILNIUS

The Tallinn – Vilnius train departed the Jelgava Station ten after three. The train was full, but there were still a few empty seats available. Sofija scanned the railway carriage and moved towards the back. There the passengers seemed a little more reserved – no one was playing cards, smoking, or shouting Russian curses. She spotted a middle-aged woman clutching a mesh bag filled with apples and sat down beside her. Sofija pulled a book out of her handbag and placed it on her knees. Would she have the concentration to read? She gazed out the train window at the long beige two-story train station with its arched windows, at the people standing on the platform, waving to their loved ones. A blonde in a white apron selling ice cream out of a pushcart leaned against the station wall. A wave of anxiety washed over Sofija. She felt a bottomless sensation of sadness inside of her.

The train jerked forwards and began to move. Chug... chug... That sound resonated somewhere deep inside her unconscious mind. Chug... Probably that sound remained with her from the days when her desperate mother, clutching her on her lap, escaped by train out of Warsaw to Vilnius. She couldn't remember anything from those days. She was too small, barely a year old. Mama never talked about it. But that sound...

That sound… And the reek of diesel fuel. That smell was somehow familiar to her. That smell made her tremble. Mama did not even consider that there would be war, that the Iron Curtain would come down, cutting her off from returning home for all times. She also could not imagine that all her attempts to find her husband – who had been taken away to Smolensk – would lead to a dead end. She could not foresee that all the letters she sent to the International Red Cross would be returned to her with a stamp from Moscow and two words written in Russian: "Not found".

The beautiful Latvian landscape flowed past her window. Nature lived its own life… Oh, how she longed to meld into nature right now – then she would not need to worry about a single thing. She would simply drink droplets of rainwater, feel how the water drips down her cheeks… *The KGB…* Just the thought of those three letters hit her like a lightning bolt… Her ears began to ring.

What could have happened? The last time they came and took Mama away was over ten years ago. Was it starting again? Sofija pondered to herself. In all those years, she had never dared to ask her mother the reason why they continually arrested her. Mama probably would not have told her anyway. She would have worried that Sofija would repeat her words somewhere outside of their home and to the wrong people. Should she tell Mama that the KGB wanted her to report to them? Or maybe she shouldn't tell her? What will she tell Mama? The strong wave of anxiety burned inside of her.

The woman with the mesh bag stood up and prepared to exit the train. Sofija slid across the wooden bench closer to the window and leaned her head against the glass. Beyond the window meadows spread out towards the sky and tractors ploughed the collective farm fields. She could not shake the image of the woman in the white apron selling ice-cream out of a cart. *Why can't I forget her?* She wondered, then shook the thought away. The image came back. *How many years has it been? Four years?*

That was back at the 1963 Soviet Championship, the *Spartakiad*[8] in Moscow. It was a painful competition that they lost not because of their own fault, but because of an untruth. She was rowing on a Lithuanian quad team with Rita Tamašauskaitė, Gaila Juodytė, Janina Lukošiūnaitė and coxswain Jūratė Narvydaitė. They finished first, but the judges placed them third. The other two quads were very close; therefore, it was no surprise that the USSR team leaders simply assigned first place to the team from Leningrad and second to the team from Moscow. Sofija's teammates, Janina, Rita, and Gaila were not that upset about it, but Sofija could never accept the lie. Jūratė agreed with Sofija. They understood their worth more clearly than the others. She was tormented with these thoughts that she could not let go: *We could have gone to the championship. We could have raced in the European Rowing Championship. We were a solid team.*

The incident she now remembered took place the day before the unlucky finals. Moscow was smothered by the summer heat. Every day the temperature was 35 degrees Celsius. There was only one free half day left before the finals on the following day. The girls, as always, wanted to go shopping. Moscow, the capital of the Soviet Union, is well stocked with goods that are not available in other parts of the Soviet Union. The girls took advantage of the opportunity to buy a few things they could not purchase at home.

However, before such an important race the coaches didn't want them walking around too much. The girls also understood that it was not a good idea to tire themselves out walking. So, Sofija, Janina, Rita, and

---

8 An internal Olympic-style sports competition held inside the Soviet Union.

Gaila decided to spend their time at the expansive exhibition grounds across the street from the hotel. In Russian, they were known by the acronym VDNCH.[9] Although there was a lot of ground to cover, they decided they could admire the flower gardens and enjoy the cool mist from the fountains. That would not exhaust them or give them sunstroke.

"Just don't stay too long, girls!" their coach warned them. "Save your energy for tomorrow."

They all wanted to see the "Fraternity of People's"[10] fountain with its eight-point pool surrounded by a circle of "golden" girls from the fifteen brotherly Soviet republics clad in their national costumes. Of course, their most important goal was to find the statue of the Lithuanian girl and to take a photograph together with her in the background.

Someone from Moscow had told them that a month ago a film director named Fellini, an Italian, had called this fountain, "Nonsense created by a drunk baker". But they all thought that the "golden" girls were very pretty. Perhaps because one of them was a Lithuanian?

They were also interested in walking around the "Stone Flower" further off in the distance. The grandiose pavilions of the republics and the branches of the economy with many columns, sculptures, mouldings, and decorations looked more like ancient palaces, churches, oriental temples than exhibition halls. However, they were not interested in visiting the exhibitions inside the buildings, not unless to spend a few minutes inside the cool buildings, taking a break from the hot sun. Then

---

9   *VDNCH in Russian: Vystavka dostizhenij narodnogo choziajstva* (Exhibition of Achievements of the National Economy).

10   According to Marxism, nationalism is only a tool of the ruling class, used to keep the working class divided and thus easier to control and exploit. With the success of class struggle, the natural brotherhood of all workers would make the idea of separate nations obsolete.

they would go inside one of the pavilions to see the elegant interiors with all its columns, mouldings, and ornaments. However, it would take a few months' time if they actually wished to visit them all. It was much more fun to wander the footpaths between the flower gardens and observe everything from the outside. The girls were accustomed to this Stalin-era architecture.

It was a Saturday afternoon and even outdoors in the park there were crowds of people, mostly families with children, tourists, Muscovites, and visitors from other parts of the USSR. Most of the visitors congregated around the fountains. There was hardly any shade in the expansive grounds and beside the fountains people could enjoy the cool mist that sprayed from the water. Children climbed onto the edges of the fountains, trying to get inside the pools to splash around. Everywhere people were taking pictures.

Two elderly men had placed a board between them on a bench and were playing chess. Three curious men stood behind them watching. They had brought along a *Sokol* portable radio and had propped it against the back of the bench. Romantic melodies blared from the radio.

"Do you hear?" Gaila squealed.

"What?" Janina asked.

"The Boatman romance!"

"Oh, yes," Rita said and smiled.

"Sofija doesn't know," Gaila said. "The Boatman at our Kaunas boathouse often sang this romance... Smoriginas... Kostas."

"He always travelled with us to our races," Rita added, "to Trakai or Klaipėda. We'd all travel in the back of the truck, stretched out on the hay underneath the boats. You know? Right? You've probably travelled like that as well? The coaches pile hay into the back of the truck and we all flop down onto the straw with the boats over our heads."

"It's so romantic," Janina said and smiled.

"He always brought his guitar," Gaila continued. "His wife used to come along with us too. The entire trip the two of them would sing beautifully together. They sang Russian romance songs! It's too bad that we never learned the words. We could only listen."

"They would bring their son along too, little Kostas," Rita added.

"Oh yes! We would all play with their little boy. They were intellectual and kind people."

"Our boatman was Zhenia and Rycha's uncle. He didn't sing romantic songs for us," Sofija said and laughed, remembering the coaches, two brothers, Eugenijus and Ričardas Vaitkevičius. Everyone called Eugenijus, Zhenia and Ričardas, Rycha. Uncle Pranciškus was the soul of the *Žalgiris* Club boathouse in Vilnius. "When we travelled to races, yes, we also lay down on the hay under the boats. That was fun. After a while you couldn't feel your side anymore, but it was a lot of fun."

"I want ice-cream," Gaila said as though in a daydream.

"Why not? Let's go get some ice-cream," Janina said.

The day was hot and there was a long queue at the ice-cream cart. The girls took their place at the end of the queue and counted their coins. "Eskimo" cost 11 kopecks. A cone cost 19 kopecks. A chocolate roll cost 28 kopecks.

"I'll go up ahead and see if there will be enough left," Sofija said, breaking away from the group and walking towards the ice-cream cart. "If there's nothing left, we'll need to find another queue," she called behind her.

Three ice-cream sellers had set up their carts in a row. There was a long queue stretching out in front of each cart. Sofija poked her head inside each ice-cream cart and saw that there was plenty of ice-cream for everyone. Satisfied, she re-joined her group.

"I borrowed two roubles from Aleksandravičius," Rita said cheerfully.

Their good-hearted coach, Leonas Aleksandravičius, looked out for the girls since their days at the Institute of Physical Education. He was like a father to them, even though he was only a few years older and no longer their coach.

"I have one rouble left, but I'm afraid I'll have to borrow from the coach," Gaila said, digging out kopeck after kopeck from her wallet. She could not decide which type of ice-cream she'd like to buy.

Janina laughed, then said: "I've borrowed so much money from coach that I don't know how I'll pay it all back. I suppose, I'll probably have to get married."

The girls burst out laughing.

"Oh, that's a new one!"

Of course, it was not really a joke. Everyone knew already that they were planning to get married sooner or later. Coach Leonas Aleksandravičius was ten years older than Janina. From her very first year at the Institute, he had his eye on her. First, he saw that she would make a good rower, although he himself had been a hang glider. Then, he saw she was a hardworking student. After working with her for a few years, they fell in love. The team was secretly anticipating their wedding.

"What kind are you buying?" Gaila asked Rita.

"Maybe, an *Eskimo*? Those waffle ones just get all soggy. Look at what a mess they are."

"Me too then," Rita said.

Rita and Gaila were inseparable from their very first day in the boat together. Whatever one did, the other followed. They went everywhere together, holding hands like sisters. All their friends had combined their two names into one: Ritagaila. Coach sat them in the boat together and from that moment onwards they were inseparable. They were both blondes, cheerful, and friendly, and not just with each other, but with everyone.

Gaila dreamed of becoming a doctor. She studied hard and passed all her exams with high marks. But then, not even suspecting anything, she ran into trouble when she submitted her documents to the university. The committee asked her what her father's profession had been. She didn't even stop to think and blurted out, "He was in the military." The committee shot back, "Then maybe he was a member of the Plechavičius army?"[11] She pondered out loud, "Maybe he was?" They shoved her documents back at her and spat out, "Then go and figure it out." That was all it took for her to lose her chance to study Medicine.

Rita was accepted into the Kaunas Institute of Physical Education as a tennis player. But, as was usually the case, there were not enough rowers on the student team, so she was told to go fill in. Once she sat down in a boat, she never climbed out. She changed her major to rowing.

"The cone tastes good, but it's so hard to eat," Gaila said as she watched a man who had just made his selection pressing a soggy cone between his fingers.

"And it's expensive. Twenty-one kopecks. For that money we could only buy one and share it."

---

11   Povilas Plechavičius (1 February 1890 – 19 December 1973) was an Imperial Russian and then Lithuanian military officer and statesman. In the service of Lithuania, he rose to the rank of General of the army in the interwar period of Lithuanian independence. He is best known for his participation in the Lithuanian Wars for Independence and for leading a Lithuanian collaborationist militia during the Nazi occupation of Lithuania, 1941-1944.

The people standing in front of them, and behind them, in the queue turned around and stared at them, curious about the foreign language they were speaking to each other in. The girls enjoyed that. They enjoyed pretending to be Westerners. They plastered wide unconcerned smiles on their faces and spoke in Lithuanian even louder. They started commenting on the people around them, enjoying the fact that they could not understand their comments. At the same time, they enjoyed listening to the other people on the queue making comments about them in Russian, believing that the "foreign" girls could not possibly understand them. They were careful not to mix any Russian slang or words into their chatter, so that the people around them would not figure out that they were just ordinary Soviet citizens just like them. The girls attracted attention not only for their language, but because of the dresses they wore. No one had seen such pretty dresses in Moscow. All the girls were experts at sewing, embroidery, knitting and clothing design. They made their own clothing, so that they looked their best and did not have to rely on the identical factory issue dresses that were the typical boring uniform of the Soviet woman.

"They are probably from the Baltic," a woman standing behind them said. She said it with a note of awe in her voice. Russians respected Baltic peoples and considered them Western. However, the girls were a little disappointed that their act had not convinced the others on the queue that they were real foreigners from the other side of the Iron Curtain.

Suddenly an inebriated middle-aged Russian man dressed in a Soviet military uniform hung with rows of medals elbowed his way into the middle of the queue and began shouting violently at the girls in Russian.

"Baltic bitches! They ought to be shot! Like those Polacks in Smolensk!"

"Comrade, you ought to be ashamed of yourself!" a woman shouted at him. "Girls, don't pay any attention to him. He's a drunk. He's bringing shame to those medals he's wearing."

Other people tried to soothe them as well.

"Can't you see that I'm a hero of the Great Patriotic War! I'm entitled to stand at the front of the queue! I don't stand in any queues!"

"And maybe you think you don't need to pay for your ice-cream either," the woman behind the ice-cream cart said testily.

"Shut up, idiot! Give me two portions for nine kopecks!"

The girls were upset, but they stayed quiet. Inside, they were burning with anger, but they gritted their teeth. It was never worth it to pick a fight with those types. They had learned to internalize their seething pain and to be quiet. Only Sofija's face was flushed. She lowered her eyes and turned her head to the side. She gazed at the flower gardens and took a few deep breaths to steady herself.

The scent of the flowers was pleasant in the heat. Sofija closed her eyes, and in her thoughts she touched the photograph that she would hold and gaze at on those days when they took Mama away, when she was left alone in their room in the Vilnius flat. In that photograph her father stood erect, shoulders back, dressed in independent Poland's military uniform. He was so handsome, proud, upright. She had never laid eyes on him in real life, but in the photograph, he seemed like the perfect man to her.

She never so much as touched the photograph when Mama was close by. That was because seeing the photograph always made Mama cry. When she was little, she would ask her mother: "Who is that man in the photograph?" Her mother would reply, "That is your father." Then she would start to cry.

When she asked Mama where her father was, she would turn away from her for a very long time. Then Sofija would be frightened. She did not want Mama to cry. Her father's eyes were so beautiful, kind, peaceful, but his eyes were gazing off somewhere to the side. That was probably where the photographer instructed him to look. His short dark hair was brushed back. There was a dimple in his chin. His face was incredibly peaceful. Sofija liked the ornaments on the collar of his uniform most of all. They looked like stars on an upside-down princess crown. Once she learned how to count, she would count the stars on his epaulets – one star, two stars, three stars... Then she would count the small medals that looked like tiny crosses from the church altar pinned to wide ribbons – one, two, three, four... Her father's hands were large and strong! She would look at his hands and imagine him stroking her head. "When is Daddy coming home?" she would ask her mother, once she understood that other children had fathers who came home. Mama would not say anything. She'd simply pull Sofija up onto her lap, hug her, and rock her for a long time. When Sofija was older, she explained: "At the beginning of the war, they took your father and the other Polish officers to Smolensk, to Russia. They never returned..."

Suddenly, Sofija felt a strong pain in her left palm. Without realizing what she was doing, she had picked open the blister that was perpetually on her left palm because of rowing. Now blood was oozing out of the blister. "Oh, that's all I need right now..." she muttered. She clenched her teeth, slid her handkerchief out of her dress pocket, folded it into a tidy triangle, and pressed it to the wound on her palm.

The drunken veteran of war stumbled off, and the crowd calmed down, although a few still muttered under their breath about "those Great Patriotic War veterans."

"Two *Eskimos* for me," Janina said, holding up two fingers, standing before the cart with the Russian word, *Morozhenoe*, ice-cream, written across its side.

The hefty woman behind the white cart, dressed in a white apron, took the 22 kopecks from Janina's hand.

"Sofija, I got yours," she called out and waved.

"Oh, I'm sorry... Thank you! How much do I owe you? Or should I pay back Aleksandravičius?"

She didn't quite pull off the joke. Sofija was trying too hard to seem as though she were not upset.

"Ha, ha," Janina quipped. "Tomorrow you can buy me ice-cream."

They unwrapped their ice-creams and headed for the first unoccupied bench and sat down. The sun slowly began to set behind the tall pavilions. It was no longer as hot as before.

"What happened to your hand?" Rita asked, pointing at the handkerchief wrapped around Sofija's palm.

"It's nothing, the scab on my blister tore open," she said, giving her hand a wave as though to say it was not worth mentioning.

"Your handkerchief is so pretty," Janina said. "What's embroidered there?"

"My mother's initials, A.G.," Sofija said, twisting around the handkerchief and showing the delicate letters embroidered in white thread. My mother's name is Aleksandra.

"Grucienė? If you are Grucaitė..."[12]

Sofija smiled and explained: "My surname is not actually Grucaitė.

---

12   In Lithuanian special endings are added to female surnames to indicate whether a woman is married or unmarried.

My real surname was Gruca, and my mother's surname is Gruca. Coach Pavilionis transformed my Polish surname into a Lithuanian one. That's why everyone calls me Grucaitė."

"What's written in your passport?"

"Grucova.." Sofija said quietly. An ever-present small sense of disappointment regarding her name washed over her. Now, she probably would have the strength of character to fight for her Polish surname, but at the time, when she was sixteen, when she had to face an official in uniform, her fear was so great and so uncontrollable, that she simply nodded obediently when her Polish surname was transformed into a Russian one. She held back her tears.

"What are these papers?" The official had demanded.

"My birth certificate."

"What language is this written in?"

"Polish."

"This isn't a document! Haven't you seen what a real birth certificate looks like?"

"I was born in Warsaw, Poland. This is the birth certificate I was given. I don't have any other."

"I have no idea what this is! No such documents exist in the Soviet Union!"

The official, who was dressed in a blue uniform skirt, wearing a military jacket with gold buttons, demonstratively tore apart Sofija's Polish birth certificate with the Polish eagle printed on it.

"This is rubbish! This is not a proper document! Go to the archives and come back with proper documents!"

"What kind of documents?"

"A birth certificate! Understand?"

"I never had any other kind of documents."

"What don't you understand? You must go to the archives!"

"I was born in Poland. There is no birth certificate for me in the archives here."

"Don't explain to me what you will or won't find! Go and bring back a proper birth certificate from the archives!"

Of course, she found nothing in the archives because there had never been anything there in the first place. Mama carried her in her arms to Vilnius. They came straight from Warsaw, where she was born. They came with refugee passports at the beginning of the war. Her mother wanted to be closer to Smolensk, so that she could somehow find her husband, the father of her child, and rescue him. The archivist handed her a paper that read: "Not found".

She handed that document to the same official.

"What kind of a surname is Gruca?" she said in an arched tone of voice. "A name like that cannot exist in the Soviet Republic of Lithuania! From now on, you will be Grucova!"

The official crossed her father's surname out of the application form and wrote in its place the Russian name, Grucova. She wrote that same name into her passport. Sofija was too terrified to say a word. Suddenly, she forgot everything that she had intended to explain to the passport official. The words caught in her throat, like when she was a child, when the soldiers appeared in their doorway.

"It could be my mother's maiden name. I'm not sure about the letter, G, what it means. It's an old handkerchief. I've had it forever. It was lying in a drawer and no one was using it, so I took it. I couldn't find another. What's the difference? My palm will heal by tomorrow. I'll cover it with a bandage. It's not the first time..." Sofija said, cutting off the conversation, so that the girls would not ask her any more uncomfortable questions. She did not know how to lie. If she even tried, her trembling voice would give her away. She had been taught since she was a child not to talk about her mother's origins.

"I'm starting to feel frightened," Gaila said and shook her head. She tossed down the wooden ice-cream stick.

"What are you afraid of?" Janina asked, pretending to be surprised. "Wait until tomorrow to worry." She laughed nervously, revealing the worry in her own stomach.

"I don't know. I'm probably worried that it'll be the same as at the Moscow and Leningrad race," Gaila said, recalling how a few month's previous right before the finish line, their boat was pushed back from first place to fourth by a wave in the Khmiki water reservoir. The reservoir was notorious for its waves. The edges of the reservoir were cement and the passage of steamboats, barges, and other motorized boats added to the swells, tossing their slender boats like feathers. For this reason, in Moscow, and more precisely, in the Khmiki, races were like a lottery that cost them a lot of nerves.

"We won't get the swells," Sofija said. "We've got the fourth lane. If anyone is going to take the swells, it's going to be the team from Leningrad. They're in the first lane, aren't they?"

"Probably," Rita agreed.

"Eat your ice-cream before it melts," Janina said and giggled, pointing at her hand at the chocolate sliding down Gaila's fingers.

"Oh!" Gaila gasped and started to lick her chocolate ice-cream, worried that the chocolate would stain her white dress rose patterned dress.

"It's good that they created lanes," Sofija continued. "It'll be easier for Jūratė to stay on course. Where is she anyway? Why didn't she come with us?"

She suddenly remembered their coxswain and glanced at the others.

"She took our shopping lists and headed out to the GUM, the department store."[13]

"We should have invited her to come with us."

"We did invite her, but she decided to shop while she still had time."

"She's a good friend. She took care of our shopping, so we didn't have to."

"She's saving us our legs, so that we wouldn't get tired before the finals."

"That's right, it's exhausting to walk around that enormous store, and it's also such a long distance to get there."

"It's awful when we're racing bow to bow. It's better when we've got some space," Gaila continued, focusing on her fear of tomorrow's race, not even noticing that the others had moved on to a new subject. She simply could not relax.

"Who doesn't? I also would rather see the others' backs than their whirlwinds," Janina agreed.

"I'm not afraid when I'm behind Sofija and Janina," Rita said and smiled. "I'm less worried in the quad than I am in a double. You know you've got four heads to rely on, even five! Besides, you don't even need to steer. You don't have to worry about being late getting to the starting line."

"A double is always worse than a quad, but not as bad as a single," Janina said. For a few years already she was the strongest single in Soviet

13   *Gosudarstvenny Universalny Magazin* ("State Department Store") In the Soviet Union, there was no free market, so every city had one State Universal Department Store where people could buy consumer items in limited supply in the deficit economy.

Lithuania. "When you're in a single you're afraid all by yourself, and you celebrate your wins all alone."

"That's right," Sofija agreed. "I was in a single all my life. At first, I liked being alone, but I'm too short. I can't compete with the likes of a Konstantinova. In a tail wind, yes, but in a head wind, no."

"None of us are that much taller than you," Rita said, looking around at the girls. "But we're fast!"

"That's right," Gaila said and smiled. "When Sofija picks up the pace, it takes all we have in us to keep up."

"You keep up beautifully! You all support me!" Sofija spoke these words to encourage the girls who she had only been rowing with since the beginning of summer.

"Who wants more ice-cream?" Janina asked. She folded her ice-cream wrapper together with the wooden stick and tossed it at the rubbish bin. "Yes! I made it!" she shouted gleefully when she saw her trash land neatly inside the bin.

"You cool down a bit as you eat ice-cream, but as soon as you're done, you feel hot again," Rita said and sighed. She ran her fingers through her short blond hair.

"We ought to get back? Dinner is in half an hour. There won't be anything left for us to eat if the men get there first," Gaila said, standing up from the bench.

"Not enough food for you, Gaila?" Rita said and laughed.

"What should I do if I'm always hungry?" Gaila said, blushing.

"Eat, eat, you need your strength tomorrow," Janina said, encouraging her younger friend.

"I forgot for a moment, but now I'm trembling again," Gaila shook and stamped her feet, pretending to be impatient.

Sofija unwrapped the handkerchief from her palm. The wound had stopped bleeding. The blisters didn't frighten her, but they were a constant annoyance. At the beginning of the season, the blisters come out after the first training session. They hurt, they itch, they tear, the ooze, but then they harden and for the rest of the summer they prevent new blisters from forming. It was a little embarrassing to shake hands with a man. The girls had learned to extend their hands only so far as to offer their fingertips in a handshake. If anyone grabbed hold of their palms when shaking hands and felt the blisters, they'd hear that embarrassing comment, "Wow, what a rough hand for a woman!" They had grown used to it. When they were younger, they were embarrassed by their ragged palms, their bruised knuckles, and their scratched up shins.

"Everything will be fine, don't you worry, it's only a race," Sofija said in a soothing voice. "Come, fellow Baltic "you-know-what's", let's go before the veterans of the Great Patriotic War shoot us," she said sarcastically and stood from the bench.

"Were your feelings hurt?" Rita asked, catching up to Sofija. "Don't pay any mind to the words of a drunk."

"Me? Oh, no! It didn't phase me at all. I've heard that kind of talk my entire life," Sofija said and waved it off.

But she was lying. Those words hurt her and confused her. And not because the drunken Russian had singled them out as enemies of the state, but because for the first time she heard spoken out loud what she had heard her mother talking about quietly, in Polish with another woman. And then, she'd seen her mother cry her eyes out after that talk. That had been long ago. She could not remember how old she was then. She lay in the bed she shared with her mother and pretended to be asleep. Although she was a small child then, she understood the familiar feelings of loss, anxiety, fear, and hurt that the women expressed to each other in their conversation, their utter hopelessness… Now those random words began to form themselves into a chain of meaning – Polish officer, Russians, her father, Smolensk, the Red Cross, the KGB.

Sofija reflected on those words: *If I wasn't so torn apart inside, I could have used that veteran to find out a lot more. I couldn't even think in that moment because my blood was boiling. Drunks usually reveal everything they know without censoring themselves. So what that he called us Baltic Bitches. I would swallow all his curses if only I could find out what it was that he was trying to say about shooting Polish officers in Smolensk?* As they walked, Sofija's eyes scanned the park, searching for the veteran. *Maybe he hadn't gone that far away? Maybe she could still find him and provoke him to say more about Smolensk and what happened there with the Polish officers.*

"Where are you going, Sofija?" Janina asked, surprised to see her friend turning around and walking back into the park. "What's going on with her?" she asked the others.

"I'll be there in a minute. I'll catch up! Just go on without me!" Sofija called behind her as she walked briskly towards the ice-cream cart.

But she did not find the veteran. He was nowhere to be found. There were different people standing in the ice-cream queue. Only the ice-cream seller recognized Sofija and asked:

"Did you lose something here?"

"No, no, it's nothing. Thank you."

CHAPTER THREE

AUGUST 1967, JELGAVA – VILNIUS

Choo-choo!

The train continued to meander through collective farms field, each territory separated from the next by woods and farm buildings. Sofia lowered her eyes and was surprised to see that she was squeezing the same handkerchief with the embroidered letters A and G in her hand. Her book lay unopened on her knees. She felt a heaviness inside. Maybe she ought to read, distract her thoughts?

She opened the book to the first page and leaned her head down on her palm. For the umpteenth time she read the first sentence, but by the time she reached the end of the sentence, she could no longer remember what she'd read.

"What are you reading?" a young man who had sat down in front of her asked in Russian. He seemed to see the worry in Sofija's eyes.

"Nothing," she said, and wasn't lying. She really couldn't read a single word. She closed the book and held up the cover for him to see.

"I only read in Russian," the young man said, clearly uncomfortable, smiling sheepishly. "I don't know what that says."

"It's Stendahl, *The Italian Chronicles*," Sofija said, translating from Lithuanian into Russian. The small book had a moss-coloured cover. She'd borrowed it from her teammates stash of books before leaving, because it seemed like the right length of a book to read in the course of a train ride.

"Are they short stories? I haven't read it," the pleasant young man asked.

Sofija lifted her head and flashed a wane smile, but she did not respond. She simply could not relax. Her body was tense. There was no way she could forget where she was headed and whom she was going to meet with in the morning.

I'll need to be up early. I've got to be there at nine. In front of the Lenin statue. Will I even be able to fall asleep? What should I tell Mama? Should I tell her where I'm going? Maybe she can give me some advice? She's been there many times. She knows the rules. If there are any rules in such a place. She could tell me how I should talk to them. But then again, why worry her? Perhaps I should tell I'm going to see the doctor? But that might frighten her even more? Maybe I shouldn't tell her anything? Maybe I shouldn't even go home? Where could I spend the night then? At Birutė's? But what would I tell her? No, I'll go home, to Mama. We see each other so seldom. I'll tell her that I missed her and that our coach gave us a day off. I'll simply go out in the morning as though nothing were amiss. No, she'll never believe me. She'd wonder why I came home late at night and left early the next morning. I could tell her I can't find my passport. No, she won't believe that...

"Where do you live in Latvia?" the young man asked.

He was probably bored, Sofija thought, shaking her head from her consuming thoughts.

"I don't live in Latvia. I live in Lithuania," she replied.

"So, you're on your way home?"

"Yes, I'm on my way to Vilnius."

"I'm also headed to Vilnius, but I live in Estonia."

"Are you a sailor?" Sofija asked and giggled.

"Why a sailor?" the young man replied, taken aback at the suggestion.

"Oh, no reason," she answered.

"And what's so funny?"

"Nothing," Sofija said and smiled. "It's just that I had this hilarious encounter with sailors in Estonia."

"Really? Tell me about it?"

"Oh, it's not that interesting," Sofija said and turned her face towards the window, so that she would not need to keep up the conversation.

She remembered the incident and had to admit to herself that at the time, it didn't seem that funny at all. Only now, whenever they remembered what happened, she and the girls had a good laugh. Perhaps just because it all ended well. Or maybe they couldn't forget how they were a little tipsy, running around the streets of Klaipėda, giggling and flapping their striped sleeves accompanied by the Estonian sailors.

The incident happened three years ago. It was the spring of 1964, only six months after the unlucky "loss" at the Soviet Championship. Their girls' quad had fallen apart. Coach Eugenijus Vaitkevičius invited Rita to row in the eight and made her into an European champion. Janina decided to leave to become a coach. Her background as a Siberian exile got in the way of her career as a rower because she would never be allowed to row in competitions abroad. The KGB would not allow her to participate in any competitions outside of the Soviet Union. Coach Jonas Pavilionis formed a new quad. Janina was replaced with Genovaitė Šidagytė and Rita was replaced with Vida Majauskytė. The weather had warmed in the final days of March. During the day the temperature reached 10 degrees. Spring always begins earlier in Klaipėda than in Vilnius. The ice melts earlier in the River Dangė than it does in the Neris. That first rowing camp for those who hadn't left for Soviet Georgia was a real joy. Everyone wanted to get out of the cold wet gyms, out of the rowing tanks that reeked of mould, and finally sit down in a boat. That feeling of sitting down for the first time in a boat after a long winter was unbeatable. Of course, you had to work together to adjust your rhythm, to heal your callouses again, and yet, the sound and feeling of the water flowing away from your oars was magical.

In the early spring the coaches wouldn't let anyone row in a single. Not while the water was still cold, and they hadn't gotten back into form. For this reason, at camp everyone rowed in big boats. Everyone wanted to spend as much time as possible on the water and not run cross-country. Besides, it was important not to fall behind the lucky ones who had a head start because they'd already been out on the water since February in Poti, Georgia.

According to the plan, on that March 30th morning they were supposed to train for an hour and a half on the water. You still couldn't row that far in the river. There was still ice along the shores in some areas and if that ice broke away and hit the boat, it could damage the fragile exterior. Usually, the coach accompanied them in a motorboat out in the Curonian Bay. Only, this time the coach did not show up. At ten thirty, a half hour later than planned, they carried the boat down to the water, waved to the boys working out on the shore, and pushed off from the pontoon.

Carefully manoeuvring between hunks of floating ice, the girls left John's Hill behind them. The distance to the bay from the River Dangė is one kilometre. After that one kilometre, the expanse of the bay opens up. Only, not the Baltic Sea. That direction was forbidden because it was the border between the Soviet Union and the West. They could not go any further than the island. The island was beside a Soviet military base, located five and a half kilometres from the mouth of the River Dangė. In this place the bay became wider, and the waves were stronger. Only the previous year those waves had swallowed up two sixteen-year-olds when their eight capsized not far from Juodkrantė. But why didn't the coach explain to the boys that the boat doesn't sink? Why didn't he explain that they must cling to the boat, as though it were a life raft, and wait for a rescue? Why did they attempt swimming to the shore? And in the dark? The two teenage boys drowned in perfect view of their friends, who could not help them. Although it was June, and the water was not that cold, they didn't make it to shore. After that accident, the coaches forbade anyone on the team from rowing out into the bay.

Another horrible and mysterious tragedy occurred in 1950. A quad and their cox never returned after a long day of training. The crew set out with a plan to row along the shoreline five kilometres to Dreverna. No one believed that they drowned. To this day people say that they didn't capsize, but that they were shot and killed by Russian border guards... Five families received a sealed zinc coffin each from the Soviet officers. The families were not allowed to open the coffins...

For these reasons, the girls were reluctant to ever venture beyond the island. They were not afraid of small waves. The wind was blowing from the west from the Curonian Spit. If they wanted to get to calmer waters, they'd need to reach the other shore. The girls headed across the bay in a diagonal and in fairly calm waters reached the island.

A trickle of water steamed into the boat through the patches that had been repaired over and over again. It was not much more water than usual. By the end of their training session, they usually acquired a few centimetres depth of water. That was nothing out of the ordinary. Once they got back, they'd flip the boat and drain the water. It usually wasn't even enough to get their shoulders wet.

The waves in the Curonian Bay were never calm. There are always waves ranging from the slightest ripple to rolling waves. This was especially true near the port. There was constant boat traffic here of all sizes, barges, motorboats.

"Just like in Khimki!" Sofija joked. "It's a good opportunity to train with waves."

The only difference was that the waves did not break from the shores like in Khimki. The cox was experienced. Just as soon as a wave approached, she'd steer the boat alongside the wave, so that it wouldn't break on the bow and the water wouldn't splash inside the boat. A wave rises and falls, and you keep on rowing. In this manner, they cut across the waves.

There are shallows a kilometre long in the middle of the bay. People called it the Hog's Back. They'd say that you'd make a mess out of your boat if you hit the Hog's Back. That shallow was slowly forming into an island.

"That's it! Stop! Turn around!" the cox called out when they were about fifty meters away from the Hog's Back.

Just as she said it, the wind picked up and the waves got bigger. The boat became unsteady, rocked by the waves hitting it from both sides. The boat began to twist and make creaking noises, as though someone were crumpling a large newspaper. The seams stretched and tore. Now water was not trickling inside through the patches, but pouring in.

"Girls! We're taking on water!" Genovaitė shouted from the bow.

"We can see that! Let's move more swiftly across the water," Sofija said in a firm and calm voice. They all listened to her command.

The waves rose. The lightweight patched up boat was tossed around like a leaf in the wind. The ice-cold water reached their foot stretchers[14] and soaked their wool socks. The breaking waves sloshed frigid water onto their knees and backs. Their fingers went numb with cold.

"Faster! Work with the water!"

"Genovaitė, take a look at how much water the boat is taking on up front?" the cox called out, her teeth chattering.

Genovaitė signalled through the round hatch: "About half my palm!"

That meant the boat was already half filled with water. They were sinking. The sides of the boat were now lower, closer to the water, and they were letting in even more water. Chunks of ice were hitting up against the boat's wooden sides.

"I don't know how to swim!" Vida screamed in panic.

"I don't either!" the terrified cox called out, clutching the rudder in terror. "What should we do?"

With every swell, more water rolled back towards the cox, then the water sloshed back towards the front. The ice-cold water sloshed around legs, taking their breath away.

"Don't panic!" Sofija commanded. "Those of you who don't know how to swim will stay in the boat and cling to the sides. The rest of us will climb out and hold on from the outside! The boat won't sink! Do you hear me? Boats don't sink! The most important thing is not to let go!"

"Vida, don't panic, you'll stay in the boat," Gaila said, seeing that her friend was pale and in a state of shock.

There wasn't much of a difference if you stayed in the boat or jumped

---

14   Wooden panels that are attached to the boat and had metal heel rests and leather straps tightened by shoelaces.

into the bay. The ice-cold water had soaked them through. Sofija, Gaila, and Genovaitė climbed over the sides and lowered themselves into the freezing water and clung to the side of the boat among hunks of ice. The boat swayed, having lost some of its weight. With their teeth chattering from cold, the girls tried to use their legs to kick and push the boat towards the shore. But it was no use. Their legs, hands, and bodies were rigid and frozen from the ice-cold water.

When Vida saw that the boat really wasn't about to sink, she began to joke around: "The captain never leaves the ship!" she called out.

At the same time, on all fours, Vida crawled from one end of the boat to the other to maintain the balance.

Meanwhile, the cox was shivering, clutching the rudder rope with one hand, and her seat with the other. Sofija, Gaila, and Genovaitė did their best to kick their legs and push the boat towards the shore, but it was to no avail. They felt as though their legs were swelling up and turning into rolls of cotton. Their wet wool sweat suits and warm jackets were taking on water and tugging them downwards.

"Calm down!" Sofija shouted through chattering teeth, trying to keep up morale. "Let's all kick at the same time, one, two, three…"

Now their seats were floating inside the boat and their oars were bumping around like spider legs. Their lips were turning blue. Icicles formed on strands of their hair.

The waves and the wind pushed the boat towards a large white wall. "Oh, where's the shoreline" they wondered.

Someone called out to them from the white wall. Then more voices joined in. The girls looked up and saw that the waves were not pushing them into a wall, but towards a large white ship. Assembled on the deck, a crew of sailors gazed down at the girls admiringly.

"Help us, please!" the cox called out. Then the others joined in, calling up to the sailors for help. They tried to wave with their frozen arms, but they had already lost feeling in their limbs.

"Help us!" they cried.

Suddenly, a siren went off. There was movement up on the deck. Commands were shouted out. Two rescue boats were lowered from the deck. They seemed to be moving in slow motion. Another siren joined the first as another, a smaller boat, sped towards them from the shore. Apparently, it received the SOS signal.

They could no longer feel the cold. They were so frozen that they probably wouldn't even feel it if someone pushed a knife into their sides.

"Save the seats," Genovaitė called out to Gaila.

"Leave them and save yourself," Gaila tried to joke, but she could barely form the words.

By the time the rescue boat reached them, the girls no longer had the strength to climb inside. The sailors grabbed onto them by their soaked jackets and hauled them onboard. Then the boat sped back to the ship. They were lucky that the rescue boat was pulled back up with a crane because they would not have been able to manage the ladder.

"Where did you beauties come from?" an older man, most likely an officer, asked in Russian.

Before they could explain, he turned to the sailors and commanded, "Get some spirits right away, and blankets! And dry clothing!"

They brought a few bottles of vodka and poured each of them half a glass. Then they poured what was left out of the bottles onto rags and began to rub the alcohol onto their bodies. The girls no longer cared that the sailors saw them naked. They didn't have the strength to rub the alcohol onto their bodies themselves. Then, the sailors dressed them in their extra sailor shirts and sweaters. As soon as they had sufficiently warmed up, they set out to return them to their hotel.

As soon as their cold and fear subsided, their cheeks grew hot. They felt dizzy and their speech slurred. They were overcome with hysterical laughter. Giggling and chortling, the five of them walked back to the hotel accompanied by the sailors. They were all dressed in the typical Soviet striped sailor shirts.

"Where did you come from?"

"From Estonia."

"Now we'll know that Estonian sailors saved our lives!"

Passers-by turned around and stared at the girls dressed in sailor shirts. And the girls waved the long arms of the shirts joyously in all directions. They forgot about the cold, the sinking boat, their fear, and their panic. It seemed as though the entire adventure hadn't happened to them. That they had watched it all in a film. They were all ravenous. All they wanted was to eat and crawl under a blanket in their hotel room beds. The girls had to run to their rooms and change their clothes and return the uniforms right away because everything was counted on their ship.

Their coach, Jonas Pavilionis, met them at the hotel door, livid with anger.

"Get out of the camp!" he shouted.

His voice trembled even more than they had been trembling from the cold. He probably thought they had drowned. Now they would have to explain to him that they'd abandoned the team boat at the Hog's Back.

The train jerked forwards after stopping at a small station. Sofija hadn't even noticed that the train had stopped. She hadn't even seen the name of the station.

"Are we in Lithuania already? Or are we still in Latvia?" she asked the young man, who had not taken his eyes off of her the entire time she was reminiscing over her adventure with the Estonian sailors.

"We are still in Latvia, but I think the next station will be in Lithuania."

Sofija opened her book and tried to read the first sentence again.

No, the coach was not angry for long. Of course, he'd been worried. He probably didn't expect to ever see us again. After all, if even one of us had drowned, he would have faced a prison sentence!

He took back his, "get out of camp" after fifteen minutes when he forgot his anger.

Once they were back in the hotel, all they wanted was to get under a hot shower, put on dry clothing, and wrap themselves up in blankets with cups of hot tea in their hands. The Estonian sailors waited patiently in the hotel lobby for them to return their clothing. They had lucked out with an unexpected pass to town. The heavy curtains on either side of the windows in the lobby were probably used only for decoration and hadn't been moved since the hotel opened. Sofija tugged on the curtain and one of the folds up on top came loose and an entire nest of squealing mice fell to the floor. It was as though that entire day was one never-ending nightmare from the moment they set out on the bay until the evening.

Women don't scream, not unless they've seen a mouse...

"Let me guess your name?" the young man said, intruding upon Sofija's private thoughts.

Sofija raised her eyes in surprise.

"Ana!"

"Why Ana?"

"Because of the letter A on your handkerchief," he said and smiled. "Letter A for Ana. Did I guess right?"

"Perhaps Ana," Sofija said and smiled, gazing at her handkerchief.

"I'm Alexander," he said, introducing himself. "And what does G stand for?"

Sofija gazed at the finely stitched letters. She ran her thumb across the white silk threads. The handkerchief was quite worn. *I need to take better care of this handkerchief. It probably means a lot to Mama.*

"Galinat," Sofija blurted out her mother's maiden name. She hadn't revealed that name to anyone before. They hadn't spoken about that name at home, and now, all of a sudden, she had blurted out the name to a complete stranger. She broke out in a hot sweat. How could she be so foolish? Then she consoled herself. *What's the difference? This is probably the first and last time I'll ever see this person again...*

"Galina?" Is that your second name?

"Yes," Sofija lied.

Good thing he didn't hear me say the surname. Then a thought came to her: *How do I know who he is? Maybe the KGB sent him here, planted him in this seat in front of me, to question me and elicit answers*

Fear washed over her. Sofija felt her cheeks burning. She lowered her head so Alexander wouldn't notice the expression on her face.

How would he have known that I am on this train? She reasoned. *They know everything. They no more than we do ourselves. There has to be one of them on our crew. Or an informer... Why did I open my mouth? Maybe they dragged Mama into the KGB basement for interrogation because of her surname? Maybe for her Prussian origins? How would they have known about my grandparents' large farm in Prussia. The farm that exported butter all over Europe. Why should they care about that? That was so long ago. They deported all those farmers to Siberia. The farm is long gone. My grandparents are long gone. I don't even know when they disappeared. The only thing left behind is a ring with the family crest on it. Did it belong to Uncle Edmund? When was the last time I saw him? When I was four? Five? I don't remember anything except for his dark hair and his incredibly handsome fur neckpiece. That was during the German occupation… When Mama brought me to a flat near the Protestant Church in Vilnius… They spoke for a long time. Now, where that church once was there's a movie theatre, The Chronicle. Mama's sister once let it slip that Uncle belonged to some underground military organization, and that the Bolsheviks were hunting for Major Edmund Galinat. She never saw him again after the war. Auntie said something about how after the war he flew to Romania and the plane crashed. Was it after that when Mama tore up Uncle Edmund's photograph with some famous marshal and tossed it into the stove? Most likely… She didn't want the KGB to find it. She cried then…"*

"My mother's name is also Galina."

"What?" Sofija asked, as though woken from a dream.

"Nothing, don't pay any attention to me," he said. "I'm probably bothering you. You seem to be daydreaming."

"No, you're not bothering me. My mind is wandering."

"Thinking about home?"

"Yes."

Home wasn't a place she enjoyed coming back to. Until the horrible neighbours finally moved out, home was a place of fear, filth, stench. When the neighbours wanted to make them leave, they cut off their electricity and they were stuck in the dark. She would have to do her homework by candlelight. When that candle was used up, they didn't have the money to buy any more.

Mama, who had earned her university degree in Berlin and spoke seven languages, was forced to work as a mail carrier. Her wages lasted them exactly two weeks. After that, they had nothing to eat. Sofija was often weak because she never had enough to eat as a child. She came down with tuberculosis. *How did Mama survive all that? How did any of us survive?* She fell into sadness. *If it hadn't been for the TB, I never would have started rowing. And I wouldn't be sitting here right now in this train, and I would not be on my way to a rendezvous with the KGB...* A lightening shock wave of anxiety wracked her stomach.

Mama sent Sofija out to the boat club to learn how to row so that she would recover from a tenacious illness. The boat club was just one bus stop away from Pervaža Street, where they lived. If she walked there, it took her ten minutes. If she ran, five. She never took the bus. She saved every kopek.

"I'm also thinking about home," Alexander said and sighed. "I have a sister. She's ill. Mama isn't working. She's taking care of my sister. After I completed the eighth grade, I had to go out and work. I really wanted to study. Then, they took me into the army."

Sofija gazed intently at Alexander.

"I also began working after eighth grade," she said. "But it wasn't so bad, I attended night school and completed my studies. Then I was accepted into the Institute. If you wish to study, you should just study. It's never too late."

"That's right... I'll try."

"Why are you going to Vilnius?"

"I have a girlfriend there. She's studying in the university," Alexander said shyly.

"It's a bit of a distance to keep up a relationship," Sofija said and smiled warmly at Alexander.

"Yes, it's far, but I'm thinking that when she graduates, I will marry her and bring her back to Tallinn. Or we could both stay in Vilnius," he continued brashly. "Ana, are you married? Sorry if my questions are offensive to you?"

"Not yet," she said and smiled slyly. *I'm already twenty-eight and I'm still waiting for my prince. My girlfriends have children in nursery school already, but I'm not married.*

"You're waiting for Prince Charming?"

Sofija laughed out loud. He seemed so childish. His eyes were as innocent as his questions. She wondered how the army hadn't broken him? Usually, when men returned from that so-called "training camp for men" they came back somehow diminished, with eyes full of sadness, depressed and suspicious. Some of them were angry and annoyed at everything. They came back like beaten down dogs.

"Do you like fairy tales?" Sofija asked.

"Or maybe princes don't only exist in fairy tales," Alexander said playfully.

"I hate to disappoint you, but princes exist only in fairy tales. In real life there are only real people. Some are good, others not." Again, she remembered where she was going and felt a tingling sensation run down the length of her body.

"But you're reading Stendhal," he said, gesturing at the book on Sofija's lap.

"Unfortunately, there is no prince in these stories either," Sofija laughed.

She opened the book and read the first sentence yet again: *Everything exquisite that Italian art can create, and the luxury of Paris and London, was created to decorate this old palace…* A chill ran down Sofija's spine. *Paris. If the KGB don't let me travel, I won't see Paris, and I'll miss the championships. It would be better to get it over with… What if the KGB don't give me permission to travel to Vichy, France? But last year I had no problems, and they let me go to the Netherlands. What's the difference between France and the Netherlands? How many of our team were yanked off because their documents were "not in order…" However, I don't think any of them were called in for a chat with the KGB? At least, as far as I've heard. They just weren't allowed to travel and that was that. In 1962 they wouldn't allow Celestinas Jucys and Povilas Liutkaitis to travel. And, I believe, Alfonsas Mikšys. They were told their documents were not in order and that was that. And then, there was Janina, another persona non grata… Foreign travel was banned for her. Gita Strigaitė lost her place in the eight in 1964. And she was already a European Champion. Gita never hid that she had been deported to Siberia, but everyone still thought she had a chance to race abroad. She cried so hard when she found out she couldn't. It broke your heart to see her cry like that. They let her out to Grünau, but only because it was in the DDR. They wouldn't allow her to travel to the West.*

The train clanged to a halt in the middle of nowhere.

"Half an hour," the train attendant growled in Russian in a rough voice.

"What happened?" Alexander asked, surprised.

"It's nothing. They always stop here. Another train needs to pass. It's probably running late," the man sitting across the aisle said.

"Let's go outside," Alexander said, standing and motioning for Sofija to follow him.

"I think I'd rather stay here and read," she said and opened her book.

Her eyes returned to the first sentence. Soon, though, her eyes wandered off the page and gazed out the window at the verdant fields, lush after a summer rain. In the distance, behind a wire fence, the collective farm cows grazed peacefully.

I wish I could simply run around in the fields, like I did when I was a child. Then, everything seemed so beautiful. Every day was so pretty... Mama would take me to the large two-storey house beside the Church of Saint Peter and Paul. From the hill I could see the River Neris. It was such a bright house. She would talk for a long time with an older woman, and I would watch two cows grazing, and then I'd go and play with the birds she kept as pets. Who was that woman? Was she my grandmother? Or an aunt? Why don't I know anything? Why didn't I ever think to ask Mama? I still didn't understand that she was doing everything in her power to hide all her troubles from me, all our poverty, so I wouldn't feel it, so I would be happy. Even when the Russians came and dragged her off to the KGB.

A chill ran down her spine.

Sofija pressed her cheek against the window and tried to soothe her anxiety. She watched through the window how the passengers climbed down the metal stairs onto the platform. Passengers stretched and shook out their legs. Mothers with small children leapt over the drainage ditch and led them towards to closest bushes. Men lit cigarettes. The train stewardesses glanced at their watches. *They are all so lucky! They don't have to go talk to the KGB. Oh, if only they knew! They probably are contemplating all their small worries. Oh, how I'd like to be in their place. I would! What would happen if I simply didn't go tomorrow? Would they not let me out? Probably. Oh God. I cannot not go. The team would fall apart. It's no game with them. Nothing to it. I'll pull myself together and I'll go.* Sofija took a deep breath and sought strength within herself. But her body was once again wracked with fear. She felt the same way she did before the start of a race. *However, at the start of a race at least she knew what to expect. I know that it will hurt. That it will hurt physically. And here? What will happen to her here?*

Suddenly, something moved on her open book. Sofija jumped. There was a toad on her book. Alexander stood beside her smiling.

"What's this?" she asked, surprised, looking up at him.

"A toad," he said and laughed.

"Why did you do that?"

"Do you know the fairy tale about the frog queen?"

"So, you brought me a prince?" Sofija asked, surprised. She started to giggle. "And now I suppose you expect me to kiss it?"

Alexander frowned. Suddenly, he felt that his joke was too boyish for an older woman.

"It's an adorable toad... I'm sorry. I was just trying to cheer you up. You seem very worried about something," he stammered.

"We ought to let him go. He's probably searching for his mama. Open the window." Sofija took the cold little toad into the palms of her hands and gentle released it out the window to the fields. "I think my little prince needs to grow up a bit."

The stewardesses began waving at the passengers to return to the train. Mothers with their small children leapt from the bushes. Men ground out their cigarette stubs with their heels. The train clanked and moved forwards.

I want to get home as fast as possible. The faster I finish this the better. The old days when they kept you in the basement for weeks on end, like they did to Mama, are over. There are some who'd rather like to see me drop out of the race. But why would they go to such lengths? I refuse to believe that. What will I tell Mama? How can I tell her and not upset her?

"Ana," Alexander interrupted her reverie again. He'd probably been calling out to her for a while because he was leaning in towards her.

Sofija stared at him.

"Don't be angry at me over that toad. It was stupid of me."

"I'm not angry. The toad is home again," Sofija said and smiled warmly.

"Do you know what? I still like to watch cartoons. Especially stories. There's a lot of wisdom in those stories."

"I agree. There are some lovely cartoons. But when I was growing up, there was no television, so I never saw any."

"I didn't see them when I was a child either. I only saw them in the movie theatre. That's probably why I remember them so well. Going to the cinema was a real treat!"

"I've seen cartoons in the theatre as well. We only bought a television at home last year."

"My parents bought a television when we still lived in Leningrad."

"Why did you move to Estonia?"

"My father is an officer in the military."

"Oh, I see, you live a mobile life."

"When I was growing up, I'd barely get used to a new school, to my classmates, and we'd have to move again. Did you live in Lithuania your entire life?"

"Yes, my entire life," Sofija said, not mentioning that she was born in Warsaw and was brought to Lithuania when she was a one-year-old. Why did he need to know anyway? She couldn't remember a thing from those times. Nothing at all. She only remembers that one day she no longer understood what people around her were saying. The most frightening part was when she could not understand what Mama was saying to another woman on the street. When she was small, she did not yet understand that not everyone spoke Polish like her and her mother. She did not know there were other languages, and that people could speak in another language and understand each other. Sofija smiled to herself as she remembered her childish ignorance.

"I'd like to settle in one place and not move around anymore," Alexander said.

"Where would you like to live most?"

"Perhaps in Leningrad?"

"Why Leningrad?"

"Leningrad is like a history book. There is so much culture and history in Leningrad!"

"That's true."

"It's a beautiful city. I love the white nights. They are so romantic... Have you ever been to Leningrad?"

"I have. Many times."

When was my first time? Maybe in 1960? Of course, most of the time we were in Kavgolovo, 15 kilometres beyond Leningrad. In the forest there is the Hepojarvi lake –the realm of rowers. How many races they had in that lake! Oh, how much rowing fun! In the winter, the skiers trained in the Kavgolovo. There is an artificial snow trampoline there. It can be used in the winter and in summer. Beside the lake there is a stadium. That's where the opening parades took place and were the medals were given out at the end of the championships. It was only ten minutes from the boathouse to the train station. And from there, it was only a twenty-minute train ride to Leningrad. After championships they always took a day to sightsee in the city.

"Did you like it?"

"It's a beautiful city. Especially Petrodvorets."

"Of course. The fountains. The gardens. Everything shimmering in gold... I love to go there for walks."

"The ice-cream is delicious in Leningrad," Sofija added.

"Do you like ice-cream?" Alexander asked eagerly.

"Who doesn't like ice-cream?" Sofija said and laughed.

Sofija remembered the ice-cream cart again. *What a shame we lost them. We could have won the European Rowing Championship in our quad. A Lithuanian quad. We were equal, if not faster than the others. But they won Europe... We also could have won. I have nothing against those Russian girls personally, but it was not fair. I hated them then!*

"Ana, may I ask you something?"

"About what?"

"You won't be insulted?"

"I don't know," Sofija said, "I'll try not to be insulted."

"Promise not to be insulted."

"How can I promise if I don't know what the question is yet?"

"Well..."

"Okay, I'll do my best not to be insulted."

"Where do you work?"

"Are people insulted by those sorts of questions?"

"I don't know... But..."

"Why are you so doubtful?"

"It's probably not very polite of me, but I noticed your hands... They're... Sort of..."

"Manly," Sofija said and squeezed her hands into fists.

"Well... Yes... I was wondering what sort of work a girl would do to get hands full of blisters like that."

Sofija opened her palms, glanced at her assortment of blisters, clapped her hands together, clasped her fingers, pressed her chin into her hands, smiled, and said: "Guess!"

"I can't imagine... I had hands like that after digging ditches in the army for three days."

"You think I work with a shovel?"

"Perhaps."

"Cold," Sofija laughed.

"You rake grass?"

"Cold."

"Your face is tanned. You obviously work outdoors."

"Outdoors..." Sofija revealed a hint.

"You're a brick layer."

"Oh, that's a good one!"

"I don't know. You don't seem like the type of girl who would be out sweeping the streets."

"Is it such a bad thing to sweep the streets?"

"No, not bad... But usually that's a job for pensioners."

"Why do you think so?"

"I've never seen a young person out sweeping the streets."

"I'm not a street sweeper," Sofija said and smiled.

"Then where do you work? Tell me?"

"I work as a courier in the energetics system," Sofija said. She was beginning to have fun deceiving this naïve young man.

"What do couriers carry?"

"Letters, correspondence."

The young man was perplexed.

"Something's not right with that. You must be doing something else after work."

"Or perhaps instead of work?" Sofija hinted.

"I give up," Alexander said, raising his hands in frustration.

"I'm a rower," Sofija said and grinned. She studied the reaction on the young man's face. His eyes widened. His lower lip quivered. He leaned in towards her."

"You? A rower?"

"Yes, and?"

"I thought that rowers are much taller and…"

"Heavier?"

"That's right."

"There's all sorts."

"Why did you choose such a difficult sport?"

"There's no such thing as an easy sport, Alexander. Anywhere there is competition between people, it's hard."

"But rowing is a man's sport! Maybe you ought to try gymnastics? How did you ever get into rowing?"

"Mama chose it for me."

"Why? Was she a rower?"

"No, my mother never did any sports."

"So, why did she decide that for you?"

"I was often sick when I was a child, so my mother decided that an outdoor sport would make me stronger."

"But there are easier outdoor sports, like track and field or skiing…"

"There was a boathouse near our home. I didn't even consider that it was a manly sport. There were always plenty of girls at the boathouse."

"How many seats are there in your canoe?"

"We don't row in a canoe. Our sport is called rowing."

"How is it different?"

"You row forwards in a canoe and backwards in rowing."

"What do you mean backwards?"

"Just like you row backwards in a simple fishing boat. Have you ever rowed?"

"Oh, yes, of course, but how do you see where you are going?"

"We turn around and look," Sofija said and smiled. "If the boat is a quad or an eight, we have cox. She sits facing front and keeps an eye on our direction and navigates by pulling a rope."

"But doesn't she row?"

"No, she navigates and shouts commands."

"So, you need to drag extra weight along."

"Yes, we do, that's why she ought to be lightweight."

"You don't give her anything to eat?" Alexander said and chortled.

"That's right." Sofija laughed at the joke.

"Interesting. So how many places are there in your boat?"

"I'm in a quad now, but before I was in a single or a double."

"What do you mean by a double?"

"There are two types of boats. There are sculling boats, where everyone has two oars, and sweep oar boats, where everyone has a single oar – on the right or on the left. The double is a sculling boat, like a single and a quadruple scull. And sweep oar boats are a pair, a four and an eight."

"Which one is easier to row?" Alexander asked.

"I don't know. I think it's probably about the same. Right from the beginning I rowed in a sculling boat with two oars, so it's hard for me to judge."

"Have you been rowing for a long time?"

"Twelve years."

"Twelve years?" Alexander seemed shocked.

"Yes, twelve years already," Sofija said, surprised herself.

"That's a long time! Where do you row? In a river?"

"In Vilnius in the river. But in the summer, we go to rowing camp on the lake in Trakai. The lakes are calm there. Just as soon as the ice melts, we head out to Trakai."

"I've not been to Trakai, but I saw photographs in a book. There's a castle on an island there?"

"Yes, a castle."

"And old castle?"

"It was built five hundred years ago."

"I'd like to see it…"

"It was crumbling into the ground, but they've been rebuilding it."

"So, you row in that lake?"

"Yes, in that lake. Near the castle, around the castle."

"It must be so beautiful!"

"You ought to go there with your girlfriend and see it for yourself."

"I'd like that."

"You can take a bus there from Vilnius. It's only an hour away."

"We will. What were you doing in Jelgava?"

"I was rowing. What else? We have a camp there."

"So why are you Lithuanians rowing in Jelgava if you have the lake in Trakai?"

"There's not just Lithuanians in Jelgava. It's a national team training camp."

"What national team?"

"The Soviet national team."

"So, you're on the Soviet team?"

"That's right."

"Wow! Are you training for a competition?"

"Yes."

"Which competition?"

Sofija did not want to brag about her accomplishments, but she was so deep into the conversation that there was no way out.

"The European Rowing Championship is next week."

"What? I can hardly believe it! I'm speaking with a person who is about to compete in the European Rowing Championship!"

Sofija felt uncomfortable. She glanced around to make sure no one was listening.

"Where is the championship held?"

"France," Sofija answered reluctantly.

What if I'm not going anywhere? Why can't the team managers help me out? How serious could this problem be that I must go and see the KGB? What did I do? I haven't opened my mouth anywhere. I've never told a single political joke. In 1961 in Kiev, they could have arrested us all, but they didn't.

In September 1961, the Soviet Championship took place in Kiev. It turned out to be a success for Lithuania. For the first time, the men's eight from Lithuania was competing for the gold medal.

"Žal-gi-ris!"

"Ry-cha! Ry-cha!"

Not even feeling how their legs were soaking in the water, on the rickety pontoon, the Lithuanians shouted themselves hoarse in support of their national team.

"Rycha, go!"

"Rycha, go!"

Then, someone seated behind their backs shouted, "Rycha, the Reds are dead!"

Nobody turned around. They all felt the satisfaction of that moment of resistance, when someone shouted out what they are all thinking – the Reds are dead! They were proud of their team out there in green uniforms with the words, LITHUANIA blazoned across their chests. Maybe it wasn't even one of their own who said it. Maybe it was a local Ukrainian, who had slipped in among them. Obviously, whoever it was, they were all proud of their courage.

Žal-gi-ris!

The pontoon swayed, pulsating with their joyous shouts. More than thirty Lithuanian national rowing team members and their coaches were caught up in the euphoria. With all their hearts, all their will, they pushed on their men's eight towards the finish line.

"Reds are dead!" one of the girls shouted and began to giggle, covering her mouth with her palm, so that no one would see she had repeated those words. Her words melted into the hurrahs of the crowd, with people jumping up and hugging each other, experiencing the immense pleasure of solidarity. Nobody could hear the commentator shouting through the megaphone. The Russian voices dimmed. Just a moment ago they'd been trying to outshout the Lithuanians.

"Žal-gi-ris! Žal-gi-ris! Žal-gi-ris!" they all chanted their winning team's name. The Lithuanian rowers no longer felt how they were soaked to their knees by the cool Dnieper River water in the bay. They felt as though together with the men in the eight all of Lithuania had experienced victory. *For Lithuania!*

"Reds are dead!" Sofija's teammates giggled as they waited for their team to return from the finish line and glide past them. The new Soviet champions did not seem tired at all. They were waving with both arms, turning towards the shore, scanning the shoreline for their friends, laughing and enjoying the moment. Of course, they were discussing all the details of the race. That's always what happens after the victorious race. It's as though everyone has an abundance of energy. All the physical effort of the race evaporates in an instant. But if you lose, then the opposite happens. No one has any energy, only agony, and a lingering sense of hopelessness.

"Lithuania!" they shouted. Their hands burned from clapping. Some team members climbed off the bridge and waded into the water to grab onto an oar and touch it, and in this manner, touch the champion himself.

Nobody even worried for an instant that the KGB could show up out of nowhere and for that "Reds are dead" throw them out of the university or out of work. Nothing happened. The coaches didn't even breathe a word about it.

"Wow! You're going to France!" Alexander could not get over the news. "Paris! I've read about Paris! Oh, I wish I could go too!"

"The competition is not taking place in Paris, but we will fly into Paris."

"Where then?"

"Vichy. Three hundred kilometres from Paris."

"I'm so jealous. Is that going to be your first time abroad?"

"No, not exactly."

"When were you abroad?"

"Last year I rowed in the European Rowing Championship. This year I was in the regatta in the DDR."

"Really? You were in the European Rowing Championship? Where?"

"Amsterdam, the Netherlands."

"Really. Is it a nice country?"

"Very nice."

"And how did you do?"

"We came in second."

"Wow! Do you have a silver medal from the European Rowing Championship?"

Sofija shrugged. "I do," she said modestly.

Some would consider that the height of success, but for our team's coaches it was a failure.

"Are you the only one from the Lithuanian team?"

"Oh no, there are eleven girls."

"Eleven Lithuanians?"

"I suppose so."

"So how many are on the team in total."

"There's a single, a double, two quads with a cox and an eight. How much is that? Twenty-two, not counting reserves."

"Wow! And half of them are Lithuanians!"

"All the women in the eight are Lithuanians. The single is a Lithuanian. And on the men's team, now, wait, four, five, no I think four Lithuanians."

"Well! Who would have thought! I don't know much about rowing."

"Most people don't know much about rowing."

"I'll have to read the papers now."

"If you read the papers, don't look for the name, Ana. My real name is Sofija," she admitted, giving up on the fake name.

"So, that's it! You're not Ana!"

"No, my mother's name is Alexandra, that's why there's a letter A on my handkerchief."

"Alexandra! Just like me! What a coincidence!"

Sofija laughed.

"And Galina?"

"You heard wrong. G is for Grucova." She was careful not to repeat her mother's maiden name.

Suddenly, she realized that this naïve young man had gotten her to reveal much more about herself than she had planned. *Oh, so how does the KGB operate if this young man managed to get so much information out of me?*

CHAPTER FOUR

AUGUST 22, 1967, VILNIUS

It was only six in the morning, but the lump in Sofija's throat would not let her sleep. She had hardly slept all night. Every hour she woke up, shivering as though a cold wind had blown through her. She could not stop thinking about the fated meeting. By morning, she was trembling. Her eyes were heavy from exhaustion, but her heart was pounding out of control.

Sofija pulled open the curtains and gazed across the street at the M. K. Čiurlionis National School for the Arts. On T. Kosciuška Street the first trolleybuses were already rolling down the street. On the trees the summer leaves were fluttering in the gentle breeze.

Mama is awake. She must be in the kitchen preparing breakfast or reading a book with a cup of tea in her hand. She always gets up very early.

Sofija lacked the courage to tell her mother yesterday why she'd come home to Vilnius. She lied. She told Mama she was missing a medical form.

Why should I worry her? If I need to, I'll tell her later. I'm an adult. I'll take care of myself. Mama also had to take care of everything herself, with nobody's help, and while caring for me. And that was during the war. She was constantly terrorized by the KGB. What's the worst that could happen? They can't shoot me? Put me in jail? What for? No, they won't jail me... If they had wanted to arrest me, they would have come themselves and arrested me. They wouldn't have invited me to their headquarters. What if they don't give me permission to travel abroad? It would be terrible, but not the end of the world. There's nothing else they could take away from me.

Autumn was approaching. The morning was cloudy. The thermometer showed 9 degrees Celsius. The weather report predicted it would be 16 degrees by midday. Only three days ago it was 28 degrees outside.

It'll take me fifteen minutes to reach Lenin Square on the number three trolleybus. I'll leave at 8:30 and I'll have plenty of time. Maybe I should walk?

Sofija glanced at the dark sky. *Maybe it won't rain? It's probably better to walk than to stand crammed between four walls. I miss the walk along the Neris. I'll walk past the boathouse. There won't be anyone there yet so early in the morning, not unless the Boatman is there already. Finally, I can get on the trolleybus at the boathouse and ride the last three stops. It's not cold outside. I'll wear my raincoat.* She glanced at her coatrack and smiled. *If it weren't for the men in the eight, we rowers wouldn't be that fashionable with our English raincoats.*

They didn't tell everyone that story, but nonetheless, it got around. It was about three years ago, in 1964, when the *Žalgiris* men's eight team travelled to the England to the Henley Royal Regatta. As always, they were only given a small amount of money, maybe twenty pounds, or maybe less. Also, the team managers would give them that small amount of foreign currency only after the race ended. What could anyone buy for that beggarly amount of money? Lemonade and chocolate? Forget about buying clothing or shoes. However, as always, the rowers filled half their suitcases with caviar and vodka. After they sold it, they'd have enough money to buy new clothing and gifts to bring home.

Imagine an ancient and lovely English town. In this town the regatta has taken place since 1839, and the oldest rowing club in the country was founded. Ladies and gentlemen would come to the races dressed as though they were attending a royal wedding, wearing hats, club blazers, elegant dresses. The elite from the entire country met there to watch the best rowers from the entire world. On the final day of the regatta, service was held in the church. On both sides of the street cosy cafes served delicious coffee and the scent of fresh rolls filled the air. Through the restaurant windows you saw respectable waiters serving ladies who lifted their champagne glasses with elegant hands. The doormen bowed as they welcomed you inside.

And through those same doors walk young, handsome, strong, men with darting frightened eyes. Men who barely speak English. They show their tins of caviar to the doorman and the men behind the bar.

"No thank you. We are not interested. No, sorry," they answer politely.

Of course, they were polite, but shocked at this black-market proposal.

One door after another, shuts in their faces. There was no time to even think about the race. They had to sell off the goods they had brought with them. Speaking with the English felt like talking to a wall. They were all proud and very polite. They were beginning to think they would have no choice but to eat all the caviar themselves. Oh, there were so many temptations in the shop windows! They had no money to buy anything. It felt humiliating to be so poor.

The first race ended in victory. That meant they would race the next day. That meant they had half a day to try to sell their caviar and vodka. The men visited every small street, every café, bar, and restaurant in town.

Everywhere they were met with the same response, "No, thank you."

Hope came on the second day of the race when after the second record-breaking win they heard some people behind them speaking Lithuanian, though with an accent. "They must be émigrés," the men agreed. Although the KGB sternly warned them against fraternizing with any of the Lithuanian war refugees or their children who had settled in England, they approached their smiling countrymen with barely contained joy. They started a conversation. They discussed the weather and the race. It was taboo for them to tell the exiled Lithuanians anything about their home country. They had no choice. They had to either ask for their help or ask them to mediate with the English to sell off their caviar and vodka. They didn't need to say a word about Lithuania. Their need to sell off these contraband items made clear the position they were in.

"Here in England no one will take anything from you. It's illegal. The English obey their laws. I'll see what I can do to help you. I know a few people," a middle-aged Lithuanian émigré said to them.

The next morning, he knocked on their hotel room door carrying a large box stuffed with bologna.

"This is all I could get in exchange for your goods," the man explained.

The *Žalgiris* men's eight won the Grand Challenge Cup. The semifinal time made it onto the record board. Everyone called the winners, "the incredible Russians," because their uniforms and oars were blood red and bore the letters CCCP, the Union of Soviet Socialist Republics in the Cyrillic alphabet. It was much easier for the commentators to pronounce the word, "Russians" than to read the name the team was entered under, the name of their club, "Zhalghiris, Viljnjus."

Black raincoats were all that they brought back from the incredible Henley Royal Regatta. The rowers back home considered the black raincoats the height of fashion and everyone wanted to buy one. They sold them all and earned back the money they had spent on the caviar and vodka and even had a little profit left over. There weren't enough raincoats for everyone. Those who didn't get one were jealous of those who did.

Sofija took a step back from the window, scooped up her clothing and her black Henley Royal Regatta raincoat, and tiptoed into the bathroom. Ever since she was a child, she had learned to walk as though she were treading on air, so that the floorboards wouldn't creak, the curtains wouldn't rustle, and the stairs wouldn't squeak. The fear of the neighbours hearing her was ingrained into her ever since those years when they lived together with the horrible Golosovs in one flat. To this day, she would only open the faucet just barely so that the dripping water in the shower would not make too much noise. If the Golosovs heard the water running, they'd shout that she and Mama has not right to waste the water to bathe themselves. For this reason, they lived with two buckets in their room. One bucket was filled with water for washing, and the other was used as a toilet. If they tried to use the toilet when the Golosovs were home, it could lead to a beating or shouts and curses.

"Oh, just look at me!" Sofija said to herself as she gazed at her face in the small mirror in the bathroom. She had dark rings under her eyes and her cheeks were pale. The anxiety and sleeplessness of one night had added ten years to her life. She turned on the cold water tap and doused her face with the icy water. Her skin tingled. She splashed more and more water onto her face. She looked in the mirror again. Her cheeks were red from cold, but livelier. The dark circles under her eyes had receded.

Everything will be fine. Everything will be fine. Everything will be fine. Everything will be fine... She repeated these words to herself in her thoughts while trying to swallow the lump in her throat.

Oh, maybe I should tell Mama? She thought, then, *No, I can't. It's almost done. Not much time is left. How terrible. I'm a knot of fear. I'm afraid of everything. I'm so scared.*

CHAPTER FIVE

AUGUST 22, 1967, THE KGB

People hurried across Lenin Square from all directions. It was rush hour in Vilnius and the city dwellers were eager to get to work. In the centre of the square stood Lenin on his red granite pedestal. As people strode past the monument, they picked up red dust from the gravel spread around the statue. They carried this red dust on the soles of their shoes onto the boulevard, leaving behind them a long trail of red footprints. With their heads tucked inside their jacket collars and hunched under their umbrellas they hurried to get out of the cold rain that had suddenly bore down on them.

Lenin's right arm is pointing straight towards the KGB headquarters, Sofija thought bitterly to herself. *Why did I only notice that now? Although, the Conservatory students might think he was pointing the way to their next class.* The two grandiose buildings stood just a few metres away from each other, but they evoked completely opposite associations – beauty and horror, creativity and destruction, fantasy and fear, fun and suffering.

Sofija killed time. She had ten minutes until her appointment, but she did not want to spend them inside that massive grey building. *What if I may never leave? What if they lock me up in the basement?* She strode past the right corner of the building and snuck a look at the barred basement windows. She had often heard talk about how people were held prisoner in that basement and were tortured there. They were arrested for anti-Soviet activities, for having a Lithuanian tricolour flag, for telling a political joke, or just because someone registered a complaint against them for nothing at all.

This is where they held Mama. Right in the centre of Vilnius. Happy pedestrians walk past this building all day long. Meanwhile, inside, someone is being tortured. Some might even die. And if they do die, their loved ones will never know where they disappeared to. How awful... Sofija trembled. *How could Mama stand it? She never talked about it. I'm an adult. She no longer has to worry that I'll blab in the wrong place. She doesn't have to hide anything from me anymore. I'm going to ask Mama to tell me what happened to her. My mind is made up. At least now I can be a comfort to her... Mama is sixty-eight years old. What has she experienced in life? From the very day I was born she has experienced nothing other than poverty, humiliation, fear, and injustice. All because I was born just when the war began. All because my father, who was an architect, was in the military reserves. Just because with me in her arms she ran to Vilnius, so that she could be closer to Father and rescue him from Soviet captivity. She should have stayed in Warsaw and not gone anywhere. She should have stayed in her spacious flat in the centre of Warsaw. The Germans didn't even bomb her building because it stood beside the water tank that served the city. We could have been living there now, just the two of us.... Her entire family is there – my father's sisters and brothers and their families. Mama must wish she could go home and be with her family again. Only, where are they? Some of them fled to England. Who knows where the others went? I don't know anything about Mama's relatives! Where are they now? Why is Mama silent about them? Why doesn't she tell me anything? Where did her parents disappear to? Where did my grandparents go? Where is Uncle Edmund? I do not have a single memory of seeing Mama happy. She must have known how to laugh and be happy once upon a time?*

Sofija glanced at her wristwatch. *That's it. Time to go inside.* She turned around but could barely tear her eyes away from the barred basement windows. She took three deep breaths and walked back towards Lenin Boulevard.

The doors to the KGB Headquarters were massive and heavy, as though they were designed that way so that they would slam shut behind you and you could never get out again.

Sofija leaned her entire body into the dark wood of the doors, but at the same time someone exiting yanked the doors open from the inside and she just about stumbled inside the cold depressing hallway. The police officer stationed beside the reception window immediately noticed that a young woman had entered their dreary hall.

"Who are you going to see?" he asked in Russian.

Sofija's eyes wandered from the Soviet militia[15] to the receptionist and back. The receptionist lifted his head and repeated the militia's question.

"Who are you going to see?"

"I don't really know. They told me to come here today at this time."

"Surname?"

"Grucova."

"Name?"

"Sofija."

The receptionist ran his pencil down the list of surnames on the register and paused at the fifth or sixth line.

"Room Fifteen. Sign here," he said, ticking off where she should sign and turning the register around to face her.

---

15   In the Soviet Union law and order was maintained not by policemen, but by militia.

Sofija felt how her hands were frozen with fear. With shaking hands, she tried to sign her name, but the shaky marks she managed to make did not resemble her name.

"Climb the stairs to the second-floor hallway and wait until they call you in."

Sofija nodded and turned towards the grey granite steps. Her feet would not obey her. She felt the way she did before the start of a race, when it was time to climb into the boat and row to the warm-ups. She took two deep breaths and climbed the stairs. She reached a narrow hallway with arched ceilings. *How many people like me entered this hallway? How many like me never exited again?*

She walked along the red carpet that extended along the length of the hallway and found the door marked with the number fifteen. *Here... Here everything will soon be clear to me. How many poor people like me stood here and waiting to learn their fate? How many of them stayed here?* The corridor was empty. The sun poked through the window at the end. *So, it has stopped raining. That's a good sign. Soon my teammates will be heading to their training session for the day. Without me. Who will take my place?* She felt her throat constrict. *And what if they travel to France without me? Oh, why did this happen to me? What did I do wrong?* She felt as though she were choking, gasping for air. *I cannot remember a single time when I opened my mouth at the wrong time or said the wrong thing. Oh, and what if they keep me here and shove me into the basement?* Sofija was gripped with an even greater fear of ending up in prison... Of never seeing the sky through the window again... Of never seeing Mama again...

She heard a door hinge creak. A few meters away a door opened. *Not my turn yet...* A stern woman in uniform with an enormous blond bob and wearing thick black glasses emerged into the corridor. A few brown folders were tucked under her elbow. She scanned Sofija up and down, then strode past her, and disappeared inside another room. Sofija breathed in deeply. *Hurry... hurry... Hurry up and let's get this over with. This feels like that awful sensation before an exam. If it were up to me, I'd be the first in line to answer questions just to get this over with...*

She heard the sound of boots clicking down the hall. The sound became stronger as it came closer. A tall well-built man in civilian clothing appeared her where she stood, outside of Room Fifteen. He looked Sofija up and down.

"Grucova?" he asked.

"Yes," she croaked. Her mouth was completely dry.

"Good day," the man said in an overly polite tone and extended his right hand to shake hers. "Please come in," he said and opened the door gallantly.

Sofija entered the room first and he came in behind her and closed the door. He directed her to a chair in front of the desk and himself sat down behind it. On the meticulously tidy table there was only a bottle of ink, a carafe with water and a glass, a table clock, and one thin brown cardboard folder. A portrait of Lenin hung on the wall behind him. Just like everywhere else – Lenin's portrait hung in every university classroom, director's office, school classroom, kindergarten, athletics hall, and in every factory. Through the window, Sofija saw the statue of Lenin in the centre of the square with four red paths running towards it and criss-crossing in the centre. However, her eyes focused on the roof and two towers of the Church of St. Philip and St. Jacob just behind Lenin Square. *Wimię Ojca i Syna, i Ducha Świętego... Amen*, she prayed in her thoughts in Polish and made the sign of the cross in her mind. Mama had told her that after the war, in 1948, the Russians closed that church and turned it into a storage warehouse for fruits and vegetables. Now, the church was used as a storage space for costumes and props from the opera and ballet theatre. Nonetheless, people still made the sign of the cross when they passed the church.

The KGB agent sat calmly behind the desk with his fingers intertwined. "My surname is Minkevičius," he said finally.

Sofija nodded but said nothing.

"You are Grucova, Sofija," he said and grinned. Sofija saw that his teeth were stained yellow from cigarettes.

"Yes."

The KGB agent unclasped the folder and peeked inside, but so that Sofija could not see the contents of the folder.

"Where were you born, Comrade Grucova?"

I wonder why he is speaking in such a sweet voice? Sofija thought.

"In Warsaw, Poland."

"How long have you been living in the Soviet Union?"

"Since 1940."

"You live in Vilnius?"

"Yes."

Why is he asking me that? My domicile registration is stamped in my passport.

"What is your address?"

"Pervaža Street 14."

"Have you lived there a long time?"

"Yes, for a long time. Since 1945."

"Who do you live with?"

"My mother. It's just the two of us."

"Do you have relatives in Vilnius?"

"No, we do not."

"I see," the KGB agent said, although he must know everything about her already. "Would you like some tea?"

"No, thank you," Sofija said and shook her head, although her mouth was as dry as it usually was in the middle of a long-distance race.

"Do you have relatives abroad?"

"Yes, we do. We have family in Warsaw."

"Who lives in Warsaw."

"My aunts, uncles, and cousins."

"Do you keep in contact with them?"

"We write occasionally."

"Have you been to the West?"

"Yes, I have."

"Where?"

"I was in Warsaw in 1961. I was in Amsterdam last year, in 1966. This year I was in Grünau, the DDR."

"As far as I know, you are an athlete?

"Yes, a rower."

"Are you preparing to go abroad again?"

"Yes, to race."

"What race?"

"The European Rowing Championship."

It can't be that he doesn't know all this. Why is he asking me?

"Vichy, France," Sofija added in a trembling voice.

My voice had to betray to this KGB agent how frightened I am.

"How long do you plan to be abroad?"

"A week I believe."

He probably wants to get me to agree to inform on my teammates. No, no, no. I won't do it! But if I don't agree, they won't let me out. No, I refuse to spy on my friends and report to them! No no...

"Are you planning on bringing home a medal?" the KGB agent asked in a falsely sweet voice.

"We are planning on it, but we can't make any promises."

"Then, I'll hope for the best – that you come home with a medal!"

Sofija shrugged.

"Thank you," she whispered.

Suddenly, the KGB agent rose from his chair and stood towering over her, staring down at her.

"Comrade Sofija, I'd like to ask you something..."

Sofija looked up questioningly at him. He now looked so tall, towering over her, so tall and almighty. Fear wracked her body. Her heart raced.

"Where is your father, Comrade Sofija?"

The question surprised her so much that she leaned back suddenly in her chair, making it creak. Her handbag slid off of her lap, spilling its contents onto the floor. Sofija bent down and began scooping up her belongings. She felt heat rising to her face.

"I'm sorry..."

"Did you hear my question?" the KGB agent said. Then he slid back into his chair and waited for Sofija to regain her voice. "What can you tell me about your father?"

"I don't have a father. I never had one."

"All people have fathers, Comrade Grucova. Without the help of a father, a child cannot be conceived."

The agent snickered at his own clever comment.

"I don't know anything. I grew up without a father." She shook her head. Her face was burning. She broke out in cold sweats.

"What do you know about your father?"

"Nothing. He disappeared at the beginning of the war. I was a baby then."

"Under what circumstances did he disappear?"

"I don't know anything except that he was an architect."

"That's all. Just an architect."

"And he was an officer, a captain, in the reserves, mobilized before the war."

"An officer of which army?"

"Poland's."

"When was he mobilized."

"I don't know."

"Did you see him when the war ended?"

"No, I did not see him after the war. In fact, I've never seen him…"

"What do you mean you've never seen him?"

"I wasn't even a year old when he left for the army. I don't remember him at all."

"What does your mother know?"

"I don't know. She knows as much as I do." Sofija did not want to drag her mother into this. As it was, back then she hardly left this building.

"Can you tell me where your father is now?"

Sofija's eyes widened at the unexpected question.

"I don't know anything. I've never seen him, and I haven't heard anything about him."

"Do any of your relatives know where your father could be?"

"No, no one has told me anything. We don't keep in contact with our relatives."

"Do you really not keep in contact, Comrade Grucova?"

"We have very little contact, and only through letters," Sofija knew that it would not be possible to hide her correspondence with her Polish relatives. The KGB censored all letters sent abroad and read all letters that were sent to the Soviet Union from abroad.

"Do your relatives write in their letters about where your father stays?"

Oh my God... What is he talking about? Where he stays?

"No."

"And your mother hasn't told you anything?"

"She said that he was an officer, and that he probably died in the war."

"Have you ever tried to search for your father?"

"We tried. But we didn't find out anything."

"How did you try?"

"Mama tried looking for him through the Red Cross. But all the answered she received said, "No such person," Sofija admitted. Only, she didn't say that all the answers came from Moscow and that the Red Cross probably never received their letters.

"Have you received any information about where your father is staying?"

"No," she no longer knew what to say. The questions were confusing her. She hardly had time to answer one before she was hit with another. "My mother said that my father was no longer..."

"No longer what?" the KGB agent asked, twisting his head around to gaze into Sofija's eyes, smiling a fake smile.

"No longer alive," Sofija said in a trembling voice. "But she didn't need to tell me."

"Why."

"Because he was never in our lives anyway."

"I'd like to warn you that hiding the truth about your relatives can have a negative effect on your athletic career."

"I'm not hiding anything."

"Comrade Grucova," the KGB agent said snidely while slowly pulling open his drawer and pulling out an envelope, "I have something to tell you."

He placed an envelope on the table in front of her. On the long white envelope Sofija saw three postage stamps with red maple leaves on them.

"How could you know nothing if this letter is addressed to your home?"

"No such letter arrived at our home address. That is, we never received that letter," Sofija shot back. As soon as the words left her mouth, she was frightened by her own daring. It was an open secret that the KGB confiscates and checks all letters that arrive from abroad. By stating the obvious out loud she risked enraging the KGB.

And he was engulfed in rage. He snatched up the letter and waved it in front of Sofija's eyes. "You want to tell me that you don't know that your father lives in Canada?" the KGB agent roared in her face.

Sofija was drenched in sweat. Her ears began to ring. The sound of her banging heart drowned out all other noise. Her hands began to shake and she couldn't utter a single word. The news was so shocking that for a moment she forgot that she was sitting inside the KGB headquarters. *Tatuś... tatuś...* she repeated in her thoughts, *daddy...* She simply could not believe what she'd just been told. That face in the photograph was so calm, and so good... The dark hair combed back neatly... And his eyes, looking off somewhere to the side. The officer's uniform. The stars on his epaulettes. One star, two stars, three stars... She began to feel dizzy. *Maybe it was a mistake? Maybe they mixed something up? Was that really a letter from her father? Could it be that he was actually still alive?*

"I didn't know, I didn't know. I really didn't know…" Sofija repeated in a trembling voice.

The KGB agent observed her reaction, took careful note of her every move, then said:

"Comrade Sofija, because you have relatives who escaped to the West, and because you are hiding that fact, you may have some trouble traveling outside of the USSR."

She suddenly raised her frightened eyes. Her cheeks quivered. Tears formed on her eyelashes. They threatened to slide down her cheeks. She tossed her back and cast her eyes up at the ceiling and prayed that her tears would dry up, that they would not slide down her cheeks, because if that happened, she would not be able to stop them. The lump remained lodged in her throat, but at any moment, she felt could burst out in sobs.

"I didn't hide anything! I really didn't know!" Sofija insisted.

"Let's just say," the KGB agent continued, "that you didn't know. But now you do know. So, what are your plans in the West?"

"I don't have any other plans besides participating in the competition. I am racing for the Soviet Union Team. It's a rowing competition. In Vichy, France. I am the quad's stroke. Without me, the team will fall apart." Sofija said all this frantically, hoping that something she said would make a difference.

"Yes, we know all that. But what are your plans connected with your father?"

"I don't have any plans. This is the first time in my life that I heard that I even have a father."

"Assuming that's true, although I don't believe that your mother wouldn't have told you."

"My mother? She really didn't know anything!"

"Can you be so sure?"

He locked his fingers and stared at her.

Sofija cringed. She felt dizzy. She struggled to remember anything from her childhood that would have indicated her mother knew her father was alive, but nothing came to her.

"I'm certain," she answered, barely hearing her own voice.

"Comrade Sofija, you are a citizen of the Soviet Union. You are a member of the Soviet Union's team."

Sofija nodded, staring at the KGB agent with eyes filled with terror.

"Therefore, we believe that you should not make plans to stay in the West," he said, then, with a pregnant pause, waited for Sofija's response.

Sofija remained silent. She was overwhelmed with too many conflicting emotions.

"You understand that you must return to the Soviet Union?"

She showed him that she agreed without uttering a single word. *No, of course I have no plans to run away! I only want to race.*

"You are a citizen of the Soviet Union. Any attempt to remain behind in a capitalist country would be considered treason. Is that clear?"

Sofija nodded in agreement.

"Sign here that you received this letter delivered by hand," the KGB agent said, making a mark on a document, indicating where she should sign. He handed her a pen.

She signed quickly, not even reading what was written on the document. With trembling hands, she picked up the thick envelope that lay on the table between them.

"You understand that when you are abroad you must avoid speaking with any émigrés because they can involve you in certain provocations?"

"I understand," Sofija said, lifting her frightened eyes to meet his.

"Good. You may go," the agent said, snapping shut his folder and standing up from his chair. "We expect you to bring back a medal from France," he said with a smile. Then, he bowed with a flourish.

Sofija jumped. She took a step forward, but her foot got caught on the chair's leg. She stumbled and almost fell to her knees. She grabbed onto the chair, to hold it steady. She righted herself, shoved her handbag under her arm, and squeezed the letter tight in the other.

"Thank you, thank you. Have a nice day. Thank you," she said and rushed out the door.

As soon as she was out in the hallway, she pulled the folded sheets of paper from the envelope. *Wait, calm down. Stop! This is not the place to read this letter. This is not the place to read my father's letter. I have to get out of here.*

She could not contain her feelings. Her heart was beating fast. Her breath caught in her throat. She wanted to breathe, to cry, to laugh, to calm down and to try to understand what had just happened. *My father... My father... My father... He's alive... I have a father!*

With her legs shaking uncontrollable, she stumbled down the granite stairs. She pulled open the heavy black doors. In front of her, Lenin waved from his pedestal. Behind Lenin she could see the red roof of the Church of St. Philip and St. Jacob with its two towers. You would never find such a sight in any postcard – Lenin in front of a church. But here, right now, everything looked so strange, as though all the symbols were tossed together into one mad carousel. Sofija strode briskly across the square, past the church, and towards the River Neris.

I just need to get as far away from that building and from Lenin. I need to get to a calm place where I could read the letter. Where Lenin won't wave to me and where I won't feel the suffering of the prisoners in the KGB cellars. Somewhere quiet and beautiful.

She knew that this would be a moment that she will remember for the rest of her life. There could not be even one shard of an unpleasant feeling in that moment. In her heart, she laughed that all her fears were unfounded. No one will stop her from travelling abroad to race. No one will lock her up in the basement of the KGB building. How could she have thought such a thing?

It's only nine thirty. I still have time. Calm down.

Sofija slowed her gait, turn around, looked at the KGB headquarters, and shook her head. Her feelings of joy mixed with anxiety and regret. She simply could not fathom what she had heard. *Finally, it was all over.* It all ended completely differently than she had imagined. The enormous anxiety had hardly dissipated when she was consumed with a completely different feeling. Her head was spinning, and her legs were weak. She had to find a quiet bench and sit down. She had to calm down and concentrate. Sofija did not feel the cool morning air. Her body was burning hot.

She walked down towards the riverbank, crossed the street, slipped under the fence, and walked down the riverbank until she was close to the river. There, she sat down on the grass. The sun had broken through the clouds and had dried out the grass. The River Neris ran past her feet. *That river's water is so well mixed!* On the other side of the river a few lone fishermen were fishing.

Sofija took a few deep breaths and began examining the envelope. It was white, long, worn, and obviously, it had been opened. Apparently, the letter had been held over steam to open it because the address and postmark had washed away from the damp. She looked at the three postage stamps with the Canadian flag and the number "5". The steam had caused the edges of the stamps to curl, but they were still intact.

Sofija Gruca. Sofija stroked the envelope.

Ignanci Gruca. Niagara Falls. Canada. That was on the edge of the earth as far as she was concerned. Where was Niagara? Was that the famous Niagara Falls she had learned about in school? *How did he get there? How did he travel all the way to Canada? Why didn't he turn up sooner? Why didn't he get in touch with Mama before? Twenty-eight years have passed. What happened? Where was he all that time?*

Sofija carefully opened the letter that had been opened and resealed. She pulled out the thick letter. She unfolded the paper. There were four pages! Oh, and his handwriting was so fine! How delicate was her father's hand. He was an architect. Some of the words were washed out from the steam. In some places, words, and entire sentences, were crossed out. Half of the text of the letter was crossed out. *That was the work of the KGB! They read everything! They only left what they decided she was allowed to read. How could they do that?*

Droga córko Sofia – My dear daughter Sofija, she read in Polish.

The knot in Sofija's throat broke and she began to cry. Hot tears streamed down her face. Those few words drowned in her tears and she could no longer read them. She covered her face with her palms. She cried and didn't even try to stop herself. Something inside of her broke... Something completely unexpected in her life... Something that had turned the twenty-eight years of her life into one never-ending legacy of loss...

Aunt Marylia wrote to me and told me that you live in Vilnius. Daughter, all those years I wrote to you and Mama. I wrote to our home address in Warsaw. I did not know that you had left for Vilnius. Didn't anyone send my letters on to you?

Sofija, again, could not see through her tears. She could not stop the unrestrained flow of her tears. She felt as though those hands from the photograph were hugging her and stroking her head... Sofija held the letter to her tearful face and felt the scent of her father – warm and masculine. It was the scent of lost years. *Tata... Tata... Father...* She sat hugging her knees, resting her head until the cool August air made her tremble with cold.

I need to go... The train leaves at twelve... I'll tell Mama when I get home... She carefully folded the letter and put it back into its envelope. She slid the envelope into her handbag. Mama gave her that handbag as a gift. And the handkerchief, which was now damp with her tears, smeared grey and dusty from the dirt her hands picked up from the door handle of the KGB headquarters door. AG. Aleksandra Galinat. Aleksandra Gruca.

Mama is sitting at the window at home. She doesn't know anything. She searched for him all these years and waited for him. She waited silently, not telling me anything. Sofija felt such pain for her mother in her heart. *She suffered so much over him! No, I cannot simply leave without telling her first. How will I feel during the race knowing that I hid such an important thing from my mother? I could not bear knowing that Father is alive and that Mama doesn't even know... I must go home. I still have two hours until my train departs. I'll go home and leave at eleven fifteen and I'll have plenty of time to spare. I must run home...*

Sofija leapt to her feet, brushed the grass from her skirt, rubbed her eyes, and hurried towards her home.

Should I walk straight along the river side? It's a kilometre to the boathouse and from there a kilometre home. If I walk briskly, I can make it in twenty minutes. Or should I just take the number three trolleybus? From the

Central Department Store its only three stops to get home. It's a five-minute walk to the station. If I ride the trolleybus, that's ten minutes. But how long will I need to wait? No, it's better to run. The wind will clear my head.

She walked briskly toward the bridge and hurried along the riverbank towards home.

* * *

"They took him away from us," Mama cried, covering her face with her hands. The letter lay open on her lap. "They took him away from you, me, from both of us."

"Who *Mamo?*"

"I felt that he was alive. All the time I felt it..."

"Mama, please calm down."

"They never liked us. From the beginning, they didn't like us. They knew all along, but they didn't tell us. That's cruel."

"*Mamusia*... Mama... Who knew?"

"Your aunts. Your father's sisters. They never liked me. But to take your father away from you? I don't understand. I simply don't understand why they would do such a thing?"

"Aunt Marylia?"

"No, Sofija. Aunt Marylia was the only one who supported us. I don't think that she knew. They didn't like Marylia either. They didn't like any of the sisters-in-law. They loved their four brothers too much to let any other women have them. The brothers never believed their good sisters could do anything immoral. Your aunts, Sofija. If you can call them that..."

"What are you talking about, *Mamo?*"

"I'm speaking the truth. They never liked us. They hated us..."

"You believe that they knew where Father was?"

"It's all written here in the letter. He wrote to them from the very beginning, only they never told us. It's my fault. I never should have left Warsaw. I shouldn't have left our home." She began to cry again. "I was convinced that from Vilnius I could find him faster and help him escape. Smolensk is closer to Vilnius than to Warsaw. Did you know how many Polish officers were shot in Smolensk, in Katyn?"[16]

"What?"

"Only no one talks about it. You won't hear about it anywhere. They say that the Nazis shot them. But the Germans hadn't even invaded yet! It was in the spring of 1940. You were not even a year old. When they took all the officers, and not a single one returned. There were twenty thousand. They blame what they did on the Nazis."

"Who?"

"Who? Who? The Russians, my child, the Russians…"

"*Mamusia*…" Sofija suddenly remembered the war veteran's words near the ice-cream cart in Moscow: *Shoot them like the Poles in Smolensk.* What was he saying? Did he know what happened there?

"Your father was among those twenty thousand, but he survived. Somehow, he survived… I will probably never find out how. They took him away from me. I searched for him everywhere! I wrote everywhere! And nothing… Not a single one of my letters brought me any information. They all went straight to the KGB. And his sisters hid everything from me."

"Maybe they tried to tell you, but their letters never reached you. See how they control everything."

"In twenty-eight years, they could not figure out a way to tell us?

16   In April 1940, some 21,892 Polish officers and other Polish citizens were shot by NKVD officers in the Katyn Forest and at four other sites.

No… They never wrote to me. Never. You visited them yourself. Did they say a word to you about your father?"

"No, but there was a KGB agent there with me."

"So what? You can find a hundred ways to pass on important news! Shove a note into your pocket. Go to the toilet together. Whisper it into your ear as they kiss your good-bye. A hundred ways!"

Only now Sofija understood what her mother had to sell, sacrifice, who she had to bow down to and how much she had to grovel just to be able to make it possible for her to visit their homeland, Poland. Six years previous, in 1961, when they allowed the first Soviet tourists to travel abroad, one group was headed to Poland. How did Mama find out? How did she manage to get Sofija's name added to the list of tourists? Where did she get the money to pay for the trip? All she said was that she wanted her to see where she came from, her homeland Poland. Sofija didn't ask any questions. She knew that Mama wouldn't tell her anything anyway. She knew that she would do everything to make it possible for her to travel to Warsaw. Then she met her aunts for the first time. For the first time, she saw Aunt Marylia and her cousin Alicia. They came to meet her at the Warsaw train station.

The delegation of tourists was handpicked: artists, cultural figures, party leaders. She was the only regular person among them. Maybe Mama managed to get her in as an athlete? They always tried to group together people into those delegations from a variety of fields – culture, art, sports. She didn't know any of them. Half the group were KGB agents. Even the one who did not even move one step away when Sofija's relatives came to meet her at the station. He went along to the home of her father's sisters. The entire time, he asked her what they were saying in

Polish, demanded translations. It was disgusting. And they couldn't slip in a single word about her father. They couldn't even tell her with their eyes. They really didn't want to tell her? Could it be?

"*Mamusia.*"

"Did they tell you anything?"

"No, nothing. Not a word."

"Do you understand? All that time they hid it from us! There were a hundred ways to tell us! A hundred opportunities. But they were silent. How much hatred do you have to have for your brother's wife and child to behave that way? Tell me?" Mama burst into tears.

"*Mamusia...*"

"And what about Marylia? She wrote to Father? How did she find out his address?"

"*Mamo...*"

"You thought that there could be nothing worse than war. Well, it turns out, there is something worse."

"*Mamo, nie płacz*, Mama, don't cry," Sofija hugged her mother, just like she did long ago, when she was a child. She pressed Mama to her just the way she had when Mama returned after weeks in prison. Then she would hold her and rock her. They would both be overwhelmed with the pain they shared, the loss. Two women who were precious to each other. The only other person they had. Neither ever had anyone else to hold them. They only had each other. They would hug each other and rock together until they calmed down, until they no longer heard what was hurting inside, until they were overcome with a sweet calm, and the trust that life would go on.

"Mama, don't cry."

CHAPTER SIX

AUGUST 22, 1967, VILNIUS – JELGAVA

Sheets of rain beat against the coupe window, cleansing the glass of accumulated dirt. Narrow streams of rain moved diagonally across the glass. A few passengers sat in the damp grungy coupe, their clothing letting off steam. Their opened umbrellas rolled back and forth in the train passageway. The entire coupe was engulfed in a fog of cigarette smoke.

If it keeps on raining like this, Sofija thought to herself, *we probably won't go out on the water.* She pressed her cheek up against the window frame and kept her palms squeezed between her knees. *I wonder what the girls are doing right now... Are they waiting for me? Are they on their way to the trials? Who is standing in for me right now? They don't know that I will return on time. I ought to be there by half past four. Boris Mikhailovich wouldn't pull anything behind my back. After all, there's only a week left before the championship.*

Although she hadn't been away a full day, she felt as if she had been gone a week, or even a month. *How much everything can change in just one single day! Yesterday I sat on this train trembling with uncertainty, terrified of what awaited me. I came up with all sorts of scenarios, only not the one that actually happened. Yesterday I thought: If only they don't arrest me and keep me locked up in jail, if only they don't forbid me from travelling to the championships, I'll be the happiest person in the world. They didn't lock me up. They didn't prevent me from travelling. Yet, I feel so unhappy. I feel such confusion inside. How one single decision can alter the course of a person's entire life! At the time, Mama thought her choice to follow Father was the only honourable choice. She believed that she was doing what was right. Oh, but had she just stayed in Warsaw! But who knows? Perhaps we would have died in the war? After the bombings in 1944 almost nothing was left of Warsaw. No, no… We wouldn't have been killed… Maybe I would have had the opportunity to study in the university? We wouldn't have been desperately poor like we were in Vilnius. And we wouldn't have been forced to live together with criminals in one flat. We wouldn't have experienced constant fear. Mama wouldn't have been forced to work as a postal carrier. She could have lectured in the university, written scholarly articles, worked as a translator… Mama speaks seven languages! Mamusia, Mamusia… How did you survive it all? What would I be doing right now if we had stayed in Poland? Would I be teaching children geography? Would I be rowing? Who knows where fate would have led me in Poland? But, if I were a rower in Poland, then at least I would have been competing for my own country. For Poland. Oh, how the war destroyed people's lives! At least they didn't deport us to Siberia. It's strange, but I never even wondered how we escaped deportation to Siberia? Because Mama is Polish? No, hundreds of Poles were deported. God must have intervened. Yes, it certainly must have been God. Someone from above must be looking out for us.*

Father… All that time Father was alive. The handsome man from the photograph was alive. Somewhere far, far away. Now he seems so distant. For twenty-eight years he lived an entirely different life that I never knew anything about. How could he have lived without us? How must he have felt knowing that we were somewhere on this earth, always looking for him? What did he know? What didn't he know? What did his sisters write to him?

Why didn't his letters ever reach us? Was it because of the KGB? Or did my aunt simply refuse to forward us his letters?

Sofija opened the same Stendhal book she could not bring herself to read the day before. She read: *Around midnight, news spread around the ballroom that sparked talk. A young carbonator imprisoned in St. Angel's Fortress, had escaped that evening, disguised by wearing someone else's clothing ... And out of an abundance of romantic courage, having already reached the last prison guard tower, he attacked the soldiers with a dagger.*

Sofija took a deep breath: *What happened to Father? How did he escape? How did he break out of there? How did he break out of that place where thousands of Polish officers met their death? How did he make it to Canada from Russia? Were they chasing him? Were they hunting him? Most likely... That is probably why the KGB kept dragging Mama in for questioning. Why? Did they know he had escaped? Were they afraid that if he escaped, he would tell the world what happened in Katyn? In school, during our history lessons, they would tell us that in 1943 the Germans shot all the Polish officers in Smolensk. Mama said that it was not possible because Father went to war in 1940, and at that time the Germans had not yet reached Russia... How did he escape? Mama searched for him for so long... Why did the KGB drag her in so often for questioning? Was it because Mama wrote letters to the Red Cross?*

Sofija recoiled from her own terrible thoughts. Her thin sweater did keep her warm and she could not stop shivering. Tears welled up in her eyes. She leaned her head back and tried to blow her tears away, so they wouldn't stream down her cheeks. Her troubled life flashed before her eyes. Her joy that her father was alive melded into her anger that he had disappeared out of their lives. *Why didn't he look for us? Why didn't he find us? Who would have stopped us from seeing each other? I simply cannot believe that during the war he left me and Mama forever. Something is not right. I must find out what happened.*

The rain lashed against the train windows.

The train twisted and turned on its course through the collective farm fields as the shrubbery that grew along the embankments flashed past. A heavy relentless rain fell from the August clouds. Even the harvesters stood motionless along the edges of the fields. *Oh, where is my frog prince now?* She smiled sadly to herself. *He probably would like such weather. At least, he could take a swim.* Sofija wished she could stand out in one of those fields under the heavy rain clouds and stand there until the water washed away all her pain and returned her to the daily rhythms of her routine. *I am going to Vichy. Oh, and I was so scared they would not let me go. Everything will be fine.*

She sighed and opened her book and read: *...My homeland and my freedom – they are like my cape, a necessity, which I must purchase, if I have not inherited them from my father.* Sofija's heart sank. ... *if I have not inherited them from my father.*

And what about my homeland? Why don't I, or my mother, or my father, have our homeland anymore? Why are we all living in foreign lands? Why didn't I receive my homeland as an inheritance from my father? Why did life place Mama and I inside a country that will not even grant us the permission to take one footstep outside its borders? A country where you must cope with the KGB if you want to live a normal life! A country that makes you sorry you have a father! What kind of a country is this? Who created such a country? Why can't I return to my real homeland?

Passengers entered and exited the train, but Sofija avoided making eye contact with them, just so no one would strike up a conversation with her, like on yesterday's trip. She snapped open her handbag. Mama's carefully wrapped sandwich and a packet of biscuits were tucked inside. *Oh, Mamusia packed the magazine "Sportas" into my handbag as well!* Sofija thought with surprise. She pulled out the magazine, which had been carefully folded eight times. The magazine was dated from August 17th. There was a photograph of the men's coxless four on the front page: Celestinas Jucys, Vytautas Briedis, Jonas Motiejūnas and Eugenijus Levickas. *That's probably why she packed the magazine for me.* She read the headline: *The Žalgiris four are Soviet champions.* On the right, there was another headline: *G. Šidagytė is traveling to the European Rowing Championship.* Sofija scanned the short article and found her surname at the end. *As we can see, the position of the Lithuanian Soviet Socialist Republic team is strong. Besides Z. Grucova, we have G. Šidagytė.*

Again, they wrote my first initial as Z...

"Is this seat free?" a man asked in Russian.

"Yes, yes," Sofija said and nodded. She slid closer to the window and eyed her fellow traveller. He was an older man with dark hair, greying at the edges, dressed in a grey suit. It was not a formal suit, but an everyday suit, although in good shape. He wore a bright tie. He set a brown leather briefcase down on his lap. It was so stuffed with papers that the clasps barely held it together. He looked like an intellectual. *Perhaps he is a teacher?* she thought.

"You're reading about rowing?" the man asked, pointing with his chin towards the newspaper in Sofija's hands.

"Yes," she said, a little surprised that he knew about the sport.

"What language is that paper written in?"

"It's Lithuanian. The title is 'Sportas.'"

"Oh, Žalgiris? Zigmas Jukna and Antanas Bagdonavičius!"[17] He pronounced the names with an accent, but correctly.

"Do you know them?" Sofija asked, surprised.

"No, I don't know them personally, but I'm interested in sports. I remember them from the Olympics in Rome. I read that no one expected them to win a medal, but they did."

"That's right. They didn't take them seriously. Their rowing technique seemed odd."

"So why did they compete then?"

"There came in second in the Soviet Championship. Then they won all the qualification races. There were many. They earned their place in the Olympics."

"They took the silver in Rome, if I remember correctly?"

"Yes, that's right, they won the silver in Rome."

"Too bad they didn't take the gold. They lost to those fascists."

This is clearly a Russian. A Latvian or Estonian would never use that word. He is no intellectual.

"It was a great achievement for Lithuania. It was the first time that rowers from Lithuania won an Olympic medal."

"What about the *Žalgiris* eight?"

"The women's eight is doing well, but the men's eight has fallen apart."

"That's a shame. It was a good team. For some reason, they can never win first place. They always come in second."

---

17   Zigmas Jukna and Antanas Bagdonavičius were Lithuanian rowers who won
      the silver medal n the 1960 Olympics in Rome. They were European champi-
      ons many times, as well as champions in races in the Soviet Union and in the
      Lithuanian Soviet Socialist Republic.

"Well, now their four took the gold. All teams fall apart sooner or later."

"Are you also interested in rowing?"

"I'm interested," Sofija said and smiled. "I row myself."

"Is that so?" The man looked her up and down with scepticism. "You don't look like a rower."

Sofija shrugged, smiled, and said nothing. The man opened his magazine, *Ogoniok,* and began to read. *Thank God, now he'll leave me alone,* she thought to herself with satisfaction.

Tatuś must be a similar age to this man. He may even look like him. I will find him. I will definitely find him! I will row until I see him. I will look for him until I hear him tell me his story. I have no other way to travel abroad except through rowing. I will write to him. Maybe he will be able to travel to see my face. I must see him. I must. Now I know why I am rowing and why I need to row...

But for now, I must return to my real life.

CHAPTER SEVEN

AUGUST 22, 1967, JELGAVA, LATVIA

"Sofija? You're back already?" Genovaitė exclaimed, opening the door to her room.

"Yes, I just came from the station."

"How did it go?"

"What?"

"You know... Vilnius?"

"Oh, that, it was fine. I've forgotten about it already," Sofija said and made a swatting movement with her hand, as though to push away any possibility of an awkward conversation.

"What happened?"

"It was nothing. I filled in the wrong paperwork. It's fixed now," Sofija said and smiled.

"I was worried about you..."

"I was too! But then it turned out that all my anxiety was for nothing."

"I wouldn't want to end up there."

"Just, please don't tell anyone. Okay?"

"Of course. Are you going already?"

"What time is it?" Sofija glanced at her watch. "We've got to hurry. My teammates are getting ready."

"Then I'll be going now."

Sofija switched to Russian and called out to her roommate, Aleksandra, "I'm leaving!"

The girls locked the hotel room door behind them and headed down the stairs into the hotel lobby.

"What's Vaupšas doing here?" Sofija asked, surprised.

"He's here to watch us train for the race. He's preparing an article for *Sportas* magazine. Šeinius is here as well, probably to take photos.

"Really? They came all this way just for that?"

Antanas Vaupšas was famous in track and field. He was known for long jump. He participated in the Tokyo Olympics. He'd already been working as a journalist for a while. He often wrote about rowers. Isakas Šeinius was a loyal devotee and photographer of rowing and other sports.

"Hello, girls," Antanas said when he saw Genovaitė and Sofija enter the lobby.

"Hello," they answered, surprised. They walked over to Vaupšas.

"Are you ready?" he asked.

"Oh yes!" the girls exclaimed together at the same time. They glanced at each other and burst out laughing.

"Well, Šidagytė, you surprised me! Congratulations!"

It was a custom among teammates and friends to call Genovaitė by her surname.

"Why are you surprised?" Genovaitė asked and burst out laughing again.

"We can expect anything out of you," Antanas said and smiled, "but you really thrilled us. When we heard that you'd won the qualifications race, we all leapt into the air for joy."

"Thank you," Genovaitė said and smiled shyly. "We'll see if I can keep this up."

"Don't be so modest. We're off to watch your time trials."

"Really? You are?"

"Yes, we are. Five o'clock, correct?"

"We're meeting at the boathouse at five. The start is around half past five."

"We'll rush back to Vilnius after the race, so we can write it up and publish the article in *Sportas* tomorrow."

"Will you mail me a copy?"

"Of course."

* * *

At five all the girls in the crew were already at their boats and working hard getting them prepared. A strong wind was blowing, and that bode well for good results.

Today's race involved a common start with lag time built in according to the class of boat.

In the language of rowers that meant that the faster boats gave the slower boats a lead, so that they'd all cross the finish line at the same time. This was a technique they'd learned from the Russians, to give one team or another an advantage at the starting line. The coaches decided whose boat was faster. They based their judgment on methodological literature and information gleaned from rowing manuals. Someone had already made all the measurements and calculations, so there was no reason not to trust the judgment of the professionals. It was obvious that the slowest boat was the single and the fastest the eight. According to how the girls finished, the coaches could judge which team was in the best shape at the moment. At this point, that wouldn't change anything, but it did show them what to work on and regulate in the last few days of training. It would also show who needed to rest, who needed their load lightened, and who needed to work on their technique.

From the boathouse downstream on the Lielupė there is a one kilometre stretch that was completely straight. It was just the right distance for the girls' race. A breadth of a hundred metres was all they needed to not get into each other's way and line up five boats: a single, a double scull, a coxed four, a quad, and an eight. The current was not as strong as on the Neris near Vilnius, but today they decided to race downstream and not against the current.

"We are rowing in Lithuanian waters, almost in Lithuania," the girls would remind themselves.

The waters of the Lithuanian River Mūša and River Nemunėlis flow into the River Lielupė. It is only before Bauska, where the two rivers flow into one that this river is called the Lielupė.

It began to drizzle. The wind calmed down. They would still be rowing downwind, nonetheless. Not all of them liked to row downwind. Such a wind was good for girls who were fast, flexible, and lightweight. The taller, stronger, girls liked to row against the wind.

"Attention!" Boris Schirtladze called out, stopping them in their tracks. "Remember that tomorrow after morning training we are packing up all the boats into the truck. It'll be here at eleven."

"Packing up the boats" meant the final phase before the trip. Once the boats were gone, all that was left for them to do to train was morning exercises and jogging. Then, the long trip to Moscow, and from there to France, began. No one knew how long they would need to wait in Moscow. Perhaps a day or two… In Moscow they would receive instructions on how to conduct themselves abroad in the West. They would be brought to the Lenin Mausoleum, where they would be forced to bow to Lenin and promise him that they would bring back medals for him.

"One more thing," the team psychologist, Leonid Gisen, added. "After dinner tonight you must come and pick up your team uniforms."

The ceremony of handing out the team uniforms was one of the most pleasant events before the competition. They would all receive brand new tracksuits and shirts. The new uniforms felt like formal wear compared with the worn-out ones they wore for training. They would be required to wear only those new shirts and tracksuits throughout the competition. The only part that was a disappointment were the Russian letters, CCCP (USSR) sewn onto them.

Beyond the hotel windows of the "Hotel Jelgava" on the opposite side on the offshoot of the River Lielupė, flowing along the avenue, in the Academy of Agriculture park the leaves were already turning yellow. Autumn would come early that year. The thermometer read only 10 degrees. They wished for warmer weather; however, the girls told themselves that maybe it would be warmer in France. If it were, they could travel wearing the dresses they bought in Grünau, in the DDR, after the regatta.

* * *

The hotel hallways were noisy with cheerful activity. Doors swung open and shut. The girls burst into each other's rooms for consultation, to return things they had borrowed from each other – books and all sorts of feminine items. They tried on their new uniforms. They passed needles and spools of thread back and forth, taking in their track suit pants if they did not fit properly. A spool of red thread was passed along for the purpose of sewing the emblem of the Soviet Union onto their red team racing shirts.

There were only two days remaining before the trip to the European Women's Rowing Championship in Vichy. Everything calmed down. The battle of nerves over who would get which seat on the team ended.

The whispering and guessing ended. The girls prepared for their journey to France, a land they had only dreamed of ever visiting in their wildest dreams. France was a country they had read about in the novels of Balzak, Dumas, Maupassant. It was a country they had only seen in romantic movies. They had only heard its melodies over the static of a crackling radio.

All that was left to do, was to pack up their boats, which would travel two or more days overland to Vichy. Before reaching them, the truck would stop in Birštonas, where the men's team would load up their boats. Among the men's team there were three Lithuanians, who, together with a Ukrainian, would race together in a coxed four. Traditionally, the men's championship started a week after the women's championship. This year it would start on September 7th. Although the European Rowing Championship races had been ongoing since 1893, for over half a century only men's teams raced. Since 1954 women's teams were allowed to participate in the European Rowing Championships, only their races took place on a different week than the men's races. Sometimes they even took place in different countries.

Sofija was carefully packing her belongings – her new tracksuit, her team shirts, her training clothes, which she would not need that day or the next, her dresses, her pumps, her film – when the door flew open and her teammate Sasha bounded in.

Sofija jumped in surprise.

"You frightened me! What happened?"

"I'm sorry," Sasha responded and began to giggle.

Sasha fell backwards onto her bed.

"What happened? Why are you so cheerful?" Sofija asked.

The girls knew her to be reserved. Bursts of emotion set her off balance. Maybe because when she was growing up in her home she could never laugh openly, talk, or even cry.

"Look, I received a letter from home. From my father."

"Oh! I…" Sofija caught herself before she said, "also."

"What? What about you?" Sasha sat up and asked.

"I… No, nothing. What did he write? Why are you so cheerful?"

"Oh, his letters are always so full of humour! I simply burst out laughing when I read them," Sasha snorted. "Sorry…"

"What did he write?"

"Nothing in particular. Just about home, our family… Only, he has this way of talking about the most ordinary things with this sly humour! I read his letter and it is like reading a good joke!" Sasha wiped away her joyful tears.

Sofija chuckled along with Sasha, infected by her laughter. Although, at the same time, sadness and regret gathered within her. *I wish that I could laugh together with my father. I wish we could laugh over simple, everyday things. I wish I knew that my father and I would meet each other soon. We'd talk about simple ordinary things. I'd listen to his advice. He would comfort me at times. Sometimes he would pull me in close and give me a hug. I would like to tell him about every race, about my trips, about the new countries I've seen. He is a man, and therefore all that would be interesting to him. I will find him. Sooner or later, I will find him. My only regret is that when I do find him, I will never be able to bring back the time that was stolen from us.*

CHAPTER EIGHT

AUGUST 28, 1967, THE TRIP TO FRANCE

The resort town of Vichy is located in the centre of France, around 300 kilometres from Paris. The year 1967 marked the first time that Vichy had been granted the honour of organizing such a high-level rowing competition. For the first time, the best rowers in Europe would convene here – first the women, then the men.

The project of building a dam on River Allier was considered before World War II. However, only in 1957 was the Allier dam project was approved. Construction was completed in early June, just three months before the European Rowing Championship. The town of Vichy with Lake Allier became a 2,000-meter rowing course. A new bridge was built at the locks on the site of the old pedestrian bridge. The bridge was inaugurated on September 1st on the occasion of the European Women's Rowing Championships. Just before the championship, a new rowing base camp with sheds, gyms and lounges was built and equipped.

The USSR women's team trip to France began, as always, with "preparations" in Moscow. The girls and their coaches had many long hours of boring KGB instructional speeches ahead of them. They were instructed on how to conduct themselves abroad, on what they were allowed to say and what they were not allowed to say, what they could bring with them and what they could bring back with them. It was drilled into them how important it was to keep a close eye on their Soviet passports, because they were valuable and there were many thieves out there with fingers itching to steal them. They were told to swear to the Communist Party that they would battle for the honour of the USSR. As every other time, their KGB handlers read to them from a standard text that instructed them that in the West they had to be alert and careful, and to never forget that agents from capitalist countries are ceaselessly working to extract important facts out of a Soviet citizen that they are useful to foreign intelligence agencies. They may even be placed in the compromising position of betraying their own homeland.

"To this end, the agents of the imperialist countries use modern technology, equipment to bug your rooms, they secretly follow you and take photographs of you, they also aim to deceive you, compromise you, cheat you and threaten you. The agents of capitalist espionage intelligence often pose as tour guides, translators, doctors or teachers, seamstresses, shopkeepers, taxi drivers, waiters, hairdressers and other service personnel," they were instructed. Once again, they were instructed that they had to inform their team leader about every single contact with a foreigner, and to not accept any offers or gifts. They must never go anywhere alone, but always together in a group. They must be dressed neatly and behave beyond reproach. They were instructed as to how to behave in shops, cafeterias, on the streets, in the hotels. They were told who they may associate with on the rowing venue and who not to associate with. They were warned that they may not bring vodka or any food products, or any other goods, with them out of the Soviet Union to sell abroad.

However, the girls were already dreaming of France. The words of the KGB agents were muted out by their thoughts about this mysterious land with all its new colours and scents, the Eiffel Tower, the Louvre, Chanel, and about the endless possibilities of window shopping. Of course, hidden beneath their sport tracksuits and uniforms in their suitcase lay all those forbidden items that they would need to secretly sell because the officially allowed sum of 15-20 roubles that they were allowed to exchange was barely enough to buy a few cups of coffee and a few postcards. But even that meagre sum would be handed over to them by the team managers only when the competition was over and they had travelled to Paris, just to rule out the temptation of running around shopping before the races began. No one planned to buy food with their food allowance. They would feed themselves on the scent of delicious coffee and baked goods that wafted out of the cafes. They would drink water out of the public fountains. After they bought their new dresses and shoes, they would hurry to tear off all the labels and price taps, so that they could pretend they were personal items they'd brought with them out of the Soviet Union when the USSR border guards checked their luggage for any items that cost more than 20 roubles. If they suspected anything, they would simply confiscate it. They all sold contraband. And not just the athletes, artists, and tourists, but those same KGB agents who accompanied them, because what was the point of traveling to the West if it wasn't to buy beautiful clothing and other things that they had never seen before. That was what everybody thought. Only, the girls from the rowing team had yet another goal, and that was to win one more European Rowing Championship medal.

* * *

On August 28, an impressive airplane took flight out of Sheremetyevo Airport in Moscow. Among the privileged who were given permission to travel abroad – the party functionaries, the scientists, the tourists who had paid a hefty bribe for the privilege – twenty-two female athletes in pretty dresses, a doctor, and a crowd of men to watch over them took their seats. Among these men were the coaches, the team leaders, members of the Sports Committee, Party leaders, and KGB agents.

The lucky ones who managed to get a window seat sat with their cheeks pressed to the glass watching as the towers of Moscow grew smaller and smaller until they eventually disappeared, and how the endless housing estates disappeared beneath the clouds.

The passed along the magazines that featured them. Antanas Vaupšas' promised article was printed in *Sportas*. They had the Russian magazine *Soviet Sport* and the Lithuanian *The Soviet Woman* with them as well.

"Girls, two hours have just been added to your lives!" Coach Vaitkevičius said cheerfully. "Turn your watches back two hours!"

Although the girls were by now accustomed to time zone changes, they always enjoyed this moment mid-flight when they ritualistically changed the time on their watches. It was as though their lives in the West were starting anew.

"Look at your photo, Šidagytė!" Sofija said, spreading open the centrefold of *Sportas*. There was the article about the rowing camp in Jelgava.

"The first-place rower!" Genovaitė read out loud and laughed.

"I'm probably nothing in Lithuania," Sofija said with a bitter smirk. "The article is all about the eight and the single."

"What are you talking about?"

"Just look. Here's a photo of the eight, and here's a photo of you, but I'm not in any of the photos. It's as though they've crossed me out of everything. It's their revenge."

"Whose revenge? What are you saying?"

"The two of them are taking their revenge."

"That's rich. Why would they do that?"

"They don't like me. They're angry at me for rowing with Russians. But what was I supposed to do? Give up rowing?"

"Of course not!"

"I'm always an orphan…"

"Cut it out! Only to yourself!" Genovaitė said and laughed. "You trained us in the quad!"

"I didn't train you," Sofija said, surprised. "I only advised you… There was no one else to do it…"

"That's what I'm telling you! I only remember you in the quad."

"There was no one else to do it… Rycha seated us, but there was nobody to train us. At first, Janina bossed us around, then I did after she left the quad. But is that coaching? You can't even see what's going on behind you. All you do is tell people what to do when and that's it."

"Good thing you have a loud voice," Genovaitė said and laughed.

"Why loud?"

"Well," Genovaitė hesitated, feeling a little thrown off, "I meant a firm voice."

"I never thought that I ever raised my voice?" Sofija said, growing depressed.

"I didn't mean that you raised your voice. You've never raised your voice once in your entire life! Even when I ruined the race the years before last."

"What are you talking about?"

"About the Union Championships finals."

"Oh, then? In 1965?" Sofija smiled.

"I was the one who ruined everything! We could have won the gold. We were far in the lead! And then, I fumbled my oar, I caught a crab, so to speak."

Genovaitė could never let go of that chance to take the gold in the 1965 Soviet Championship. They were just a few lengths from the finish, but her mistake cost their quad the gold and placed them in third place.

Sofija smiled wryly.

"You didn't say a single word to me... Not a single word. Nobody did."

"What can you say when you can't change anything anyway? Why create more stress for someone?" Sofija shrugged her shoulders. "What happened, happened. We need to move on and not blame each other."

"I'll never forget it, as long as I live..."

"Forget it!" Sofija laughed.

"I was so angry at myself! And I felt sorry for the crew. We were supposed to win. We were supposed to be headed to the European championship."

"What of it? We're sitting in a plane right now flying to the championship. Does it matter if we get there a year sooner or later?" Sofija said in a soothing voice.

"That crab back then always comes back to me like a nightmare."

"But you still do some crabbing in your single, don't you?"

"That's my technique," Genovaitė said, chuckling. "But seriously, I don't know what's up with that. Probably there's been an error in my stroke from the very beginning. The oar just flips. I have the strength of a horse, but my technique is weak. I'm self-taught."

"We're all self-taught. When I started rowing, there were so many people on the water that the coaches could not give all of us their attention. They let a group out on the water and then met another coming back in. There weren't enough boats. They didn't have motorboats. They had to shout out instructions to rowers from the shoreline. I remember how Pavilionis would shout from the shore, "Stronger! Longer!" I had this really long stroke, but I didn't have any technique. I'd just dig in with all my strength."

"And you dug yourself out?" Genovaitė laughed.

"Rycha helped me a lot."

"But did he train you?"

"Officially, no. Pavilionis was my coach. He still is. He's a great organizer. He keeps a close watch on the time. It was always interesting to travel with him. But it was Rycha who taught me technique. He would watch me from the shore. Like he watched everyone. If he saw that anyone was having a hard time, he would come over and give some good advice. He knows how to assemble a crew. He glued together our quad in 1963. I was with Rita, Gaila, and Janina."

"Why didn't they seat you in a bigger boat from the beginning?"

"I didn't want it. All I really wanted was to row in a single."

"Like me!"

"Yes, but then I reached my limit. I saw that with my height and weight I couldn't achieve much in a single. The only way I would get anywhere was on a crew."

"So, you see, we're both loners! I don't even want to be on a crew. I love rowing alone. I do as I please."

"Does it ever feel lonely?" Sofija asked.

"All the time I was in good company with the eight. At first I was always around the four with older girls. After that at the camp in Trakai I always lived with the girls from the eight. I never felt that I was alone. Of course, when you win a race it's much more fun to celebrate with your team. You have others to share the joy with. In a single it's just you out there on your own." Genovaitė laughed, "I don't have those problems!"

She had no problem making friends. She was always cheerful and talkative. Genovaitė would talk to anyone.

Suddenly, Sofija became serious: "You know, I'm very happy for you. Last year I felt so guilty that they hadn't taken you into the quad."

"Why?" Genovaitė asked, surprised.

"They truly believed that you would make it into the championships…"

"Who did?"

"You know who. From then on, they wouldn't have anything to do with me… My conscience was gnawing away at me all the time."

"Why? What did you have to do with it?"

"I didn't help you."

"And what could you do about it if I was always off rhythm and couldn't keep up? I'm the one who always manages to catch a crab."

Sofija sighed and turned towards the window.

"I had no interest in being seated in the quad," Genovaitė continued. "I'm perfect for the single. I'm much better off on my own."

"I'm very happy that you won," Sofija said quietly and lowered her eyes.

CHAPTER NINE

SEPTEMBER 28, 1967, PARIS, FRANCE

Their plane landed in the early afternoon in the Le Bourget Airport. The girls were disappointed that they hadn't seen the Eiffel Tower through the airplane window. The airport was only 11 kilometres from Paris, but the centre remained somewhere in the distance.

The girls from Moscow whispered among themselves about how in 1961, in the Le Bourget Airport, the Soviet ballet dancer, Rudolf Nureyev, had defected to the West. Of course, the team of KGB handlers accompanying them were thinking about the same thing. They were on high alert that such a defection would never happen again. To that end, as soon as they had all disembarked, their eyes were constantly making a head count of the girls on the team and the other members of the group.

Together with the other passengers on the plane, the Soviet rowing team had to pass through passport control. After that, they would say that their trip to France had begun. The championship organizers would be waiting for them in the Arrivals Hall. It was their job to greet the group and to transport them to Vichy, where the most important championship of the year awaited them. Everything around them was bright and beautiful. Even the passenger waiting lounges seemed to be scented with perfume.

The girls were dressed in suits and dresses and did not resemble ath-

letes at all, much less rowers. However, because of their height they tow-
ered over the French passengers. That and the strange language they con-
versed in caused many heads to turn.

Jūratė heard a French passenger spit out the word, "Russe." She re-
acted by speaking very loud in Lithuanian, inviting her team to gather
around her, just so that no one would think that they were Russians.

"Soviétique," someone behind them said. Apparently, people were discussing them amongst themselves.

*Maybe they don't mean us? The entire plane was full of people from
Moscow. They couldn't mean us... It can't be that it's written all over our
faces that we're from the Soviet Union.*

They passed through passport control quickly. The girls made sure
to bury their precious identity documents deep in their purses. Then
they entered the arrivals hall where people were crowded together waiting for their loved ones along with the taxi drivers. Some people waved
bouquets of flowers at the crowds walking through the gates while others
held up sheets of paper with names written on them. Everyone was waiting for someone. When people were reunited, they walked towards the
exit, holding each other by the waist, or carrying on animated friendly
conversations.

The team managers and coaches strained their necks searching for a
sign that read: *Championnats d'Europe d'aviron.* The girls were full of
anticipation and could not wait to get on the bus and travel to Vichy.

"*Tata?!*" Sofija froze. Her father?! Her legs gave out and she was bathed
in cold sweat. Her carry-on bag slipped out of her arms and fell onto
her feet. Among the people in the arrivals hall stood a middle-aged man
dressed in a brown military uniform. He looked just like her father in
the old photograph. His dark hair was slicked back. There was a dimple

on his cheek. His smile was reserved, and his eyes were peaceful. He was gazing off somewhere to the side. Her heart beat against her chest and a lump squeezed her throat. Her friends and teammates walked beyond her. One of them rammed into Sofija's back. There was a ringing in her ears. Her head was spinning. *"Tata..."* She could not believe it. *How? How did he get here?* Sofija's face burned red. Her feet were rooted to the floor. *How could he have found out that I was flying in on this plane? What will I say to him? Will he recognize me? No, he won't, truly he won't... I have to get up close to him... He is waiting for me... He came here for me! What will the coaches and girls think? Nobody knows that I have a father...* Only a few seconds passed, but Sofija imagined that she had been standing there for a very long time. She had to do something. Walk over to him, say something, introduce herself.

Suddenly Father raised his hand and waved to someone in the distance. He smiled a broad smile and called out in French, "Bonjour Papa!" He hurried towards a grey-haired old man in a grey suit. He hugged him, patted him on the back, took his case, and they both headed towards the exit. Sofija's feet trembled and tears rose in her eyes. *How could I have made such a mistake? That man looked so much like my father! How could I have imagined that Father would show up here? This is France, not Canada. That man looked so much like my father! I made a complete fool out of myself. I hope nobody noticed? How could I know what my father would look like now? I've never even seen him. I've only seen him in that old photograph. And in that photograph, he was wearing a Polish uniform and not a French one. How could I have been so confused? Father would be over seventy man, but that man couldn't have been over fifty. He looked just like Father in that photograph. Oh, how confused my poor mind is. I'm such a fool...* She bent down and picked up the handles of her bag and looked around for her teammates. Her camera dangled from her shoulder. Sofija looked down and thought: *Good thing my camera didn't slip off my shoulder. I could have broken it.*

"Why are you just standing there, Sofija, let's go," Rita said as she walked past her. "What's up with you?"

"What?" Sofija shot back.

"Your eyes are red, as though you've been crying."

"Really? I've been rubbing them. Something got in my eye."

Sofija hurried to catch up with the rest of the group. She was always strong and reserved. No one had ever seen her cry. But now a lump was forming in her throat. Her hands and legs were trembling. She could not shake the feeling that she had been only a few metres away from her father. All she had to do was to stretch out her hand and he would have recognized her. She lifted her head and scanned the airport. Maybe she would see the officer again. Beyond the airport glass wall, she saw the back of the brown uniform for a moment. A taxi door opened and closed, and then he was gone.

Oh, what if a miracle had happened? Miracles do happen sometimes. But not in my life... They happen in the movies. My life is not a movie. Although, if he wanted to, my father could fly to France to see me.

Sofija walked towards the Soviet delegation. She lowered her eyes and stood behind everyone else. She waited for the tears that had filled her eyes so unexpectedly to dry. She leaned over and for a long time acted as though she were adjusting her camera. She breathed deeply, struggling to regain her equilibrium. Her body was still trembling.

The women's rowing team stood in a circle around their cases and bags, waiting for the organizers to come and collect them. It felt good to get up after sitting in the plane for so long, but after a while they grew tired. The girls gazed all around them, chatted, and were in general thrilled to have made it to France. But the team managers were uneasy. The Lithuanian girls, as always, stood in their own circle chatting together. The Russian girls didn't understand a word they were saying, although they did manage to learn how to say hello, thank you, and goodbye in Lithuanian while at camp.

Usually, when they arrived at a championship, the organizers would be there waiting for them. But this time no one was there. *Could they have confused the airports? The time? The date? Or maybe no one was planning to come and pick them up at all?*

"Go and sit down, girls," Vaitkevičius waved at the girls, "save your legs."

"Will we be waiting for much longer?"

"I don't know. We must wait. They are supposed to meet us here. Don't wander off!"

Time crawled slowly. At first, the scent of coffee and delicious foods from the cafes delighted them. But now, those scents teased them. It had been a long time since lunch was served on the plane and their athletic high metabolisms were feeling the hunger. The piles of croissants and chocolate biscuits in the windows drove them out of their minds. The scent of coffee, which you could never taste in Lithuania or in the entire Soviet Union, tempted them, but their pockets were empty. When they did receive their money after the competition, they would use it to buy new shoes and dresses, but not coffee or small treats.

The girls from the eight sighed and searched for empty chairs in the arrival's hall.

"I wonder if this seat is taken" Rita said, pointing to a chair with the magazine *ELLE* placed on it. She took a look around her.

The French couple seated on the chair beside shrugged their shoulders, signalling that they didn't know. They flashed a kind smile. Rita glanced around to make sure nobody was coming back to reclaim the magazine they had left behind.

"It's probably free," Irena, a veteran of the eight, decided. "Just sit down."

Irena took a seat beside the chair in question.

Rita sat down, holding the magazine in her hand.

"What kind of a magazine is that?" Irena asked.

"I don't know. It says *ELLE* on it."

"That is not your *Soviet Woman*. What a pretty magazine!"

"Yes, see, its glossy."

Rita opened the magazine. "Oh, look, what fashions! And just look at the hairstyles!"

"Show me the cover," Irena said and took the magazine from her. "Oh, what's this?"

There was a photograph on the cover of a woman in an elegant violet dress.

"What?"

"This is Grace Kelly!"

"Grace Kelly? The actress?"

"Yes, look, see, it says, Grace, right there. She married the prince of Monaco."

"Lucky her," Rita said and laughed.

"Her brother is a rower. He won the gold in the single in the Rome Olympics. John Kelly. Their father was a rower as well. I think that he won two gold medals in the 1920 Olympics. He won in single and double. In 1924 he won the gold in the double."

"How do you know all that?"

"I read about it. And Rycha told me. He showed me a photograph from Tokyo with John Kelly, her brother. He was there."

"Did he race for America?"

"She's pretty, isn't she?"

"Pretty, but rather sad."

"Really… But she's got everything. She's beautiful, rich, and her husband is a prince. What more does she need?"

"Maybe this a picture from some film. She's an actress after all. Maybe she's in character for a role?"

"I doubt it. She hasn't acted for a long time. Not since she got married."

"What are you looking at?" Aldona asked, joining the group.

"It's a magazine. See, Grace Kelly is on the cover. Have you heard of her?"

"That's the sister of that rower? The actress?"

"Yes, the princess of Monaco. Her brother won the gold in Rome," Irena said.

"Oh, yes, that's right. May I take a look?"

"In a minute, I'd like to take a look first."

Rita began to flip through the pages of the *ELLE* magazine, starting from the back.

"It smells of coffee everywhere. I can hardly stand it," Jūratė said, walking up from behind them.

"Just don't breathe in the scent of those rolls," Rita joked, "you need to keep your weight down."

"Are you afraid of gaining weight just by smelling those rolls? I know I can gain a kilo just by smelling them," Jūratė said.

"That's right, Jūratė, don't listen to them," Genovaitė chimed in. "You'll lose that weight when your nerves get to you right before the starting line."

"Look who's talking, Šidagytė, you're not the one who has to haul her around!" Leokadija quipped. She was the third seat in the eight.

"Those poor coxes," Genovaitė said and laughed. "They won't have the strength to yell if they haven't had enough to eat. Sofija, do you starve Natasha as well?"

Genovaitė turned towards Sofija. A Russian girl, Natasha, was the cox on her quad.

"What?" Sofija asked absentmindedly, "where you saying something to me?"

"Why are you standing over there all by yourself, Sofija? Come and join us," said Sofija Korkutytė, who occupied the sixth seat on the eight.

Sofija attempted to smile, but her gaze wandered off into the distance.

"You're not yourself," Sofija from the eight said to Sofija from the quad. "Are you worrying about the race?" She touched her elbow.

"What?"

"I asked you if you're afraid of the race?"

"Why?"

"You're not yourself, that's why."

"Oh, it's nothing. I suppose you caught me daydreaming."

"About the competition?"

"About love," Sofija said and chuckled. She shook her head, took two deep breaths, and felt as though she'd released all the tension she'd felt over "seeing" her father.

The girls chattered on about all sorts of nonsense. They commented on what they saw around them, cracked jokes, and kept glancing over to make sure no one was looking for them. Arriving and departing passengers hurried through the airport, but no one even gave them a glance.

After two hours had passed, the team managers decided to look for a telephone. When nobody picked up the call, they began looking for different means of transportation to Vichy. Seven hours after they landed, the entire team piled into an intercity bus headed for Vichy.

The distance from the airport to Vichy was 300 kilometres. The trip would take five hours.

The scenes that rolled past their bus windows bewildered them. The girls drank in every patch of the France they'd dreamed about all those months. They gazed at the buildings, the advertisements, the shop windows, calling out to each other in glee, until one by one, sleep overcame them.

The Soviet delegation reached Vichy just as the city's lights were dimming and dawn was approaching. Then, from the bus station they had to find their way to the international student sport town beside the rowing course where they would live. An hour's walk on foot dragging their luggage would not have been difficult for a group of rowers, if only their managers knew which way to go. It was difficult to read the street names on the map in French in the dim light. Many wrong turns added a few more kilometres to the trip.

They chose the widest street that led away from the station. The entire group walked towards the bridge over the river. The street was crowded. The shop windows tempted them with beautiful clothing, handbags, pumps, dishes. In the souvenir shop windows they admired lovely knick-knacks with French labels on them. The last partiers were laughing and talking in the cafes. The starving girls could no longer bear the scent of the closing restaurants. They were already planning how they would sneak away between training sessions and races, maybe without even telling anyone, to wander among the shops and admire the city.

They walked for a half hour along the streets until the shoreline of the river opened up before them. "Here it is…"

The girls caught the scent of the Allier first. That was how it always was when they arrived at a championship. The scent of the water always brought on anxiety over the upcoming races. The rowing course always had their own specific scent, but you could never miss it. It was the scent of the damp, and of refreshing water, of grass and wind, of the sand along the shoreline and the water lilies. Always, their bodies tensed when they caught the scent of the water, their hearts beat more quickly, and their heads began spin just contemplating the upcoming races.

The streetlights reflected off the water of the River Allier. And each of the girls, although they tried to push away their thoughts about the race, began to quietly count to herself the lengths and metres, measured the wind and the waves. If they had arrived in Vichy earlier in the day, when it was still light outside, they would have seen their competitors training, the girls who arrived earlier in Vichy. Then, they would have felt even more anxious. They would have devoured with their eyes their competitors' every stroke. They would have watched and evaluated their build, their technique, their moods. They would scan for signs that their rivals were weaker than they were, less dangerous and then they would convince themselves that it would be easy to win against them. Even when they saw the rowers from East Germany, they would have searched for the slightest signal that this year their greatest competitors could be beaten.

CHAPTER TEN

AUGUST 29, 1967, VICHY, FRANCE

In the morning, the Soviet team woke up inside a construction site. Beyond their windows construction workers laboured in a cacophony of noise, newly laid asphalt steamed, tractor engines hummed. They had walked to their accommodation in the pitch black of night and were so exhausted that they hadn't even noticed that the last stages of construction were still underway. After they were assigned to their rooms, they hardly noticed that the walls smelled of fresh paint. All they wanted was to fall into bed, stretch out, and rest their swollen feet.

Sofija was happy that they managed to get single rooms. But not because she could avoid unnecessary socializing and take time to lie in bed by herself and read a book. She mostly needed to hide all the anxiety that was building up inside of her before the race. On the exterior, Sofija seemed perpetually calm, cool, and ready to do what it takes to win a race. Yet, before every race Sofija battled her own anxiety before the start. No one in the team even suspected such an inner battle was taking place inside of her. *You have nerves of steel! Not a single muscle on your face twitches. How did you become so strong, Sofija?* Her teammates were in awe of her. She was their support. She set an example for them on how to concentrate and not worry before the start of a race. Sofija did everything she could not to show her weakness to the team. Her weakness may have even been greater than theirs; however, it was her role to lead the team and inspire them, and not just for the thousand metre distance, but even before that, in those moments when they felt the slightest unease before the race. Sometimes that anxiety would take over when they arrived at the regatta, but other times she could feel a sense of uneasiness taking hold as she was packing her case. Every day her fear would grow stronger and stronger, until the last day before the race. Then terror would form as a hard lump in her throat, transform into mood swings that were difficult to control, which she would struggle to bury deep inside of her so that no one would notice. Then her legs would grow weak, her hands would tremble, and if anyone around her asked her anything their words would fly past her ears until she gathered herself together to respond. Then, she would be engulfed in her own doubts: *Why am I doing this? What for? Why am I putting myself through this? What will I get out of this?* She could not find enough positives to justify her experience... But she couldn't just drop out and run away now... The races themselves felt like a toothache, an ache that would only stop when they crossed the finish line... But before that there would be heats, and then, God Forbid, the repechage. She would suffer inhumane physical pain, when her muscles screamed for oxygen, when her head felt as though it were about to split with pain, when her soul would leave her body. And you can't stop. You'll move back and forth forty times a minute, like a wind-up toy, and you won't even be able to control how neatly your oars hit the water... Of course, afterwards all that would be over, and you will forget the pain. And that's when the question will come back to haunt you – why am I doing this? But if you manage to win, then the very next day you'll be eager to sit back down in your boat and go through the pain all over again. But for now... Oh, God... Why?

Father… Now that she has found her father, the only way to ever be able to see him was to row and to win and to travel. That was a positive thought that was stronger than her endless anxiety.

Will it ever happen? Will it be enough to see my father to know and to feel that he is mine? I don't know anything about him. I don't know him at all. We share our blood. I came from his body. And that's all. Will he accept me? Will I be able to accept him? Will I ever understand him? I won't know until I meet him. I will not meet him until I am able to travel to see him. I won't be able to travel to see him unless rowing makes it possible. There is no other means possible to travel the world, and there never will be. I will never join the Communist Party. The Communists can travel more easily. I am not an artist, and I will never become one. I must keep on rowing. There's nothing else I do as well as rowing. Oh Lord… How many more times must I suffer this unreasonable anxiety just so that I may visit my father? What if they never allow me to travel abroad again? After all, now I have relatives in the West. From now on, I will need to report that on all my paperwork… This time I was lucky. They gave me a hard time, but they let me out. Maybe someone on the inside protected me? Maybe they were afraid that if they detained me at the last minute, the team would fall apart… The KGB…

Sofija shook off the memory of her train trip from Jelgava to Vilnius, she tried to forget the fear that she felt then, a fear that was much stronger than any anxiety before a race, a terror stronger than any she experienced as a child. *It's amazing how a person can stress themselves to such a degree. Just through my thoughts and my imagination I had worked myself into such stress. A person concocts so many frightening things in their head and then they are no longer able to control themselves or to think straight. Or perhaps it wasn't my imagination, but my experience? Was I afraid when the KGB came and took Mama away the first time? I don't remember. Probably not... Just like I didn't fear my first day at school, my first visit to the dentist... I wasn't afraid of my first race... I wasn't afraid because I didn't know what to expect. I didn't know it would be this hard, but now I know. And I'm afraid. And I'm afraid of the KGB. I must pull myself together. I must focus. I must so that the girls aren't suspicious.*

Autumnal sunlight fell through the windowpanes. She wanted to leap out of bed and go see everything in daylight. Her legs were relaxed and felt wooden. Her body longed for work. She wanted to stretch her tight muscles, exercise her back. But most of all, she wanted to eat. Through the entire long journey, they did not have the time to eat. Every minute it seemed as though they had almost reached their destination. A biscuit or two here and there did nothing more but arouse her appetite.

The lush green around the sporting centre showed no signs of autumn approaching, unlike in Lithuania. The river ought to be just beyond the trees, along with the racing lanes.

The first thing the girls did was to hurry off together to the new cafeteria on the sports centre territory. The spacious beautiful hall could seat all the championship athletes all at once. For the moment, they were all alone in the cafeteria. Feeling uncomfortable, they glanced over in the direction of the most distant tables. They were disappointed that breakfast consisted of one croissant, a pat of butter, and tea. Back home they were accustomed to a generous breakfast.

"Is this how everyone eats breakfast in France? One roll and that's it?"

The young athletes were shocked, but they didn't dare complain. They would have liked to see how the other teams ate breakfast, but there were no other athletes in the hall. They probably had arrived first.

"That's all?" they kept asking each other and glancing around.

"That's why French women are so thin," one of the girls said and laughed.

"I'd agree to join a cake eating contest, here and now," Ala Perevorucho-va, the stroke on the eight, said, flicking crumbs off her fingers. She smiled a wane smile. She was known for her reserve.

"Me too," said Sofija Korkutytė, "although, for the life of me, I never could understand why men cram that much cake into their mouths."

"Ugh, the sweetness would make me sick," Irena said and shuddered.

"How you ever participated in a cake-eating contest?" Rita asked, surprised.

"No, but just watching one turns my stomach," Irena said and laughed.

"I think only men participate in cake-eating contests," Ala said hesitantly.

The girls remembered the Trakai *Žalgiris* rowing base cake eating contest of 1961. The idea came from their teammate Rimas Derkintis. The contest lasted for a month and not a single person could manage to eat an entire cake by himself. The rules were simple. The courageous contestant received a cake and a glass or water or lemonade. Then he had to eat the entire cake. Then, once he'd eaten the cake, he had to sit and wait in front of everyone, so that he couldn't just go around the corner and vomit out the entire cake. Every single person who tried, gave up before they could finish the entire cake and take their last bite. All of them, would get up and run for the bushes and vomit, just before managing the last bite. Their punishment afterwards was to buy a large cake and to share it with all the spectators. Rimas had promised the winner a monetary prize five times greater than the price of a cake.

"Zinkevičius says that to this day he cannot eat cake," Rita said and giggled.

"The cake they bought him was hard. He chewed and chewed... But he won! Remember?" Irena said, reminding them of the details of Coach Zinkevičius' story.

"He was the only one that didn't leave us a single bite of cake," Sofija said and laughed. "We would have so much fun eating cake when somebody lost."

"It wasn't the same as chewing on bacon lard! Oh, cake!" Ala said and laughed.

"They used to have eating contests in the cafeteria. They'd all toss their ration coupons together and then compete to see who could eat the most..."

The girls gazed at the crumbs in their plates and smiled, musing over their youthful memories. Only Rimas Derkintis organized such fun games. He probably got ideas from watching his father, Valerijonas Derkintis, who was an actor, and his friend, Rimas' god father, the theatre director Juozas Miltinis. Rimas spent his entire childhood and youth in the theatre, with his father. Their home was filled with actors and directors.

"Let's go. Nobody's going to serve us cake here. This is France, not Lithuania," Sofija said and laughed. She stood up to leave.

"Let's go, girls," Vaitkevičius urged them, walking into the cafeteria. "Let's go to rig the boats!"

The new building on the shores of the River Allier stunned the girls and their coaches. A number of boats fit inside the enormous modern architecture building with its wave-shaped roofs. Lined up on either side of the central part of the boathouse were nine doors to large halls filled with racks for boats. The ceilings of the amazing wooden constructions reminded them of the inside of a huge ship and took their breath away. There were already places ready for the boats of all the participating teams – not only the women's teams, but also the men's. On the second floor there were changing rooms with showers and massage rooms for every team. The girls had never seen such a beautiful and comfortable rowing base.

They found their truck and launched into their usual ritual. They needed to untie their boats from the metal frame, carefully take them down, place it onto the slings, remove the canvas covers (these were not used by everyone, only by the members of the team, and only to protect the best boats), check for scratches or cracks that could have happened during the trip, then bring out the tools and fasten the riggers. The oars still needed to be untied. And the coxswains needed to gather the seats and the rudders from the trailer.

The girls swiftly set to work because they all were eager to get out on the Allier and to test the waters. Already from a distance they could see that the waters were rough. The concrete shoreline along the lake was steep, and the motor-boat traffic was intense. The entire scene reminded them of the Khimki where waves hit up against the shore and roll backwards towards the opposite shoreline. There, those waves mix with the waves moving from the opposite direction and return even larger. In this way, the waves bang against each other, tossing the lightweight boats up high and then back down. They hoped that the motorboat traffic would subside during the race. Although they were accustomed to rowing through waves, they could only show off their expertise when their oars did not catch on the ridges and didn't toss their boat from side to side.

"I've never raced this close to a city centre before," Rita said.

"It's really close," Irena agreed. "The entire course from start to finish is inside the city."

"The spectators don't even need to buy tickets," Aldona said and laughed. "They can watch the entire race, from start to finish."

"It's good here," Leokadija agreed.

"I've haven't seen many races, so I'm fine anywhere," Jūratė said and smiled. "All I care about is that the lanes are straight, and that the waves don't get so high."

"Maybe the waves won't be so high during the race?" Aldona considered. "You don't think they'll be out in those motorboats on the water on the day of the race?"

"As far as I know, it's a dam," Leokadija said, waving her hand for emphasis, "so there's nowhere to go. So maybe they won't be out in their boats?"

The girls eight team quickly assembled their boat and were prepared for their first training session. Beside them the quad and the coxed four worked on their boats.

"We won't wash the boats now," Vaitkevičius said, "we'll wait until after training." With a wave of his hand, he indicated the direction to carry the boat to the pontoon.

Although construction was taking place all around them, the excitement of the upcoming competition was in the air. The walls were decorated with posters that showed oars from every country tied together into a bouquet and flags with a rooster holding an oar. The caption read:

Championnats d'Europe a l'aviron 1967 Vichy.

Everything is written in French... In Canada do they also speak French? Sofija wondered to herself. *Canada is a bilingual country. English and French. That's interesting. I wonder which language they speak in Niagara? Maybe English? Does my father speak English? Or maybe he speaks French? It was difficult to image her father's life, but she so wished that she could. He was completely foreign to her, a stranger... But he must have learned one of those languages back in Poland? At least English. Mama speaks seven languages after all... He's an architect. He must have studied at least one foreign language in university. Or maybe several? And what about Polish? Has he not forgotten his Polish? Of course, he speaks Polish... What a foolish thought. His letter was written in Polish, and without a single grammatical mistake, and with good style...*

A small poster written in French and English invited athletes to come and participate in a ping-pong championship right here in the sports village. Anyone who wished could participate.

Why not? Sofija thought. *I know how to play ping-pong. It'll be a good opportunity to relax and forget about my anxiety. I can't focus on books, I'm too anxious. It's just like when I took the train from Jelgava to Vilnius... There are three days until the race starts. I won't tire myself out. The important thing is not to sprain an ankle.*

CHAPTER ELEVEN

AUGUST 1967, VICHY, FRANCE

The sunny hot days in Vichy brought back memories of summer for the girls. They were pleased with the smooth glasslike surface of the water, but they longed for a light breeze to refresh them. The good mood that they always felt when they went abroad was eroded by anxiety as each day brought them closer to the start of the race. More competing teams appeared with their boats. The coxes called out their commands in foreign indecipherable languages.

On August 30th the student athletes' town was abuzz with activity. The men's teams began to assemble for their championship in a week's time. To be honest, only one men's team arrived, the Australian team. However, it seemed as though there were ten times more Australian athletes than any others. In the athlete's town there was so much loud and open laughter, so much boisterous conversation, that the Soviet girls felt as though the Australians weren't rowers, but circus clowns. They simply were not accustomed to such freedom of expression. The girls would throw surreptitious glances at the tall handsome Australian athletes and would quickly avert their gaze if their eyes met. The Australians were just looking for an opportunity to talk to, to flirt with, the engage with the shy "Russians" as they called them. Their teammates had warned them that it didn't take much to get pulled into some sort of pranks with the

Australians.

The European Rowing Championship was an open competition; therefore, there were a few teams who were not European. The World Championship was held only every four years (and it was only for men) and therefore there was no opportunity to compete against the world's strongest teams except for the Olympics. Again, at that time, only men's rowing teams could compete in the Olympics. They'd monopolized that privilege since 1900. Would women ever have the opportunity to participate in the World Championship? Nobody knew, although there was talk.

The day before everyone was intrigued by the girls they had never seen before, not in any race. They'd never seen the emblem on her tracksuit before. It was an American flag. The Lithuanian girls glanced with curiosity, but with reserve, at their new competitors. It was clear to them that their eight and the quad would race. That meant they would meet on the water and test their strength against each other. The American girls were younger than them, and they were also shorter and more petite. But they were unknowns. They had no idea what they would pull out on the water. They knew that men's rowing had high standards in America. Three years previous their eight had won in the Olympics. There were all sorts of talk then, that they just happened to get the best lane and so on. However, weak teams do not make it into the Olympics. Those girls had to be of a similar level.

"They said that the same girls would row the eight and the quad!" the girls said in surprise.

"Two different classes? Wow!"

"They must be very strong if they can race twice in one day?"

"Why else would they travel this far to race?" the Lithuanian girls wondered out loud.

"Somebody said that this is the first time that women from America have travelled to race on an international team."

"What?"

"They only brought the men's team before."

"Why?"

"I don't know."

"Jukna said that they have separate boat clubs, and that the men are separated from the women. They said the men have it much better."

"What do you mean, better?"

"The men have better equipment, and their buildings are in better condition."

"They discriminate?"

"Why is that?"

"They say that in America they didn't allow women to row before. Antanas said that we should be happy that we have equal rights with men and that we row together because in America they don't allow women into the men's club! In 1962 in Philadelphia, they took the men on a tour of the clubs and told them everything."

"That's nonsense."

"I heard that they paid their own way here."

"Who said that?"

"Boris Mikhailovich."

"Really? How much money do you need to have?"

"They said that they have to pay their own way everywhere they go. They only fly them to the Olympics for free."

"Are you serious? So, what kind of stipends do they get?"

"They don't receive stipends. They work. They train after work."

"Where did you hear that?"

"The men told me. They go out and train on the water at six in the morning. Then, they go to work. After work, they go out and train again. Students train before classes or after classes. They don't allow them to miss classes like we do."

"I don't believe you!"

"That's how it is."

"So, when do they rest? How do they find all that time?"

"I can't imagine... I barely get a nap in between training sessions, but they have to go to work."

"I don't believe you... It's probably the same as for us – they assign them a job, but they only work 'on paper.'"

"Perhaps..."

"And look at their uniforms."

"They have to pay for that themselves too."

"You're talking nonsense! You mean to tell me that the government doesn't pay for your uniform? You even need to buy that too?"

"I wouldn't."

"I wouldn't either. I wouldn't have the money. As it is, I live on borrowed money. When we get our prize money after the championship, I'll pay everybody back."

"If we win..."

"That's right... If we win. Then I'll have enough to live on and to pay back my debts. Otherwise, I only have enough to pay my debts."

"Oh look, the Germans have arrived!"

"Yes, they look happy."

"Maybe they're counting on an easy win?"

"We'll see about that!"

"They look powerful."

"Are you afraid of them?"

"No, not at all."

"I feel sick to my stomach when I just think about the start of the race."

The girls had been leaning into their boat and speaking softly, so that the American girls wouldn't suspect that they were talking about them. They counted nine of them, and their cox. *They really will race twice, at least a few of them will*, the Lithuanian girls mused.

"Girls!" a voice thundered in Russian. "What's this?" It was coach Jevgeni Kabanov, a Russian. He was angry to see the girls dressed in their Lithuanian tracksuits.

Leokadija, Rita, and Aldona shot glances at each other and bit their lips. They had worn their Lithuanian tracksuits with Lithuanian logos on purpose because they were ashamed to be seen as "Russians." The other girls lowered their eyes and pretended to be washing the boat.

"You know the rules! You may only wear the Soviet tracksuits with the emblem of the USSR!"

"We know," Leokadija lied, "but we didn't want to get our tracksuits dirty before the opening ceremony."

"Go and change right away! Don't let me catch you out of uniform again!" Kabanov said in an aggressive voice, just so that the girls would not try it again.

"Yes, we will," they said, lying again because they knew that they would not pay any attention to his commands.

Coach Natalia Sanina watched the quad row past from the shoreline. As always, she worked calmly, quietly, without making loud commands. Once the girls climbed out of the boat, she'd say a few words to them, and that would be it. That was how she worked, always. Even at the training camp. She would sit in Boris Schirtladze's motorboat and quietly observe them. During one training session, you might hear maybe three to five sentences from her. But each and every one of her comments was to the point and timely. Her ability to observe even the tiniest of technical errors was amazing. In this manner, she was similar to Ričardas Vaitkevičius.

"I'm only your consultant," she'd say to the girls, "you know how to do everything else yourselves." That was why they would train, and writetheir training plans, themselves. More accurately, not all of them, but Sofija. She had become her own coach ages ago.

Most likely, coach Sanina didn't have much to teach adult experienced rowers. It had been a long time since anyone had to chase after them and control them, make sure that they wouldn't hide away from difficult or tiring lanes, like young rowers are often apt to do. Young rowers are often petulant and impatient because they do not yet know why they began to row, because they did not know how to suffer, because they quickly lost their breath, and didn't realize that training sessions were not for the coach's benefit, but for their own. They knew that feeling sorry for themselves during training and avoiding physical suffering would only lead to greater physical pain and suffering during races.

Galina Konstantinova adapted to the crew very quickly. Rowing in the seat three, just behind Sofija's back, she supported her stroke perfectly. The four-time European champion was probably expecting to hold the most important position in the team, and not to end up sitting behind the stroke. However, she never said a single bad word about her situation. Galina, although she did not display much mirth, tried to be an equal teammate to the rest of the crew. She wasn't just a rower; she'd become friends with the girls. They respected each other, trusted each other, and experienced wins together. Theirs grew into a strong friendship. Only, the girls had dubbed Sofija as "our foreigner." But they said it nicely, in good fun, and not to humiliate her. They simply felt the girls from Lithuania were foreign, not Russian.

"Natalia Sergeyevna, we're making our last circle to five hundred and back!" the cox Natasha called out as they passed the pontoon.

The coach raised her hand and said, "good!" She covered her eyes with her palm, watching the strokes of the quad, and the water sparkling in the light of the sun.

Behind them were white skyrise hotels, an alleyway of green trees along the shoreline, and a wall of dark mountains in the distance, protecting the city.

CHAPTER TWELVE

SEPTEMBER 1967, THE EUROPEAN ROWING CHAMPIONSHIP

On September 1ˢᵗ the shoreline of the Allier was filled with crowds of city dwellers. Inside the Athlete's Town not a single construction vehicle remained, not one pile of cement, no ravines of dug up earth. All the construction work was complete, and the championship venue was impeccable. A row of flags flew from the flagpoles. There was the French flag and a blue and yellow flag.

"Could that be the Vichy flag?" the girls wondered.

Beside the flags there was a board that would display the racing results. On the opposite side of the river there was another renovated grandstand for spectators to watch the races.

The opening of the championships was a real holiday for the girls. Although, at the same time, they were all anxious. That day the races would begin. The one and only race that would be held the next day was the eight. Only six teams arrived to compete in that race so their start would be on the final day, and the final was scheduled for Sunday. On the one hand, that was good because it meant that all their anxiety was reserved for one day. On the other hand, there was no way to shake the fears every rower felt before the start of a race. That fear would only grow stronger.

The French were especially prepared for the opening ceremonies. In earlier championships there had not been any opening ceremonies. They probably decided to revive an old tradition. At two thirty all the teams assembled for a parade. They were all dressed in the sporting uniforms of their countries. Rowers from fourteen countries waited for their championship to begin.

The Soviet rowers and their coaches were dressed in blue tracksuits with the letters CCCP in white letters emblazoned on their chests. They all wore identical white athletic shoes. They stood in a long column assembled in rows of three. They watched as young girls dressed in red jackets, white pleated skirts, and wearing red berets handed out signs with the names of countries.

Those girls are dressed up in the colours of the Polish flag, only upside down, Sofija mused to herself. *How is it that all these signs fall together into one place: Father, Poland, what next?*

A girl carrying a sign that read USSR gazed around her, looking for the Soviet team. An old woman, perhaps her boss, pointed her in the direction of the team of the USSR.

"It's all so pretty here," Irena said. "I've never been at a nicer formal ceremony."

"I agree, the mood is entirely different," Leokadija agreed.

"Who is that?" Genovaitė wondered out loud, watching another group of girls in uniform, only their jackets were not red, but blue.

The identical white skirts, blue jackets, red berets, identical shoes, the red, white, and blue coloured scarves tied around their necks, and even their identical purses, made them all exceptionally elegant.

"Listen, could that be the American team? Isn't that their cox?" Jūratė wondered out loud.

"What emblem are they wearing on their jackets?" Aldona asked, lifting her sunglasses.

"I can't see," Jūratė said, standing on her tippy toes, straining to see the light-coloured emblems on the girls' jackets. They turned around every once in a while to see what was going on around them.

"Right! That blonde is their bow rower. I remember seeing her during training. See, the little one!" Leokadija indicated with her chin.

"You only noticed her because she's a tow-head like you," Genovaitė joked.

"That's right, a blonde always spots another blonde," Leokadija said and laughed. "I would not be at all surprised if she spoke Polish."

"Look at what's written on their sign, *Ét... États-Unis.* What does that mean?" Jūratė asked, turning towards her team. "Who speaks French?"

"It really is the Americans! Look, it's the tall blonde is from the eight," Leokadija recognized another girl who had turned around to glance at them.

"Oh, but just look at how they're dressed!" Genovaitė gasped. "Coach, when we will get uniforms like that?" she asked, turning towards Vaitkevičius.

"When you buy them yourselves," the coach joked back, "or when you make it to the Olympics."

"What Olympics? To race with men? When will there ever be women's rowing in the Olympics?" Genovaitė shot back.

"Then buy them yourselves," he teased.

"Why should I buy my own uniform?"

"They buy everything themselves – their plane tickets, their hotel, their meals. That means that they must have bought their uniforms themselves."

"If I spoke English, I'd go and ask them myself. But now you can just make up whatever you want, coach," Genovaitė pouted, pretending to be angry.

"Don't get upset, Genovaitė, one day you'll go to the Olympics. You'll get a nice suit, well, maybe not quite so nice, but you'll be dressed from your head to your toes."

"When will that be, coach?"

"Who knows, but see, now you have something to row for. If you row hard enough, you'll get a nice suit," Vaitkevičius joked.

"Coach, cut it out, I'm so scared I can barely stand."

"Don't worry, Genovaitė, you've learned everything you need to know. Today, you'll just repeat it all."

It's the officers again. Sofia remarked excitedly as a group of championship participants marched to the sound of the military orchestra. On the other side spectators waved at them. She trembled thinking of the upcoming race, but also when she saw the men in uniform. They reminded her of Father.

Stop imagining things, Sofija berated herself. *Father no longer looks like those young men. He could be a father to most of them, maybe even a grandfather. You can't get upset and start looking for your father every time you see a group of officers. He hasn't been an officer for decades. He lives on the other side of the world. He's old and I don't even know what he looks like. Some day I will see him, but not here. I've got to push the thought out of my head... We're racing tomorrow... I've got to pull myself together...*

After the opening greeting in French, which not a single Soviet girl understood, young men dressed in navel uniforms raised the flags of all the participating nations. *Biało-czerwona. Moja Polska... White and red. My Poland...* Sofija realized that she was not watching the Soviet flag go up, but the flag of her own nation. *Someone here is racing for Poland... It's just a single. Oh, I could have been in her place… I'd probably race better than her. Now I'll have to race with a red shirt. Under that nation's colours I grew up without a father. Under those colours my mother was dragged in for interrogation by the KGB. They almost shot my father. They shot thousands of officers. How many families suffered with their heads of the households gone. How many children grew up without fathers? Even those who survived were torn away from their homes? And I'm racing for this country… Oh, if only I had grown up in Poland… How different everything would have been. Perhaps I wouldn't even have known a thing about rowing? Perhaps I would not have grown weak from tuberculosis and Mama would not have sent me to row? Maybe I would have become a musician or ballerina?*

Sofija chuckled to herself. *What kind of a ballerina would I have made? I was made to race and to suffer…* Suddenly she remembered: the race was scheduled to start in an hour and a half! She had to find the time to change. In an hour, she'd be launching her boat… She glanced to the right and watched the ripples of water on the Allier. Her legs felt weak, and her heart banged against her chest.

* * *

How many times did I tell myself that I will never sit in a boat again, and then I'm back. How did I manage to forget everything so quickly after the finish? Every single time before a race the fear is so overpowering that she just wanted to run without looking back, but then, she'd go back and do it all over again. *What for? What was behind this? Why did all these girls come here from all over the world to suffer? And they all feel so proud of themselves, and their team, and their sport, even as they can all barely stand the suffering involved.*

Two crews feared the start of the race the most. That was Genovaitė and the coxed four from Novgorod. They were all new to the international arena. They all replaced European champions on the team. That was why they carried the heavy weight of responsibility. When they came to Vichy, the girls understood that to win all meets and take their place on the team was only the beginning. Now they had to gather the remains of their energy, which they spent on all the training sessions, and show those who did not make it onto the team that they had rightfully earned their places on the team. The pride, and the curiosity, of their first days in Vichy were clouded by their fear of the races. They all had dry mouth and their stomachs were twisted in knots.

The old saying: "Even the walls help you at home" was not helpful before the start of Sofija's quad race. They were racing against a team of French girls. That meant that there would be an enormous crowd of supporters cheering for them.

"Our foreigner is as calm as always," Tania said, surprised. "Where did you get your nerves of steel from, Sofija?"

"Really, Sofija, I envy you," Sasha agreed. "I wish I had your calm!"

Sofija smiled. "We can change places," she said, but in her thoughts, she ranted: *If only you knew… I would love to give away my fear.*

Sofija could barely contain her anxiety which threatened burning her out. That was the worst thing that could happen before the start of a race. If the anxiety ate up her reserve of energy, she would not be able to cover the distance. *Try not to think… Don't think… I'm not afraid… I'm not thinking… If only it were over faster… If the wind turns, we won't beat the Germans… Don't think about it… The wind won't turn…*

The heats had calmed her down and had given her confidence. The quad, the coxed four and the double finished first. Only Genovaitė, who was not accustomed to the Albano system, which used buoys to separate lanes, was left in fourth place. Lake Albano was 20 kilometres southeast from Rome and was destined to go into rowing history for all times. There, during the 1960 Olympic Games, for the first time the rowing lanes were separated by buoys.

"I counted all the buoys with my right oar. There were maybe three that I didn't hit. It was as though a magnet were pulling me to the right," Genovaitė narrated after the race. At least she was able to laugh at herself. "I'm fit as a horse, but I can't steer. I caught many a crab, as always."

"Don't worry, you'll do better," Sofija calmed her friend.

"I was in fifth place the entire distance. Only at the end I passed one boat... Crab after crab... It's a good thing I didn't capsize."

"Tomorrow you'll make up for it. Don't worry!"

"Why do you even bother trying to calm me down? I'm constantly catching crabs! From my very first race!"

"Stop making things up. You'll convince yourself."

"At least it's a good thing that I'm in a single," Genovaitė said and smiled wistfully. "At least I can't ruin anyone else's race."

"You didn't harm yourself either. You got some exercise, you tried out the course. Just consider it one more training session."

"As though I don't train enough..."

"Rest, sleep it off, you'll be fine."

"How did you do?"

"Good. We came in first in the heat. We had some trouble with waves at the start. The French girls had a lot of support. The whole embankment was cheering for them. We were bow to bow with them. Just before the finish line we passed them. Last year's single was in the boat with them. She made that team faster. Like us."

"Are you going to town?"

"I'm thinking of going out. Tomorrow I'll need to rest before the finals."

"I'm also thinking of going out."

"That's good. It'll take your mind off things."

"Only, I'll have to hide from my coach somehow. He won't let me off. I need to take my mind off everything. Otherwise, I'll burn out."

CHAPTER THIRTEEN

SEPTEMBER 2, 1867, THE EUROPEAN ROWING CHAMPIONSHIP

The last day before the finals passed especially slowly. The girls were up early and spent the day wandering aimlessly. They could no longer hide from their fear. On the water the mood was frantic – the repechages were still on. All that tension was exasperated by the men's teams who had arrived and were now assembling for the men's championships. They were hard at work unloading their boats, moving all over the area, not respecting the fact that the women's teams still had precedence until the following evening.

The Soviet men's team was due to arrive that day. If they didn't run into the same problem as the women's team, and if the organizers picked them up from the airport, they were due to arrive that afternoon around four or five.

It was even worse in their rooms. They could not escape from their nagging anxious thoughts by leafing through a book or hopelessly attempting to fall asleep. Even with all the windows closed, they could still hear the race commentator's voice coming through over the loudspeaker. That presented a problem. When the windows were shut, they suffocated from the heat of the Vichy sun. When the windows were open the noise drove them mad.

Why didn't I bring Father's letter with me? Sofija suddenly remembered. She had left the letter with Mother. *I could have read the letter over again and not thought about the race. There is no way I could read a book right now. I just stare and stare at a sentence and after I've read it, I cannot remember what I've read. But the letter... That was something else... I could focus completely on the letter. But Mama needs the letter more than I do. Or maybe not? Maybe she doesn't want to see Father or read his letter? Mama's life was destroyed. How does she feel? I cannot even imagine what she suffered...*

I don't even know how everything played out. How did Father leave to fight in the war? How did he disappear? How did Mama search for him? Oh, I should have at least taken the envelope with me! Then I would have had his address with me. I could have written a letter and mailed it from here. No one would tear open my letter and read it if I sent it to him from France. I can write to him anyway... But if I mailed the letter from Vilnius, I would need to consider every single sentence carefully, not let a single word slip that could cause the KGB to stop my letter or destroy it. Or they would never allow me to travel to the West again in my life... So many people have lost their ties with their loved ones simply because their letters are held up and end up stored away in KGB files or are tossed into the trash? People are still searching for their loved ones even though twenty years have passed since the war. The people on the other side of the Iron Curtain are afraid to write to their families in Lithuania because they are afraid their loved ones will then be arrested and end up in the KGB interrogation basement. How could I have possible forgotten to write down my father's address? Niagara Falls... Canada... What else? Oh, I can't just send a letter like people do in Lithuania, addressed to Grandpa in such and such village. There was some sad Russian story about something like that. But maybe I should try it? Maybe the letter would somehow reach him? Maybe someone in the post office will search for him by his surname? Maybe they would deliver the letter to him? What a silly thought. That could happen in a town like Trakai, but… How big was Niagara Falls? I don't know anything about that place. Would I make a fool out of myself? What if they don't find him and they return my letter? Then I might get in trouble with the KGB. But maybe I don't need to write a return address? No, here, you don't have to! If my letter gets there, it gets there. If it doesn't, it doesn't. I don't have anything to lose, except for a few Francs to pay for the postage stamp… How will I know if he received my letter? Should I wait for a response? Or write another letter from Lithuania? Oh, why didn't I bring his address with me?!

"Shall we go watch Genovaitė's repechage?" Ala asked, interrupting Sofija's train of thought. They were good friends.

"Oh yes, of course. Is she racing already? What time is it?" Sofija looked at her wrist, where she usually wore her watch.

"She is already on the water. The start is in fifteen minutes. Are you coming?" Ala asked impatiently.

"Of course, I'm coming!" Sofija exclaimed. She was thrilled to have something to take her mind off her anxieties for at least half an hour. Although, she felt a lot of tension watching her teammates race. Her stomach would be filled with butterflies wondering, where is Genovaitė now, what is she doing, how is she preparing for the start, how is she making her first strokes. *She really needs to win,* Sofija thought to herself, and then, *if she steers well, she'll win.*

"You ought to," Ala agreed.

The girls rushed down to the shore to occupy the best seats near the finish so they could cheer Genovaitė on.

More and more people filled up the seats around them. Probably all the men's teams had arrived by now.

"*Labas!*" a girl from the American eight greeted them in Lithuanian.

"*Labas!*" Sofija Kurkytė shouted back and waved.

"Who's that?" Genė Galinytė asked, surprised. She was the quietest and most modest girl on the eight.

"She's a rower on the American eight."

"Does she speak Lithuanian? Or did you teach her?" Sofija asked.

"She's Lithuanian. Her name is Jenny."

"How do you know her?" Ala asked.

"We met her yesterday. She heard us speaking Lithuanian and she approached us."

"Are you serious? She's a Lithuanian?" Genė observed the American out of the corner of her eye as she whispered questions.

"Yes, she is."

"And she speaks Lithuanian?"

"She does. She said that she attended Lithuanian school somewhere over there in Philadelphia."

"Lithuanian School?"

"Yes, Lithuanian. She said that there is a Lithuanian Church there and beside the church, a Lithuanian language school. Lithuanian children attend the school and learn how to speak Lithuanian."

"Has she lived in America for a long time?"

"She was born in America. Her parents are Lithuanian."

"She looks like a Lithuanian for real. She's tall and blond."

"She said that she noticed us right away because we're taller than the Russian girls."

"What did you talk about with her?"

"We talked about everything. She said that they paid their own way here."

"That's what Zhenia said, but I didn't believe him."

"Yes, they paid for everything themselves, their airplane tickets, the hotel, their meals."

"Really?"

"They bought their uniforms themselves and their tracksuits."

"It's good that they have uniforms like that over there."

"She said they bought the dresses from a medical supply store and the blazers from a shop that sells school uniforms."

"You're kidding!" Klavdija Koženkova said, astonished. She was the youngest member of the eight.

"I don't, not unless they're joking."

"We are so accustomed to everything being given to us that we cannot even imagine what would happen if we had to earn it all ourselves," Klavidija said and shrugged.

"Maybe we could find the money, but where would we find uniforms like that?"

"I saw in the locker room the Bulgarians and Germans were asking the Americans if they could trade team shirts."

"If I could speak English, I'd ask the same thing. Their clothing is very nice," Klavidija said and sighed. "It's the custom for the athletes to trade team shirts at the end of the competition – it's a lot of fun. Then everyone proudly goes home wearing team shirts from other countries. But the American uniforms are the best. The girls want everything that the girls from overseas have. "I even saw someone asking to trade bras," Klavidja said and giggled, covering her mouth with her hand.

"Is she the only Lithuanian on their team?" Genė asked. She wanted to find out more about this Lithuanian girl.

They were all curious about the Lithuanian girl. They felt sad seeing a Lithuanian girl who was just like them living somewhere far away, living a life that was so distant and different from their own lives. They imagined that her life must be much more beautiful than theirs.

"She's the only one."

"Did you ask her what her family name is?"

"I didn't ask. It might be in the race protocol though?"

"Oh, they've signalled the start!" Sofija said, standing up to get a better view. She shaded her eyes from the sun with the palm of her hands and squinted. She gazed into the distance, searching for her friend, Genovaitė Šidagytė.

"She's racing against a German?" Ala asked.

"Yes, Kukle."[18]

"Is she strong?"

"All Germans are strong."

"I think Genovaitė is leading," Ala said, shading her eyes from the sun, squinting to judge the opportunities Genovaitė's position offered.

"Oh, yes, she is! If she doesn't hit any of those buoys, she'll come in first."

"And if she catches a few crabs along the way, she'll still win somehow."

The girls laughed good-naturedly.

All the Lithuanian girls began shouting at once: "Ge-no-vai-tė! Lie-tu-va!"

Genovaitė turned around to catch a glance of her fans. Then she picked up her pace even more, going from twenty-six to thirty strokes a minute. She soon took the lead.

---

18   Anita Kuhlke, a rower from the DDR.

"Hold on! Lie-tu-va!" the girls shouted.

"It's fine, she'll hold the lead," Irena said, thrilled to see that Genovaitė held a confidant lead.

"She gave it to those Germans," Aldona said and smiled. "Well done! Genovaitė just made it to the finals!"

"We'll show those Germans too!" Rita said bitterly. "Tomorrow's our chance."

"Did something happen?" Sofija asked.

"We met the DDR federation president," Leokadija explained.

"And who is that?"

"He's convinced that the German's eight will win tomorrow!" Leokadija said angrily.

"He said they were afraid that the Soviets were bringing a serious team, but they showed up with *Žalgiris* again. He said we were no competition for them," Aldona explained, not able to hide her hurt feelings.

"They say that the DDR's eight is even stronger than last year's team," Leokadija continued.

"We'll win on purpose just to show them who's who!" Rita said, taking a combative stance. "Maybe it's a good thing they were so rude. They've inspired us to fight to win."

"They walk past us and don't even say hello! They turn their backs when we walk past," Leokadija said, pointing in the direction of the Germans with her chin.

"They're not at all like the American girls. They always say, "hi" and "hi" whenever we walk past them," Aldona said.

"It's a different culture," Jūratė said and nodded. "Americans are very friendly. It's a shame I can't speak their language."

"There's a Lithuanian on their team!" Sofija Korkutytė explained to the girls who had joined them and had not already heard her story. "I met her yesterday. I just haven't had a chance to tell everyone. Her name is Jenny. See, the tall one, that's her."

Sofija Korkutytė indicated the tall blond American girl dressed in a tracksuit, standing below them on the bleachers, speaking with a young man.

"Really? Where is she from?" Leokadija asked.

"Her parents left Lithuania before the war. She was born in America."

"And she speaks Lithuanian?" Jūratė asked, surprised.

"Yes, she speaks Lithuanian. How else would I have been able to speak with her? She heard us speaking Lithuanian and approached us."

"What's their team like? Did she tell you?" Irena asked.

"We didn't talk about their team. She just said that they had to pass all sorts of trial races to qualify to race here."

"So, we also have to pass all sorts of trial races to get here! Probably more than they do!" Jūratė exclaimed.

"They are also the club team, and not the national team. They're all from one club."

"Sometimes club teams are very good, right?" Aldona said and smiled slyly. Her eyes scanned all her teammates.

* * *

Evening did not come quickly. Minutes of flooded apathy turned into hours. That's how time passes just when you want it to end as soon as possible. The girls scattered into their rooms immediately after dinner to wait for tomorrow. They didn't want to talk, spend time together, or go for walks. Reading became an exercise of emptily flipping through books. It was absolutely impossible to concentrate on a book. You forget the beginning of a sentence before you have finished reading to the end of it.

Sofija closed the window so that she could not hear the sounds coming from outside, although they were not as loud as earlier in the day. The men indulged themselves enjoying their time outdoors before returning to their rooms to go to bed. The sounds of their loud animated voices and laughter beneath her windows began to annoy her.

It's a good thing they housed us in singles. If we were living in pairs, we'd definitely start talking about the competition, make each other even more anxious and expend too much energy before the race.

Tonight, she could no longer allow herself to enjoy any of the recreational activities organized by the athletic town. It was absolutely necessary to conserve her energy and take time for sleep. On Sofija's table lay a diploma from the ping-pong tournament and a prize from wine tasting. She had played ping-pong for a long time and she played well, so winning that sport was a commonplace experience for her. But she had never drunk wine before and did not know what wine tasting meant.

I never tasted wine in my life! I didn't know anything about wine... I was lucky. Sofija smiled to herself. *Why am I always successful when I try something for the first time? Everything just works out so easily without much effort. Success just falls from the heavens. But then, why am I never successful the second time I try something? Or the third time? Is that because I become paralyzed with fear? With self-doubt? Is it fear of what's coming? Why is it that anything I try for the first time I take on playfully and with good emotions? That was how it was before my first race. I didn't have any fears, any doubts. I was simply excited and curious. How could I hold onto that feeling the second and the third time? How do I get back that feeling I had on my first race?*

The fear Sofija felt strangled her. Sofija stretched out in her bed and tried to relax. Beyond her dark window the stars in the sky shined brightly and then more softly.

The sky in France is just like the sky in Lithuania, she thought to herself, trying to shift her thoughts away from race the next day. *And the sun shines just the same way as in Lithuania, and the moon is the same. The stars are the same. Mama is probably gazing at the very same stars in Vilnius right now. What is Mama thinking now? Maybe she's asleep already? What time is it in Lithuania? Midnight? Of course, she's sleeping. Father doesn't see the same stars… It's day for him in Canada. It's a Saturday for him in Canada. What does he do with his Saturdays there? I don't know anything about him. Nothing… Why do stars disappear? They're here and then they're gone. Is it because of the clouds? Probably because the clouds cover them. All week the weather has been clear. Are clouds gathering? The stars are shining so brightly. And then they're gone again. Yes, it must be the clouds. The weather is changing… Maybe they'll be rain tomorrow? That wouldn't be so bad, as long as the wind doesn't pick up. What direction are the clouds moving? We've got the first lane. If the wind blows from the direction of the city, we'll encounter some waves. If only it's not a head wind… Like in Amsterdam. The Germans will take the lead again. They're bigger and stronger. The wind does not slow them down…*

Sofija rolled onto her stomach and pushed her face into her pillow. *Don't think about it, don't think about it, don't think about it. One sheep, two sheep, three sheep. Nonsense. I'll never fall asleep like that. All is well… This is only one more race. It's not the end of the world.* Her heart was beating hard. It was impossible to fall asleep. She had to do something to calm down, to not think about the start tomorrow.

The day after tomorrow we'll see Paris! We will spend the entire day in Paris! That will be amazing. Everyone says Paris is an amazing city. I've only seen Paris in the movies. And I read about Paris in novels... Few people from the Soviet Union ever have the chance to travel to Paris. Only artists, actors, or communists. And athletes... Those who make it to the European Rowing Championships. Only after they've passed dozens of trials and qualification races. And only if everything is in order with their documents. Only if the KGB doesn't stop them from traveling. But Paris will be miserable if we lose. We must win... But what if we don't? We must win. I'll suffer through it. The most important thing is that the girls keep up the stroke rate. Oh no, just don't think about it, don't think about it...

Sofija took a deep breath and rolled onto her side. *What time is it?* She took the clock from her closet and turned on the lamp beside her bed. *A quarter past eleven. I must fall asleep right away... If I don't get enough sleep, I won't have enough strength to row tomorrow. That'll be bad.* Her thoughts spun wildly in her head, returning over and over again to the finals. She couldn't take it anymore. It was always like this before a race. However, this time, her emotions were many times stronger. It seemed as though she'd never be able to close her eyes and relax her body.

All is well, all is well... I'm in France... I dreamed so much about this... This isn't the DDR, this is the real West... It's so beautiful here! The city is gorgeous... I'll bring home plenty of photos... I've shot three rolls of film already... I've photographed every corner, every house... It's a good thing that the centre is so close... All I need to do is to cross the bridge to the other side... Rarely are races held so close to the city centre... The starting line is right next to a restaurant on the water... The start... *Étes-vous prêts? Partez!* Attention! Go. Oh, just as long as we don't fumble the start... And that we don't start too fast. We don't want a false start... We don't want to catch any crabs... Six and ten[19]... Then ten more... At five

---

19   Six starting strokes and ten strokes are needed to enter into the race, when the

hundred – power ten, ten more...

Sofija suddenly up in bed, leaned her forehead onto the palm of her hand and sighed deeply. *It's no use...* She pulled on her tracksuit, slid her feet into her slippers, and padded quietly down the corridor. She stopped at room 18 and knocked softly.

"Whose there? Come in!" the men's team doctor, Tatyana, called out.

Sofija pulled open the door and stepped inside.

"What happened?" Tatyana asked, surprised to see the fear on Sofija's face.

"Good evening, Tatyana Mikhailovna. I need your help. I cannot sleep," Sofija said and sighed. "Give me something to help me fall asleep."

The doctor gazed at the quad stroke who was always the picture of calm stoicism and leaned in towards her.

"I'm not surprised, Sofija," she said, "really, I'm not. But sleep pills won't help you. To be more precise, the pills will help you fall asleep, but there is no telling how they will affect your body tomorrow. You may be sleepy all day long and then you won't be able to row. You'll fall asleep on the water."

The doctor stood from her chair, walked over to her closet, opened the door, and pulled out an opened bottle of red wine.

"The wine will evaporate by tomorrow, but it will help you fall asleep."

She poured half a glass and extended it towards Sofija.

Sofija raised her eyebrows.

"Seriously?"

"Drink it. Don't worry. That much won't get you drunk," Tatyana said and laughed. "This is not vodka. Red wine will relax you. You'll fall asleep quickly and you won't dream."

---

boat takes on maximum speed.

Sofija took the glass, gazed into the dark cherry coloured liquid, took a deep breath, and drank it all in one gulp. *One more wine tasting*, she mused.

"Thank you."

"You're welcome. Go back to bed now. You'll see how quickly you'll fall asleep. Good night."

"Good night, Tatyana Mikhailovna. Thank you. I'll try to fall asleep."

"You'll sleep like a baby!"

"Thank you."

Warmth spread throughout her body before she even reached her room. *As long as this doesn't make things worse*, she thought. She had barely lay down in bed when her body went still, and she gradually fell into a deep sleep. Soon, she could no longer hear all the sounds coming in from the outside.

CHAPTER FOURTEEN

SEPTEMBER 3, 1967, THE EUROPEAN ROWING CHAMPIONSHIP FINALS, VICHY, FRANCE

The day of the finals dawned differently than all their previous days in Vichy. First, the weather had completely changed. The sky was filled with clouds, the weather had cooled, and a wind created waves on the River Allier. Second, it was the day of the finals. It was the day that would divide their lives into "before" and "after." It was the day when they would either be jubilant with glory or eat themselves up with disappointment if they didn't win the gold. The worst part was that the glory would be short lived. However, the pain of losing the races would torment them their entire lives. The disappointment of losing would be intensified by the angry remarks they'd have to take from the team managers. Then, it would seem as though after this day the entire world had been turned upside down.

"We got a good wind today," the girls noted to each other.

The first thing they did when they awoke that morning was to run to their windows to check the direction of the wind. They could judge the wind by the direction in which the flags were flying. Then, they checked their bodies. Were they stiff? Did they have back pain? Have the blisters on their palms scabbed over?

"We're rowing down wind," Sofija whispered to herself and sighed in relief.

Such a wind was perfect for their crew. It was easy to keep a high stroke rate rowing downwind. *Oh, if only the wind doesn't turn,* Sofija found a new worry. *That wine was good. It helped me fall asleep. I barely noticed how I drifted off. And it's true, it's gone without a trace. I hope...*

Sofija felt a wave of anxiety wash over her body. There was only an hour left until the start of the final race.

"Only victory is acceptable!" their team managers commanded in stern voices. They made it clear that coming in second was an unforgivable offence. That would ruin the Soviet Union's teams plans to win. During competitions such as these, the athletes did not worry much about the Soviet team plans, but that was what was most important to the Soviet team leader delegation. They were told that it was imperative that their team defeat their worst enemy, the DDR team.

The girls met in the cafeteria for breakfast. No one was in the mood for small talk. They picked at their food and had a hard time swallowing anything. The only sound in the cafeteria was the sound of spoons banging against the edges of their cups as they mixed their tea. Even the coaches did not say anything. They sat stone-faced and silent, although they tried hard to appear relaxed and in a good mood. The wrinkles on their foreheads were deeper than usual. There was a strong sense of anxiety in the air. The girls knew that they had to force themselves to eat; otherwise, they wouldn't have any strength left before they even made it to the warm-ups. They knew that eating would ease their stress, but if anyone were to observe them in that moment, they looked like disobedient children who needed to be coaxed into taking each bite.

The quietest of them all was Aldona. Her eyes were filled with fear, but not so much about the race, but because she was running a fever and her throat hurt. She had even lost her voice.

"What's wrong?" Sofija asked when she saw her.

"I caught a cold…"

"After the opening ceremony journalists invited us to sit down on the grass for an interview," Rita said. "The earth was so damp. They kept us there for a long time asking questions and Aldona caught a chill," Rita explained.

"I heard her coughing yesterday."

"It wasn't so bad yesterday, but after the training session my temperature went up."

"You've got a temperature?"

"It's almost thirty-eight," Aldona said and bit her lips.

"Did you take anything to bring down the temperature?"

"I can't take anything before a race. The only thing I can do is drink tea."

"Does Zhenya know?"

"He knows."

"What did he say?"

"Nothing. What can he say? We don't have any stand-ins. There's no one to take my place. I felt sick yesterday as well. I was hoping I'd be better in the morning."

The girls in the eight were in a complete state of panic. It was a risk to race with a high temperature. Anything can happen in the space of that distance. Aldona could get dizzy, row coughing, catch a crab, even faint… Then what? There were times when the girls went to a training session with a cold. But the coaches had a strict rule against rowing with a fever. Nobody hoped for a miracle at that point. It was simply tragic.

As always, the day before the most important event something unexpected happened. Just like in childhood, when you got sick right before

Christmas or a class outing, or before your first race and Mama wouldn't let you out of bed. It seemed then as though you were about to miss out on the most important day of your life.

The television in the corner showed scenes from some big city clogged with automobile traffic. The cafeteria workers kept glancing at the screen and making comments to each other and then laughing. The girls did not understand what they were saying in French, but they were curious. Although even this small incident could not block out the fear of the upcoming race.

"What are they showing there?"

"I don't know... I don't understand..."

"Is that an accident?"

"What are they showing there?" Sasha, who knew a little English, asked a waiter who was walking past them.

"Sorry? Did you ask me something? Oh! The television? Today Sweden changed the driving direction from the left to the right," he smiled and pointed at the screen.

"Oh, thank you," Sasha said gloomily.

"What did he say?"

"Sweden changed the driving direction. They used to drive on the left side, but from now on they will drive on the right, like we do."

"Why should we care about their problems?"

"Just look at all those autos?"

"How do they ever control all that traffic?"

"I'm going to my room," Sofija said and stood up. "What time do we meet?"

"Our race starts half past one?"

"Yes. Let's meet in the foyer at half past twelve," Sofija glanced at the clock. There were only three and a half hours until the race. Before them the coxed four raced, then the single, and then the double would race.

I'd like to watch those races, but I need to concentrate on my own start. I've got to rest. It's better not to watch, to save my nerves.

When it's three hours before a big race, everything just seems to slip out of your hands. But not out of your head. Thoughts are painful. And there's no escape from them. As much as you try to think about something else, just as soon as you try your thoughts drift back to the race and that knot in your stomach just grows stronger. Sometimes I wish they'd just call off the finals! Sometimes I wish a natural disaster would stop them or some other unprecedented occurrence. I wish they would just hand out the medals based on yesterday's results. It wouldn't even matter what those results were. Just so that I wouldn't have to race! If only I could shake off that terrible anxiety – that stress that stopped me from talking, from being myself, from even seeing what was going on around me... But then, later, I always feel that without the finals I'd feel as though I'd left the job half done... Then I gather myself together and repeat to myself: Everything will be over soon... Everything will be just fine... There's not much left now... In four hours it'll all be over...

The coxed four had it good. They start first. We've got to wait another hour. When we row to the starting line, they'll be finishing. Then, they'll be standing on the awards pontoon. It'll all be over for them then...

"What a disaster..." The team leadership exclaimed after the first finals.

The coxed four, a crew of newbies from Novgorod, finished second. The DDR team took first place. For the managers of the Soviet team, who cared most about winning team standings, considered this "loss" the beginning of a catastrophe.

I feel sorry for them, Sofija thought to herself. *It'll be like it was for us last year in the European Rowing Championship in Amsterdam.* She re-membered how their crew was brought straight from the airplane to the Soviet Communist Party Central Committee to explain why they lost. *Or maybe we'll lose as well, and then all of us together will stand before them with our eyes lowered in shame, listening to their lectures on how they pay us money and how we cannot live up to their expectations.*

"Did you notice, the wind shifted," Sasha said, interrupting her train of thought.

"Really? Are we rowing upwind now?" Sofija asked. She glanced up at the flags. They were blowing in the opposite direction than they were in the morning.

"Half against the wind. Its blowing crosswise from this shoreline," Tanya observed.

"It's not that bad. We're in the first lane. We'll get the most tail wind," Sofija explained, doing her best to keep the crew's spirits up.

"You always find something positive in any situation," Sasha said and smiled. "Oh, but I'm so nervous!"

Sofija, as always, appeared on the surface calm and ready to go to battle. Although, as always, her legs gave out beneath her and her hands trembled. She avoided saying much because her mouth was dry and there was a large lump in the back of her throat.

"What lane did the Germans get?" Tanya asked nervously.

"The sixth, I think," Natasha, the cox, answered.

"They'll catch the head wind, but that's fine for them, they're big."

"We all got what we wished for," Sasha joked. "Not like last year."

"The Novgorod four was in the sixth lane. That's probably why they lost," Tanya observed. "I feel so bad for them."

"They're just beginners. As beginners, they've done really well!"

"Yes, but try explaining that to them over there," Tanya said, indicating with her chin the group of senior coaches and the team managers standing off to the side. "For them, it's a step backwards."

"Well, yes, you're right. All they care about is the gold."

Sofija lost herself in thought: *Genovaitė is out on the water already. She's got to handle all this by herself. There's no one for her to lean on. How does she cope with her nerves? All alone like that... No one else will steer the boat for her. No one will adjust her pace for her.* Sofija shuddered inside. *I never want to race a single again. It's probably because of the singles racing that I've become so anxious. It's much better to be with four others together throughout the race. But that's responsibility... Responsibility for yourself is one thing, but responsibility for the team is something else altogether. After an hour, everything will be over. But only after an hour... Oh, how I wish I could be a spectator up on the bleachers right now. Or just some passer-by. I'd watch casually as someone out on the water was racing. I'd drink coffee in one of those restaurants along the shoreline. I'd listen to music, and I'd wave, as I sat their relaxed with my legs crossed. I'd lean back under the sun and listen to the rustling water of the river.* The sound of the commentator's voice returned Sofija to the present and to the unavoidable routine before the start of the race.

"That's it, time to go," she said. Sofija plastered a cheerful and determined smile on her face, turned towards her crew, picked up her shiny wooden oars, and said, "Let's go."

The water out on the Allier was rough. The wind skittered across the surface. The further away it was to the opposite shore, the steeper the waves. She saw that the conditions were not at all good in the sixth lane.

At least for once we got lucky with our lane. If only the wind doesn't turn again... As she rowed away from the pontoon, Sofija surreptitiously glanced at the flags blowing across the course, as though she feared that in an instant, they could change direction again.

The girls from the eight stepped onto the pontoon carrying their oars. They were racing last. There was only half an hour remaining before the start of the race. Then, it would all be over. All their fear and anxiety would come to an end. Someone will celebrate, and someone will be disappointed. However, all that would pass sooner or later.

Behind her back she heard the engine of the umpire's motorboat as it approached. The cries of the spectators grew louder.

The singles race is halfway over... Sofija glanced for a moment to her right. *She is doing well. There wasn't much left to go. She'd win something. If only she didn't catch a crab.*

The anxiety that gripped her entire body would not let go. Her hands and legs felt weak. Her lips were dry, and her throat was parched. The usual warm-up strokes – arms, arms and waist, one third drive, half drive, didn't seem to bring her sleepy body to life. Behind her back she could hear the silent rolling of the wheels of three more seats on the slides and the precise squeaking of oars into the water. No word, no sigh. Sofija didn't try to predict how the girls would feel. There was no time and no reason for that. She was the team leader and she had to inspire her team with her strength and calm.

It's never like this during training. Not even before a qualification race do I get anxiety attacks like this. How should I cope? Perhaps I can imagine that I am at the training?

Sofija closed her eyes and tried to remember the feeling she had when she rowed on the Galvė or Skaistis Lakes. *You carried out your boat and the castle gazed down at you. And the people beside the castle watched you, and the people out boating. You push off from the pontoon and with your arms, with your arms and your waist, you row towards the curve to Žydiškes. Before the bay, the water has a specific scent – it is refreshing and at the same time sweet. It's so calm and so smooth. You hear the gentle rustling of the rushes, and you see the pretty yellow water lilies as you glide past. Oh, it feels like a miracle when you see a white-coloured water lily, they're so rare! The birds sing up in the trees. Ringlets in the water ripple outwards and away as you row. You glide your boat further and further away from those ringlets. You pull harder with your oars... One length, one and a half, two... You check yourself and your distance against those ringlets. Is it bigger than yesterdays? Are you faster than you were yesterday... It feels so peaceful, so good, to be out rowing on the water then, when the water is flat, and not rough from the wind, when there are no any motorboats to ruin it! You take a stroke and you glide across the water as though your were skidding over glass...*

The crowd's cheers in French returned her to the present, to the inevitable challenge of the race.

Everything is so grand and so lively here! In Trakai, everything is much simpler. The nature is pure and natural. People don't get in your way. There are no concrete shorelines, no houses. On the right there is the white touristic base. It was once the manor house of the Tiškevičius family, but the Soviets nationalized it. We measure distance from island to island, from bay to bay. The start is in the silty area on the edge of the lake and after twenty-five strokes you reach the island. And that island blocks the wind and the waves. Thirty more strokes down is the castle island... Then only half a distance remains... The men's start is two kilometres at the very end of the lake, near the Pioneer's Camp. Half of their distance is not protected by any island from the southern wind. The water forms waves like those in the sea...

"*Partez!*" The starting command in French echoed through the megaphone. The motor of the judge's boat burst to life.

The doubles have started their race... We're next... Fifteen minutes remaining... There's less and less time remaining... There's no were to hide... I've got to face it... We're next on the starting line...

The girls grew even more restless. They could barely control their jerky movements and compensated by taking deep breaths. The anxiety was evident in every single boat, in every quad that had made it into the finals. This was the most important start of the entire championship. Thirty young women were drawing ever closer to the dividing line between "until" and "after". Fifteen of them would celebrate with medals today. The other fifteen would suffer defeat. Five of them will experience the bitter disappointment of not making it to third place. Five will feel relieved simply to have not placed last. Perhaps those who win the medal will not rejoice as they should. Everything depended on fulfilling expectations – one's own and others.

The coxes' voice grew ever louder, and their commands became sterner. They felt the weight of responsibility on their shoulders. And now, just when their mouths were the driest, they could not remain silent, like the rowers. It was their role to inspire them, to pick up their spirits before the start, for the entire kilometre length of the course, they would have to call out encouragement, courage, and take control.

At the far end of the distance, not far from the finish, where the flags were waving. and the six doubles were gliding into the distance, they could see the eights out on the water. One crew stood out from the rest because of the bright red colour of their team shirts.

Those are our girls out there... The doubles are lucky – they're almost at the finish line. There's not much left, less than half the distance. The eights are in a good position too. They still have time. Almost half an hour. But we're on the spot now. That's it, we've done all that we could do. No, we can

say "that's it", only when they start calling out the names of the country...
Until that moment comes, so much can still happen... A storm could blow in
that would make them postpone the race. An oar can break... Or a boat...
Oh, fingers crossed, nothing will break. Not for us. Someone could be late
getting to the starting line. The Germans could be late? No, nonsense, they're
right here already. They will call out our name soon... That's the worst...
When they take hold of the stern of the boat, when there's just a few minutes
remaining... Oh, we've got to keep the boat straight in the lane... There's a
crosswind... Oh, those boat holders who have to do nothing more than hold
the stern steady have it good. There's no stress on them, no nerves... All they
have to worry about it lying on their bellies on the stake boat and watching
everyone else eaten alive with stress. I'd like to be one of them right now. I
wonder if they feel any worry at all? If they're rowers, they must worry, at least
a little. If they're just random people doing a job, then what do they know
about what it takes to row in a race? They release one boat and wait for the
next one. The only thing they've got to worry about is eating and going to the
toilet...

She heard Galya coughing behind her. One of the girls splashed some
water onto the handles of her oars. Another took a deep breath and ex-
haled three times. They were all anxious, even Galya, who won the European Rowing Championship four times already.

The concrete shoreline separated people who lived normal lives from
these young women, who chose the life of a rower, a life that had no
comparison. Just a few dozen metres beyond those massive walls, there
were beautiful, elegant hotels, shop windows, fragrant cafes and baker-
ies. Elegant women navigated those streets clacking away on their French
high heels. Meanwhile, in the boats women who were as young and beautiful as though navigating the shops and cafes, fought an inner battle in

anticipation of the pain they were soon to endure.

"Sports are war during peace time," the Communist Party instructor in Moscow strictly admonished them. "We must win that war. We must show them that we are the strongest. Only victory is acceptable. Anything else you will take responsibility for. All the Soviet Union is cheering for you!"

The wind has died down. Now not a single team has an advantage. Oh, I wish it were all over already… If we win, then I may one day see my father…

CHAPTER 15

MAY 1975, VILNIUS – MOSCOW

The Vilnius-Moscow train departed from the Naujoji Vilnia station, and curved towards the western forests. The twelve-hour journey on the night train always brought back many memories from when she was young. Back then Sofija would travel to races and her legs would begin to tremble just from the thought of the race as soon as she stepped out of the train. A lump would form in her throat that would subdue all the enthusiasm of training, and those times when she felt that her crew was getting faster, when she imagined easy victories. Despite her anxieties, those trips were a lot of fun. Her fears would be tempered by the good company of her team friends. They would share stories, tell jokes, sing, make dares. The time on the train passed swiftly. Sleeping in the coupe was nothing to a young rower – the only thing any of them had to worry about was not sliding out of the top bunk when the train headed into a curve. Any sudden jolt departing from a station along the way felt like an earthquake and woke you out of your sleep.

But now, she was all alone. Ever since she had made it into the So-viet Team, she travelled on her own. She travelled to the training camps alone, and not in a group, like the girls on the eight. "Go, go to your Muscovites," the team leaders in Vilnius would say to her bitterly. *I don't need you anyway,* she'd shoot back in her thoughts, *I'll be fine.* She saved her kopeks to be able to buy train tickets to travel to the training camps. She never understood why back in Lithuania they had pushed her away and didn't need her anymore.

The bright May sunshine fell straight into her eyes. *I should have taken a seat on the opposite side. Why didn't I think of that? Now it's too late. All the empty seats are taken. Anyway, soon the train will head north, then the light will warm my jaws and not my eyes.* Sofija pressed her hand to her forehead to shade her eyes from the bright sunlight. She began shivering with anxiety the moment she stepped into the train. This trip was going to be different. She herself was different now. She had other worries and other thoughts on her mind. She was thirty-six. She had spent sixteen years rowing, and the last five years working as a coach. Everything she experienced she compared with her experience as a rower. Right now, she felt as anxious as she did before a race. Second place was not a possibility. She had to win. Life would not give her a second chance. The hardest part was that she did not know who she was up against.

This can't be any worse than the time when I had to travel from Jelgava to Vilnius to meet with the KGB, Sofija thought, comforting herself. *This time I know the people, they're like family... Although, who knows what's in their heads and what they can do...*

Without realizing what she was doing, she tapped her fingers against the train windowsill. She counted the tree trunks as they flew past. She must assemble her words correctly.

"Aleksander Nikolaevich, I know that in August..." No, that was no good, it was too direct. *"Hello, Alexander Nikolaevich, how are you? How are the Olympic trials going? Perhaps you know the team structure already?"* No, that wouldn't work either... *I'd heard something about how he might not even be the Olympic team coach... I'll insult him, get him upset, and*

*ruin everything... Or, he'll get into a drawn-out explanation, we'll run out
of time, or someone will interrupt us, and he'll need to leave, and I'll be
left with nothing.* "Hello, Alexander Nikolayev, I took the train from Vilnius to speak with you about an important personal matter..." *That's probably better. If he understood that I had travelled from Vilnius, especially
to speak with him, then he'd know that the matter is urgent...* "Alexander
Nikolaevich, I absolutely must make it into this group..."

Alexander Nikolaevich Berkutov, champion of the Melbourne Olympics, prize winner in Rome, and many times European champion, was
now the man who the fulfilment of her greatest dream depended on.
When Sofija started rowing, Berkutov was already a well-known Soviet
rower. Soon, he became a celebrated rowing star. He was only six years
older than Sofija, but it seemed as though she could never catch up to
him. That was how it was. Women were not allowed to compete in the
Olympics and did not have the same opportunities to achieve what men
could. The highest accomplishment a woman rower could achieve was
to become a European champion. Over the years, Sofija had won a few
European Rowing Championship medals of her own. That gave her
the right to dare to approach two-time Olympic champions like Yuriy
Tyukalov and Alexander Berkutov. As they all grew older, the age difference between them diminished. But this time she had to gather all her
courage and self-confidence. It didn't matter what anybody thought. This
time it was imperative that she achieve victory.

A lump rose in Sofija's throat just contemplating the difficult conversation. That anxiety mixed with the pleasant sensation that flooded her
body just thinking about a positive response from Berkutov. *"Alexander
Nikolaevich, I came especially from Vilnius to speak with you... Yes, yes, I'm
working as a coach... It's going well... I have a great team of girls... The*

Olympics? No, not yet, they're not quite ready yet... Someday... Finally, women can compete as well... It's too bad that it happened when I'm already too old to race... My family?... Yes, of course he'll ask me about my family, he's that type of a person. I won't be able to hide anything from him... No, it hasn't been going well... Unfortunately, we divorced three years ago... It's better for both of us that way...

Sofija's marriage did not last long. Just as long as she was able to put up with her mother-in-law's intrusion into her son's marriage. They simply couldn't make the marriage work. Sergey's mother's control over them was overpowering. She did not allow him to live in Vilnius. Sergey's inability to pull himself away from his mother's apron strings deteriorated their relationship day to day. Finally, Sofija gave up and said: "Enough, you live with your mother and I'll live my own life." She slammed the door and left. Her life of commuting between Vilnius and Moscow ended then and there. However, that wasn't the end of it. Sergey had a fight with his mother and left her home. His mother was in despair. She sent a "delegation" of the relatives to Vilnius to try to reconcile their marital differences. The only problem was that due to macabre coincidence, they arrived in Vilnius on the day of Sofija's mother's funeral. There was simply too much emotion for Sofija to handle all at once. She said, "No" and that was final.

"Alexander Nikolaevich, I have to speak with you about an important matter... I heard that the pre-Olympic week isscheduled take place in Montreal a week after the World Junior championships... I know that a group of coaches are traveling with the group... I really need to be included in that group... It's very important..." But then he will obviously ask me why. Or maybe, he'll hear me out and that will be enough. I haven't told a soul... How will he react?... My father, who I've never met in my life, lives in

Canada… I very much wish to meet him… He is seventy-nine… "How did he get there?" Or maybe he'll know enough not to ask that? He ended up there because of the war… I'm afraid that this may be my one and last chance to see my father… Can you please help me?… I'm not planning on defecting to Canada. I simply really want to see my elderly father…" I want to see my father and to look into his eyes. I want to see in his eyes the answer as to why Mama and I lived for years alone and in poverty, with no knowledge of what happened to him. I want to find… No, I will return… That feeling between a father and a daughter that my heart feels, even from such a distance, that's what's pulling me towards him… They say that a blood bond is stronger than anything else… I only wish to feel my father close to me… I want to hug him and feel safe in his arms… I've never in my life have experienced what it feels like to have a father's love and protection… I've forgotten how to even image such a thing because I've never experienced it… If I were still rowing, I might have gone to the Olympics next year… Then I might have seen my father… Finally, women may race in the Olympics. And, as it turns out, the Olympics are in Canada this time… But no one can row that long… I'm already thirty-six. Next year I'll be thirty-seven… Who knows if I could have survived that long on the team… No one wants an old lady on the crew… You turn thirty and you're done… Unless you are twice as strong as everyone else… It would be hard to get out of sports then… But maybe I would see my father…

Sofija pulled her sweater over her shoulders and rested her head against the train window. She remembered the day she received her father's first letter from the KGB as though it were yesterday. Back then she felt as though she could reach out and take hold of her father. She felt that if they had found each other, then it should not be a problem for them to meet. She secretly hoped that he would look for ways to meet her. No, he would have never travelled to a communist country, but he could have travelled to a free country. Over the past seven years since she received her father's letter she'd been to many countries – Germany, Austria, Vichy… That trip to Vichy from the distance of time felt like one enormous confusion of emotions and thoughts. So much had taken place over a few weeks, that she had a hard time understanding how she could have managed to not cave in to all those emotions. Sofija remembered her last thought before the start of the race: *If we win, maybe one day I'll see my father.* And then there was the start and three and a half minutes empty of any thoughts, forty-two strokes a minute, hearing only her own breath and a word or two shouted out by the cox. They didn't allow a single other team to stick its bow out ahead of them… All she wished for was to suffer it through to the end…

"Would you like some tea?" The train stewardess' harsh voice broke into her thoughts.

Sofija raised her eyes and looked up at her. "Yes, thank you," Sofija said.

Soon three metal tea holders with glasses filled with sugary black tea rattled on the table beside their window. The two other cups were for the other passengers in the coupe. The stewardess entered the next coupe and barked out her question.

Why is she shouting like that? If there were a foreigner traveling with us in this coupe, I'd be so embarrassed. Oh, I remember when we took the train from Vichy to Paris! We felt so wonderful. I get goosebumps just remembering it. That was a good race! All the girls were in such a jubilant mood afterwards. We all received medals. We started at forty-two strokes a minute and did not decrease our pace the entire race… To Paris… Nobody on that train shouted. Soviet people who have never travelled outside of the Soviet Union have no idea that it is possible to speak to another human being without anger, without shouting, without hatred and threats.

Then, it seemed as though our entire lives had changed and from then on everything could only get better. In the Soviet team plan we earned first place in team standings, and that was what was most important. Although, there were two "catastrophes" – the coxed four's silver and Genovaitė's bronze. The team leaders were happy, though, because their heads were not going to roll because at least we were bringing home the first place as a team.

"I could care less what they have to say! I'm satisfied with my medal," Genovaitė had said to her, then added, "although, maybe I could have fought harder…"

"Don't worry," Sofija had comforted her, "you did well. This isn't your last championship. You're an incredible rower. Don't listen to what they say to you."

"I don't…"

The sadness in Genovaitė's eyes slowly subsided into calm. She was pleased with herself, but she felt sad about the way the team coaches pressured them. They did not have a single good word to say to her after she won the bronze…

The tea cooled and it no longer burned her lips when she took a sip from the glass cup. Sofija stared at the silver-coloured glass holder with the image of the Kremlin embossed onto it and for the first time pondered to herself: *What a strange object. I wonder if other countries have some such thing? Do people drink from these tea holders at home? Or just in the train? I cannot imagine the train coupe without these ideologically decorated tea glass holders.* Some of them are made especially for an anniversary, like USSR 50, for example. Sometimes they are decorated with flowers or grapes. All three cupholders on the table had different designs. *There must be a separate state-run factory that makes them. To design one of these, you need not only an artist to create the image, but also a committee to approve it.*

The warm sweet tea soothed her, but her anxiety over the upcoming meeting prevented her from dozing off to sleep. She felt the same way she did that night before she had to meet with the KGB.

The train rattled forwards, making a mechanical sound. The sun set behind the shrubbery outside her window. The monotonous rhythms of the train made her sleepy, just like they had that fairy tale September when they took the train to Paris. Only now, the cushions were not as soft as in that French train.

Then, in 1967 in Paris, when all the other girls rushed around the shops picking out new shoes and clothing, Sofija only wanted to see as many famous sites as she could and, silly as it seemed, go to see a Disney film. It didn't matter which one. Together with Alexandra Bochiarova they bought tickets and ended up in a movie theatre. They'd never experienced such a cinema in their lives – the seats were soft and felt almost like armchairs. Reclining in those soft cushioned chairs was so relaxing that they fell asleep immediately just as the film began.

If everything works out tomorrow, I may finally be able to meet my father… Oh, but what if it's too late…

Eight years had passed since she had first heard from her father. In those first days after she received the letter, her feet would give out from under her if she so much as thought about him. Not a single day passed when she didn't think about him. She ruminated constantly on what it would be like to meet him. What would he be like? Where would they meet? When?

After her trip to France, she occasionally received a letter from him. The letters were delivered already torn open and with entire passages crossed out. In some parts of the letter the ink was blotched and unreadable because the censors used to steam the letters open. Father wrote long letters in delicate neat handwriting. He was an architect… But he didn't write anything emotional, not at all. He wrote about the weather, and he wrote about nature. Sometimes he shared some life advice. He probably knew that anything else would be crossed out or that if his letter were too revealing, it would end up in the KGB rubbish bin.

Whenever she received a letter from him, Sofija would count the years and think about his age. The more years passed, the less hopeful she felt. After every race in the West, as hard as she tried to convince herself that it hardly mattered, she would be overcome with disappointment that he had not come to meet her. Within three years her career as a rower was over, and her trips abroad were over. The hope of meeting her father grew ever more distant. Sofija accustomed herself to that sense of resignation and no longer felt goosebumps run through her whenever she thought of her father. Then her mother died, and he seemed even more distant. The situation seemed hopeless. Only Mama had known him, not her, and now Mama was gone…

CHAPTER SIXTEEN

MAY 1975, MOSCOW

"Hello, Alexander Nikolaevich."

"Oh, Sofija Grucova? Hello, how are you?" Berkutov extended his hand, surprised to find Sofija standing on the threshold to his office.

"I'm well, I was just passing through," Sofija blurted out, forgetting everything she had rehearsed beforehand in her head on the train.

"Yes, of course, you were only passing through," Berkutov said and laughed. "What's going on?"

"I wanted to talk."

"What about?" he asked, patting her on the shoulder. Berkutov pointed to a chair beside his desk. "But first tell me how you are doing? How's life been treating you?"

"Everything's going well for me. I work as a coach for the Vilnius team, *Žalgiris*."

"*Žalgiris* is a solid team. Well, it was. It's too bad that Jukna's eight fell apart. They were good men, admirable men. And the women's eight was strong too. But there's nothing we can do about it... The years pass and we've got to step aside and make room for the young. That was a good championship back then."

"There are some good rowers now too."

"Maybe a few... Who do you coach? Boys? Girls?"

"Girls. Scullers."

"Of course. Why did I even ask? You must be good at it."

"I've got a group of good girls."

"Are they as little as you?"

"Exactly like me," Sofija said and laughed. "That's the only kind I know how to coach."

"I never could understand how all of you petite women won against those huge Germans."

"We didn't beat them every time. We could never beat them in a head wind."

"Yes, that's right, I remember… I know what that's like. I had to battle even being one metre eighty height as well."

"At least being small we're faster."

"True…"

Berkutov was lost in thought for a moment, then he suddenly looked up and asked, "So why did you come from Vilnius? I thought you really were just passing through?"

"I did come from Vilnius," Sofija said quietly and smiled shyly, "but I wasn't just passing through."

"You came to see my all the way from Vilnius?" Berkutov asked, raising her eyebrows.

"Yes."

"Well, tell me, what's going on?"

"I have an important personal matter," Sofija said and her voice broke. "I want to travel to Montreal" she rushed to finish her sentence.

"To the Olympics? Yes, that's right, finally women may compete. That's good."

"I would like to compete in the Olympics, but I'm too old. I would like to travel to the Junior championship. This year."

Berkutov grew serious. The lines between his eyebrows deepened. He squinted and stared at Sofija, as though trying to read her thoughts.

"And?"

"I'd like to go to the pre-Olympic week… I heard a group of coaches was going."

"We're planning on it, but nothing's certain yet."

"I'd like to be a part of that group. It's important."

Berkutov raised his eyebrows and stared at Sofija, waiting for her to explain herself.

"I haven't told anyone… But…"

"But? What happened?" Berkutov asked impatiently.

"It's like this… My father lives in Canada. I've never met him. I would very much like to see him. He is seventy-nine."

"Really? How did he end up in Canada?"

"He ended up there during the war, but I don't know how. My mother never told me. She died three years ago."

"I'm sorry."

"I'm afraid that this may be my one and last chance to see my father. Can you help me somehow?"

Berkutov turned his gaze towards the window. Sofija's heart sank. What would happen now? What was he thinking?"

"I really don't have any plans to stay in Canada. I'm not planning to defect," Sofija said, barely holding back her emotion. "I just want to see my father…"

"I don't doubt you for a moment," Berkutov interrupted her suddenly. "Of course, I'll add your name to the group! Let's just hope the KGB allow you to travel. I'll back you up with my word. I don't think they'll give you a hard time. You'll go!"

"Thank you," Sofija said feeling how dry her mouth was.

"The list hasn't been finalized yet. I'll find a place for you."

"Thank you so much…"

"By the way, how is your family? Will your husband be alright with you traveling?"

"I don't need his permission. We divorced three years ago."

"Oh, I didn't know…"

"We're better off this way…"

"I see…" Berkutov was lost in thought again. "Let's just hope they let you out. They're more reluctant to give singles permission to travel. Do you have any other relatives in Lithuania?"

"No one. My mother died. I don't have any brothers or sisters. The rest of my family is in Poland."

"You see, if you're married, you have a better chance to get permission to travel. They figure you'll go back because of your husband."

Sofija shrugged.

"I know… But what should I do? I won't have enough time to get married before we leave," Sofija said and laughed.

"Let's just hope they let you go," Berkutov said and smiled. "I'll back you up. Also, just so you know, the trip won't be fully funded. Save your money. You'll need to contribute three hundred roubles of your own money."

"I understand," Sofija said and nodded. *I'll borrow money if I'm short, I'll save every kopek…*

CHAPTER SEVENTEEN

JULY 1975, VILNIUS

Sofija heard her telephone ringing while still climbing up the stairs of her building. She had only made it to the third floor. When she heard her phone ringing from her fifth floor flat, she took the stairs two at a time. She turned her purse inside out until she found her keys, grabbed them, quickly unlocked the door, and collapsed inside. She snatched up the receiver.

"Hello," she answered, panting to catch her breath. "Yes, this is Grucova, good day, I'm listening…"

Her eyes roamed around the flat as she struggled to compose herself. *Someone has been in my flat again… They moved my belongings around… And the door was only locked once, and not twice, the way I lock it… They were searching through my letters again…*

"Yes, fine, I'll be waiting for you at six."

Here we go again… Sofija plopped down onto the edge of her sofa and glanced at the clock. It was ten of five. She had to stop and take a deep breath, like she would after a race. She had to focus. A lump rose in her throat and clouded her mind. *This is probably how Mama felt when she saw the KGB agents in the doorway. Why do they always come to your home? Why don't they make you go to them? No, it's better this way. What do they want from me? What will they ask? Will they ask me to inform for them?*

Good luck. They won't get anything out of me… I'm not their type.

Sofija stood, walked over to her desk, and slowly opened the drawer. She always kept her documents and Father's letters arranged neatly. Now, the letters were scattered haphazardly throughout her desk drawer. No one had the keys to her flat, no one except her. Sofija trembled just thinking about it. *You're not even safe in your own home.* She wanted to wash her hands, cleanse herself of the intruders' fingerprints, burn all the papers they'd touched.

She approached the window and carefully lifted the corner of the curtain and glanced out onto the street towards street. The trolleybuses were half empty. But in half an hour, they would be crammed tight with city dwellers rushing home from work. *There aren't as many people in the city in the summer. Most people leave and take a vacation, but not them…* Sofija observed the men climbing out of the trolleybus. She watched and tried to guess which one would walk towards her building and ring her buzzer. *I've taken on Mama's terrible fear of the KGB. Mama never recovered from her fear of the KGB. She took that terror with her to the grave. The experiences she lived through in the basement of the KGB headquarters affected her mind. She developed such anxiety that she began to confuse reality with her nightmares, she experienced panic attacks, and then her memory lapsed…*

Nonsense… I'm wasting my time… Sofija turned away from the window and stepped into her small kitchen to heat the kettle for tea. *This is my home. I'm the boss here. The walls will protect me. Everything will be fine.*

Sofija glanced around at the walls of her tiny flat. The walls were filled with her photographs. She gazed at her collection of medals and honorary badges pinned neatly onto a wooden bulletin board installed on the wall. *That is all the wealth I've got to show for sixteen years of hard work… I've earned nothing more than that. All I have are my medals and my memo-*

ries. I have a few friends abroad… A few photos from my trips… But maybe that's what life is all about? My impressions, memories, trips, the euphoria of winning? Nobody can take that away from me. My memories cannot burn up, rot, disappear, no one can censor them. My memories will remain with me to the very end. Should I hide away my medals? If I did, would I forget what they represented?

Sofija walked over and ran her fingers over her 1968 bronze European Rowing Championship medal. With her thumb she rubbed the shiny FISA badge. *For someone else, these medals would have felt like an enormous accomplishment. The girls who came in fourth, fifth, sixth would have been thrilled to have won a bronze. But for us, it was an enormous disappointment. We rowed against a head wind and staggering waves that reached to our shoulders. The boats were like in Khimki. Our oars flew up into the open air, then plopped down into the water, we caught crab after crab… All it took was the barest tenth of second and we lost to the Germans and less than two seconds to the Romanians. After we'd won first place in Vichy, taking third felt humiliating. But it wasn't a tragedy. The girls in the eight experienced a real tragedy… Somebody convinced them – or maybe they convinced themselves – that they only had luck on an odd year. It was a strange pattern: 1963, 1965, 1967, they won the European Rowing Championship. Then, in 1964 and 1966, they came in second place. After they noticed the pattern, they began to worry about the 1968 championship.*

The host city of the 1968 rowing championships was verified only in March. The beautiful Olympic scale rowing course in the Langer See (The Long Lake) was well known to them from their experience in the Grünau Regatta. The men raced on the Langer See in the 1936 Berlin Olympics. However, their anxiety proved greater than their resourcefulness at controlling it… From the shoreline, the coaches and teammates thought that the scoreboard was malfunctioning. It only showed the results of four crews, and the USSR team was not listed among them, although clearly five eights were racing against each other.

It turned out that the Soviet team with nine Lithuanians aboard was disqualified for a false start. *Perhaps they didn't understand what the judges were saying, or perhaps they were hoping for a miracle, but they fought hard to the very last stroke... All for nothing... They came in second, just like on every even year. It was as though they weren't there. The hard work of that year was all for nothing... After that, the never-ending threats and accusations that they had to endure from the team leaders hurt more than what they put themselves through for fumbling the start.*

1969, Klagenfurt, Austria... Sofija clutched the gold medal with the stylized five oar blades in the palm of her hand. *That was a hard gold to win... Only four tenth of a second... The lake was amazing, the water like glass, it was surrounded by majestic mountains, there was not the slightest hint of wind... Around a hundred metres before the finish line it was as though I'd lost consciousness... Tamara, the cox, told me later that it was as though something had bit me... I began to furiously pick up the pace. The coaches watching from the grandstands couldn't see the finish line... They gave up and stood up to leave... Somehow, the crew managed to find the strength to pass the Romanians in the final metre... Genovaitė also came in first that year... Only, our Žalgiris eight girls weren't there... After their tragic loss the preceding year, they simply could not go on...*

I have nothing to lose, Sofija thought, *if they don't let me go, then fine, life will go on as usual... What am I so worried about? They can't throw me out on the street. They can't fire me from my job. I don't need anything more than that in my life, work and home, that's it. I have a roof over my head, I have a job I love, I have clothes to wear and food to eat. If they don't let me out, they don't let me out. All I really wanted was to find Father for Mama's sake, but she's gone now…*

The sound of the doorbell ringing ran through her body like a thousand needles. Sofija made a movement towards the door, tripped on the rug, and with an awkward movement ran her left hand across her medals, causing them to ring like bells. She quickly pressed her palm to her medals to silence them. Usually, she enjoyed this sound, but not right now. She took two deep breaths and unlocked the door. A man in his forties dressed in a dark grey suit and crisp white dress shirt stood on the threshold. He was smiling.

"Comrade Grucova?"

"Yes, please come in. No need to take off your shoes," Sofija said, indicating her living room with a sweep of her arm.

"Thank you. I'd like to speak with you. Where may I sit down?"

The man's eyes roamed around her living room, surveyed the view from the window, examined every detail in the small room. He settled into an armchair and pulled out a cigarette.

"Do you smoke?" he asked, extending the pack towards Sofija.

"No."

"Do you mind if I smoke?"

"Not at all…"

"We know that you are planning to travel to Canada."

Sofija's heart was beating quickly. She knew that this is what he'd come to talk to her about.

"Well, yes, I was included in the group… I'm going to the World Junior championship."

"I know. Is your team competing?"

"No, they're not."

"Then why are you going?"

"Well, ah, they assigned me a spot together with the others on the team."

"Yes, I heard that already."

"I'd like to see the races. I'd like to witness where for the first time in history women rowers will race in the Olympics." Sofija had prepared her reasons ahead of time, just in case…

Sofija was pleased with herself that she had answered so well, but she'd been naïve to think that this KGB agent didn't know about her father.

"Is that so? And what do you plan to do during your free time?"

"I don't know… I'd like to see Canada. I heard the nature is beautiful there…"

"Will you visit your relatives?"

"What relatives?" Sofija tried bluffing, pretending she didn't understand the question.

"Comrade Grucova, we know that you have relatives in Canada."

Sofija grew quiet.

The KGB agent rubbed out his cigarette in the ashtray and bore his clever eyes into her.

"I came here to warn you that you had better not have any ideas about trying to stay there."

"I don't have anywhere to stay there," Sofija said, surprised.

"You didn't understand me correctly. If your case, any attempt to remain abroad may cause serious problems. As far as I'm informed, you weren't born in the USSR. Therefore, without any problem, you have the legal right to exit the Soviet Union and return to your homeland. However, any attempt to remain in a foreign country will bring with it painful consequences for you. Is this clear?"

"I have no intention of staying there!"

"Well, well, good for you then," the agent said and leaned back comfortably into the armchair.

Sofija sat down and waited for the KGB agent to leave. However, he was in no hurry to go anywhere.

"We have another request. To put it more precisely, it is a requirement. During your trip there may be some foreigners who will approach the team and try to establish contact with people in your group. They may even attempt a provocation. I would like you to monitor the others carefully and take note of any suspicious behaviour."

"No," Sofija said firmly and shook her head. "That I will not do."

"Oh yes you will, Comrade Grucova. If you wish to go on this trip, then you will need to collaborate with us."

"I refuse to spy."

"It's not spying. You are being asked to protect our homeland from enemies. You must observe them and give us a report upon your return."

"I refuse to report anything!"

"Comrade Grucova, here are your choices: Either you work with us or someone else will take your place on this trip. Do you understand? Without the signature of the Soviet Security Services you are going nowhere. We will simply hold up your documents. Without our signature, you're not going anywhere. So, the decision is yours."

The KGB agent smiled cynically and in an ironic tone of voice said, "If you want to see where women will race in the Olympics for the first time, then you better do as we say."

Sofija felt weak. Her hands trembled. She felt the same way she did before a race. A terrible anxiety overpowered her. Her heart was beating so hard she wondered if the agent could hear it from across the coffee table. *I will not inform... I will not spy... I will not rat out my fellow passengers...*

"I want..." Sofija muttered, but then turned towards the window, her back facing the agent. Tears pooled in her eyes. Her ears were ringing. Her throat hurt from the nasty stench of the cigarette. *I want to see my father. Either in Canada, or not in Canada, I must see my father. I must see him if only that one and only time. I won't write any reports... I can say I didn't see anything, didn't hear anything, nothing happened... But if I do, will I betray Mama, who suffered so much from the KGB. She suffered so much at their hands that just before she died, she lost her mind. She feared the KGB and hated them with a passion. She would never forgive me. But I must find Father for her... Only for her... I must see my father...*

"Comrade Grucova, I trust you. I will allow you to fulfil your obligation. I take responsibility for you. But, when you return, we will meet, and we will talk. Is that clear?"

"I'm not much of a spy..." Sofija said evasively.

"Don't worry, there's a first time for all of us. You'll be fine."

"I don't know... I... I..."

"You'll know what to do, Comrade Sofija," the agent cut her off.

He lit another cigarette.

His gaze softened and he squirmed in his seat a moment uncomfortably, as though he wanted to ask her something more.

Sofija fixed her eyes on him and nodded slightly.

The agent rubbed out his cigarette, locked his fingers together, and hunched over.

"You'll be away for a long time. You'll probably have time to do some shopping..."

"Probably, but I'm not going there to shop. I'd rather see the sites."

"Yes, of course, that's what they all say, but then they return with their suitcases stuffed. My only suspicion is where do they get the money?"

"What are you saying?" Sofija asked, thinking to herself that now he'll ask her to follow the others around and keep track of all their purchases and what contraband they brought with them to sell abroad.

"That's not what I had in mind," the agent said in a sugary voice. "My son plays Ping-Pong... Could you bring back a paddle for him?"

I wonder if I won't need to report anything to him if I bring him a ping-pong paddle? Sofija thought and smiled inwardly.

"Fine. I'll look for one. I play ping-pong myself, so I know how to pick out a quality paddle."

"Have a good trip then," the agent said and stood up to leave. "We'll be in touch when you return."

CHAPTER EIGHTEEN

AUGUST 4, 1975, VILNIUS – MOSCOW

Sofija arrived in the Vilnius Airport far too early. There were two hours remaining until her flight. *No matter,* she thought to herself. Her greatest fear was to run into an unexpected problem and be late for the plane. She had with her, her purse, her suitcase, and her constant companion, her camera. Sofija pressed a few magazines under her arm, so that she wouldn't be bored while waiting for the plane. She scanned the departures board searching for "Moscow." She'd made plans to meet Algis from the *Žalgiris* team central committee who will travel together. However, he would only be arriving in another hour.

Beyond the waiting hall windows she saw a row of white planes with a blue stripe on the side and the words, *Aeroflot.* A few years back, the government ordered all the airplanes painted identically. You had to look carefully to discern their model number and to see the small hammer and sickle symbol. Sofija played a game of trying to guess which airplane she'd be flying on.

This was probably the first time in her life that she had worked towards achieving her goal with such courage and determination. Now, reflecting back she saw that she'd never find it within herself to be this bold to make the impossible happen if it weren't for Father. She secretly travelled to Moscow, borrowed money, took time out at the height of the rowing season... Only, this time everything came together into a happy ending, just like in the movies. Her need to see her father, to feel him wrap his arms around her, to see the tears in his eyes, probably sent her all the right people, their assistance, the extra money she needed, so that today she could fly out and return lost time.

All the anxiety of the last few days caused Sofija to feel the way she did before a race. Just the thought that she would climb out of an airplane and step onto the same land where her father walked made her weak in the knees. On the one hand, she was grateful that she would not be racing this time. She won't have to go through all that. On the other hand, her heart was beating just as hard. She could not decide which was worse – to suffer, but to do what you've done hundreds of times before, or to delve into the unknown, which was terribly frightening and alluring all at the same time.

Sofija had never travelled across the Atlantic Ocean. *What a coincidence,* she thought. *In September 1967, when we returned from Vichy, the first plane departed from Moscow to Montreal. I remember it all so well. That was when I'd just found Father. I thought to myself then: One day I will fly on that plane to see him. And now, I'm doing it. How strange. Dreams really do come true. Is this my dream, really? Yes, it was... But eight years had to pass first... Everything is different now... Mama is gone... I'm different. I'm calmer. Then, I felt as though, if it were possible, I'd run headfirst to see him... Mama took so many secrets with her into the grave. There is so much that I didn't ask her. What did she know about Father? What didn't she know? Maybe she understood that he was alive, but she knew they could never meet again. Or maybe she didn't want to see him? Was that why Mama would cry? She can't tell me now... Not anymore... Either I find out the truth now, or I block it all out and move on. And, so what, if I do find out?*

Who will I leave that legacy to? I have no brothers, no sisters, no children.
But still, that need to understand my family story burns deep within me.

* * *

Tu-124... Sofija noticed the model as she climbed the stairs into the
plane. *That's the plane that crashed two years ago carrying those doctors...*
They were also flying to Moscow... Horrible... What did they live through?
What did it feel like? As always, the government kept it quiet. But everybody
knew and everybody talked about it... All the top paediatric specialists of
Lithuania were on that plane and they all died. Did they hide it because
the people who died were famous? They must have known that they couldn't
keep the deaths of so many important people secret? They gave the doctors a
bombastic funeral. Lithuania's Communist Party General Secretary Antanas
Sniečkus himself attended the funeral. The urns holding their remains were
placed inside coffins and there was a wake for them at Vilnius University.
Lithuania mourned them for a long time afterwards.[20]

Sofija settled into her window seat. She leaned back and closed her
eyes: *Today I will be in Moscow. Tomorrow I will be in Canada. The day*
after tomorrow, we may meet... No, probably not. The distance between
Montreal and Niagara is quite far. No one will allow me to travel alone.
We'll only be allowed to travel after the competition. They will probably take
us there. Niagara Falls are an important touristic destination... Do I have
Father's telephone number? Yes, I do... I have his address...

"You're here already, Sofija?" Algis said, sitting down and securing his
seatbelt. "I didn't notice how you got ahead of me."

Sofija was feeling nervous about the long flight. Her throat was dry,

20   On December 16, 1973, in Russia, approximately 100 kilometres from Mos-
     cow a Tu-124 Lithuanian civilian airplane crashed. Many Lithuanians died in
     the crash – six crew members and 45 passengers, among them four of the most
     famous paediatricians in Lithuania at the time.

and she was not in the mood to chat. She smiled politely and smoothed out the magazines she'd brought with her on her lap. She didn't feel like reading either. She glanced down at the smiles of the famous actors Regimantas Adomaitis and Vaiva Mainelytė. It was as though they were smiling up at her from between her fingers.

"What are you reading?" Algis asked politely.

Sofija pulled up her hands so Algis could see the magazine title.

"Oh, *Švyturys!*"[21]

Then he added, "And it looks like the latest issue. That's a nice photo. I've only got the July issue with me. I haven't had the time to finish it yet."

Sofija smiled again and glanced at the cover. *It really was a nice photo. She had to read the article that went with it. Where was it? Oh yes, page 28... But later... Now she had to calm herself down. There was a long and difficult journey ahead of her...*

Behind the porthole, the airport building grew smaller, she saw smaller and larger planes, mechanics waving at them as they slid away. The stewardess strolled slowly down the aisle, offering a basket with hard candies for them to suck on to help balance their ears during take-off.

Sofija's heart slid down somewhere into her stomach. *Oh, this is just how I used to feel before a race... Êtes-vous prêts? Partez!*

Sofija closed her eyes. The sound of the wheels on the tarmac grew louder... *We will take off soon... When I return again I will have already met my father. What will my life be like then? What will I be like?* Suddenly, the rattling noise ceased, and she felt herself sliding back into her seat. *We're taking off...* Sofija opened her eyes, leaned her cheek against the porthole rim and watched as Vilnius became smaller and smaller and

---

21   *Švyturys (The Lighthouse), a popular Lithuanian magazine during the Soviet era.*

eventually vanished. Often, flights originated right over the Old Town. Then, she could clearly see Gediminas Castle and the Soviet Lithuanian red, white, and green flag waving in the wind. Then, scenes of the green earth would take over, and then clouds.

Sofija opened the magazine and the first page already reminded her of home. Among the most important news events she saw her friends Genovaitė Šidagytė-Ramoškienė and Vytautas Butkus smiling up at her. They were the VI Soviet Spartakiad Champions.

How wonderful for Genovaitė. I hope she can hold on until the Olympics... Last year she came in second at the World Championship. If she doesn't win this year, the team leaders will start looking for someone to replace her. They will simply begin to ignore her. They won't invite her to the training camps... The trials... They won't give her the better quality boat... They won't assign her a place on the team... Or they'll put her through so many qualification races that she'll tire herself out and lose. The usual. That's how they got rid of me in 1970. In my case, it had to do with my teammates' ambitions. What false friends they were... They weren't getting enough attention, or so they thought. When the news writes about the crew, mostly they write about the stroke. Or maybe I'd reached my limit? The first sign that you are on the out is when they assign you as a stand-by. Then, either you get the message and leave on your own, or... Thank God, I figured out what was going on and took myself out of the situation in time. I had no intention of playing along in their nasty games...

The conclusions that the team's "scientists" came to regarding a rower's age were difficult to comprehend. A second or third place win in the World Championship was hopeless. Already in 1967, one of the best Lithuanian rowers, Zigmas Jukna, was almost left without a seat in his crew's boat. Even when he was already in France, at the very last minute, they tried to switch him out... They claimed he was too old. Thirty was the limit. At thirty either you've accomplished all you're capable of or you won't amount to anything anyway. As it turned out, Zigmas would not give up his seat. But it seemed that at the time they needed Zigmas' seat for a Russian. Good thing he stood his ground and did not back down. If he had, he wouldn't have attended the Olympics in Mexico and won the bronze, and he wouldn't have won the silver in the 1969 European Rowing Championship.

Butkus is strong... He came in second the year before last in Europe. Maybe he'll win this year? But will they let him race a single? They'll probably place him on a crew. He's only twenty-five so he's got a chance. In 1970 he made his mark – he won the USSR Championship and the Cup of the USSR in Kiev. Still, they put him through a special set of trials. They probably expected him to lose. Good for him for holding on!

"Is that about rowing?" Algis asked, interrupting Sofija's reading.

"Yes, but there's not that much, mostly photos."

"In your days they would fill up the whole page."

"Yes, but generations change. There's new people now."

"I wonder if anyone from Lithuania will compete in the Olympics?"

"You have a better idea of that being in leadership... Maybe Šidagytė will make it onto the team. Butkus has a chance. We'll see."

Sofija spread open the magazine, searching for interesting captions. She found one: "The World in the Year 2000." The article predicted that in the year 2000, people would live to 100 or 150.

She turned back to the cover. "Page 28..." "The First Lithuanian Musical is Galloping Onto the Screen on Horseback..." *Hum, that might be more interesting...* She didn't usually see photographs of paradise in a Soviet magazine. They made her happy.

"What's that?" Algis asked, pointing at the photo.

"It's about a musical called, *The Devil's Bride.*

"Is it playing already?"

"Not yet…"

Sofija spotted a familiar name and her face lit up.

"A musical and a film by Arūnas Žebriūnas."

"If it's Žebriūnas, then it will be good. I like his films."

"Žebriūnas was a rower."

"I know."

"When I started rowing, he was still on the team. He rowed and he coached young people. He's tall, built like a real rower. He seemed so mature. He was about twenty-five then. I seemed tiny standing beside him! He's intellectual, and very polite."

"Many talented people were formed through sports."

"Rowing especially. Maybe that's because rowing is a student sport. Most rowers come to the sport through the university. That's when they have visions about the future. They're intellectual, educated. Many of them come from families of artists."

"How many years did you row?"

"Sixteen. Half of my life."

"How do you like coaching?"

"I like it. You do what you do best, and the work is interesting. And it makes me happy."

"That's true, and then you enjoy seeing the results of all that work."

"I'm not only interested in results in sports. I like to see how the girls develop character. All my girls are very different. I must work with each one individually. Some need encouragement, others need to be reigned in."

"Is it difficult to pull a crew together?"

"It's not difficult to get girls to join, but it's a challenge to get them to stay. Around twenty to thirty girls usually come to the first training session. Then half come back to the second session. Then, after the third session I lose a third more. Rowing is an endurance sport. Not all of them have the stamina. Others believe all sorts of nonsense – that rowing gives you broad shoulders and a thick body. I'm lucky if four or five stick with it. You can form a quad with them. But those who do stay are dedicated. They learn to love rowing."

"I've heard that your girls fall in love with their coach," Algis said and smiled.

Sofija shrugged and smiled.

"There are times when they compete for the coach's attention. I don't really want that to happen, but I am pleased that they trust me and that they appreciate me. Sometimes, I'm like a mother to them. Sometimes, I'm like a sister. Sometimes I need to be a stern father."

Sofija shrunk into her seat, remembering her first group coaching session. She had gone to all the schools in Vilnius and had talked thirty high school students into joining her at the Žalgiris Hall in Vilnius. It was February 16, 1971[22]... It did not even occur to her that there was something wrong with the date she had scheduled. She was nervous, but the coaching session went well, and the girls had a lot of fun. At least, that's what she thought. The young people were in a celebratory mood. The very next day Sofija was called in by the team leadership to explain why she had organized a training session on Lithuanian Independence Day, a holiday that was strictly banned according to Soviet Lithuania's law. On

---

22   February 16th is the date Lithuania declared independence from Tsarist Russia in 1918. During the Soviet occupation it was against the law to gather or celebrate on February 16th.

that day in particular, all mass meetings and celebrations were forbidden. She had forgotten about the date and what it had meant.

Oh, and then there were the night activities at training camp. One of the girls, either Birutė or Gintarė, decided she wanted to take a walk about the Trakai Castle at night. As their coach, she didn't want to let the girls out on their own. They all sat together in a wooden boat and rowed towards the castle. The full moon that night lit the way. It was beautiful. They feared that the guard of the castle would not spot them in the moonlight. The girls were not satisfied with exploring just the castle moat, they wanted to see the inner courtyard. As their coach, she could not show them that she was afraid. They went inside together. They climbed over the fence and entered the castle, but then when they had to climb out, they were afraid to jump down over the gate in the dark. They had no way out... The guard was patrolling the gate... *Oh, good thing it all ended well...* Sofija shivered just remembering that night. If they had been caught, they would have all been thrown out of camp, but her especially...

"Oh, I read an article in an issue of *Švyturys* about how doctors have patients recover after heart attacks by rowing. There was a photograph of patients in a hospital rowing on these rowing machines," Algis narrated, interrupting Sofija's thoughts.

"I read that as well. What a shame that we athletes don't have those rowing machines."

"But you have the rowing tank!"

"Yes, we have a tank, but it's old. We built it ourselves together with our coaches. It's damp and cold..."

"Don't tell me damp and cold is something new to a rower? You can't choose the weather, not even in summer."

"That's true... We row in the rain, and in the snow. I have this photograph of myself from when I was young.... Probably from my first training session. I'm wearing mittens and a knit hat with a pom-pom. There's snow everywhere. The shores of the Neris are covered in snow. The boat was wide and heavy, a gig boat. But it's a different type of cold in the tank. That cold gets into your bones. And you don't see the shoreline moving past. All you see are the same dark boring walls as you row. It gets very monotonous.

"You could produce electricity," Algis said and laughed.

"I've said the same myself often," Sofija said and giggled. "We could be one more electrical station in Vilnius. However, it's the only way to row through the winter if they don't take you south."

"Well, for you rowers, of course, water is important. You can't train just anywhere. This isn't basketball or track and field, then your fields and gyms are pretty much the same everywhere."

"Do you know how wonderful it feels to sit down in a boat after a long winter? It feels great to go south in February or March – your hands are just itching to make the first strokes. Georgia, Azerbaijan... Oh, when you've rested well, when you're not sick and tired of your boat just yet, when your blisters have healed over. Oh, I feel wonderful just remembering it all."

"Do you row on rivers or lakes there?"

"In Azerbaijan, Mingachevir we row on a river that flows down from the mountains. In Georgia, Poti there are two rivers and a lake, but the lake is enormous and often has choppy waves. It's a completely different feeling to row in calm waters after a rushing river. When we return to Trakai, we really appreciate the pleasure of calm waters, even when the rowing is harder."

"Harder in a lake?"

"Yes, in the sense that you can't blame anything on the current," Sofija said and burst out laughing. "Really, it's an entirely different type of rowing. When you row against the current, you work with a tempo. When you row with the current, you need force. When you hook into the current, it's like pushing off of a wall... The speed is faster with a current, but the rowing is tougher. When you row against the current, you need to be quick to catch the tempo. In a lake the conditions are altogether different. You slide as much as you pull.

"But all the races take place in still waters."

"The main ones do, yes. All the international regattas and championships. But there are many regattas in rivers as well. I've raced against the current and with the current."

"Is it a lake or a canal in Montreal?"

"As far as I know, it's a canal. A new one. We'll see," Sofija bent down into her magazines. This time she opened up *Jaunimo Gretos.*[23] Again, she saw the smiling faces of her friends, Genovaitė and Vytautas.

"Rowing here as well?" Algis said, glancing over at the magazine.

"Yes, Butkus and Šidagytė."

---

23 *Jaunimo Gretos (Among the Youth),* a Soviet era Lithuanian magazine for young people.

CHAPTER NINETEEN

AUGUST 5, 1975, MOSCOW - MONTREAL

The Cabin of the I1-62 was abuzz with the joyful anticipation of enthusiastic travellers. Almost a third of the airplane's seats were occupied by athletes, their coaches, and members of the delegation traveling to the FISA junior rowing championships in Montreal. Everyone was in a jubilant patriotic mood. They were all fired up by the training, and by personal conversations on how to conduct themselves in the West. They were all sufficiently on their guard against the capitalist world and its dangers. For some reason, they were flying on a route with two transfers, one in Paris and one in New York. That was strange considering that there was a direct flight to Montreal.

When I read eight years ago in 1967 that Aeroflot was flying to Montreal, I could never have believed that I would be flying there one day myself. Although, at the same time, I really wanted to, and I knew that it was the only way for me to reach Father. As they say, God works in mysterious ways. Perhaps someone up in heaven is helping me? Maybe it's Mama... After all, the information about this trip came to me as though out of the sky. And all the paths came together to make it happen. I'm so pleased that I did not doubt myself somewhere along the way...

The Soviet rowing team was taking the junior rowing team – twenty-three rowers. For the time being, the FISA junior championship was only for men. Girls were not yet allowed to compete in regattas at that level. However, there was talk that in two or three year's girls would be able to compete in the championships as well.

It's too bad there aren't any Lithuanians on this team. What a shame… The next generation hasn't come of age yet. It would be more interesting if I had someone to cheer for. Sofija sighed. *Maybe one day my girls will be able to race… When there's a girls' championship.*

But there were Latvians. Six of them. There might have been nine… Our neighbours, the Latvians fought their way in to race with their eight. They won all the trial races against last year's champions, the ASK military sports team. Of course, as usual, their team was "strengthened" with the addition of three Russians. For athletes from the Baltic republics, the requirements were much higher than they were for Russians. They participate in one qualifying race after another until they lose one. Then the Russians are brought in to replace them. If they stubbornly keep on fighting to hold their place and are eventually invited to the championships, by the time of the competition they are exhausted and not in top form. In other words, they reach the end of their endurance because all their attention is focused on the qualification races and the absolute necessity of winning them. For young rowers it is more difficult to "maintain" their form in the first place. They cannot handle as much as adults can. If they race twice in a competition, they're exhausted. And if before that they must endure three or four qualification races they're done.

The three young athletes who were left behind will never know why they were the ones to be replaced. They'll carry this sense of injustice with them all their lives. They'll blame themselves and this inferiority complex will be imprinted onto their everyday lives. There was no guarantee that the addition of the three Russians would make the team any stronger. It almost never worked out well. It takes a long time to fine tune a crew. It takes many hours of rowing together. Neither height, nor weight, had anything to do with. It took almost a year to work out a rhythm when team members came with different technical styles. They only had a week. The other boys who remained on the team were also upset, they wanted to cause trouble, to make amends…. That was how strong and unified teams were transformed into the average crew…

For now, they were all in a good mood. Right now, their most important goal was to fly to Canada, to see the capitalist world, to meet the foreign rowers, to buy some nice things. The race was second place, so to speak.

In Canada they would all wear red team shirts and they would all be called Russians. But that wasn't so important in the moment. Maybe they'll think about it when they see all the other young men from the other national teams and they'll hear themselves being referred to as "the Russians."

Every crew travelled with its own coaches. Then there were at least five more state coaches. The doubles coach was Raisa Shiriayeva, the 1958 Soviet singles champion. She was petite and short like Sofija. She probably never would have become a champion if it hadn't been for an unfortunate accident, after which she gave herself her word that she would win first place in the Soviet championships. That happened around 1955 when Raisa was rowing in a double scull. The girls rowed out to train on the Khimki in the height of summer when a storm blew up. They were far from the shore when they heard thunder and then lightning struck the water. They thought they would have enough time to row to shore, but destiny had its own plans. Lightning struck directly onto Raisa's feet, paralyzing her legs for a moment. Then, the lightning bolt passed through her and to her partner, the stroke, and hit her body. Her friend shuddered and then collapsed. Raisa was in shock and still thought she could save her. Sobbing, she rowed towards shore, pulling only with her arms because she could no longer feel her legs. She rowed back with the burned body of her teammate lying in front of her in the boat. It took a long time for her to recover from the shock of what she lived through. It took two years for her to regain feeling in her legs, to feel alive again, and for her to cope with her feelings of guilt. She made a promise to her friend who had died that she would win first place in the Soviet championship in her honour. And she won. Now she coached young people. She found the strength within her to keep on going.

Besides the coaches and team leaders, thirteen more people were traveling with them. That group was assembled "through bribes" as they liked to say. Strange as it may seem, those extra seats were allocated to people from various Soviet republics, and not just the chosen ones, the Russians. Out of those thirteen, five represented rowers. Four were from the Baltics.

There were only two women in the group – Sofija and a Georgian, Nina Dumbadze, a discus thrower and two-time European champion and winner of a bronze in the 1952 Helsinki Olympics. Her name was really Nino, but everyone called her Nina. She was born in Odessa, in Ukraine, but later, when she was 18, in 1937 they left to live in her father's home country, Georgia.

It feels as though we're all just watching each other closely, Sofija thought to herself, glancing around her. *I'm probably not the only one who had a little visit with the KGB… More than likely, everyone is afraid of each other…*

The airplane had barely moved when she was overcome with exhaustion. *It's probably all the stress,* she thought to herself and sighed. *Finally, we are about to take off. No one can stop me now. Oh, how much I had to deal with... Filling out forms, having little talks, receiving instructions... Everything will be fine. Finally, I will meet Father.... What a wonderful coincidence that he lives in Niagara Falls. We will surely travel to Niagara Falls. There's no way that we'd miss that. Niagara Falls are the most important touristic site in Canada, and in the world. Once we get there, I'll find the way to my father's home. Even if just for a short time... Now everything will be fine. Soon I will be able to hug my father...*

As Sofija drifted off into a pleasant nap, she saw fragments of her life pass before her eyes. She saw herself as a child, counting the stars on Father's lapels in the photograph. She saw Uncle Edmund's fur collar. She saw herself walking along the Hill of Tree Crosses – and God Forbid anyone heard her saying that name out loud... She saw the sunsets at the Trakai *Žalgiris* boathouse when the sun expired behind the castle towers. She saw herself making friends for the first time with the other girls from the team. She saw the races in Pärnu, Moscow, Kavgolovo. She saw the girls she was training – the girls who she'd left in the capable hands of Coach Stasė Dragūnienė until she returned.

I have a wall full of medals at home... And, so what? Who needs them? I spent the best years of my life torturing my body, but I never thought about why. For months I'd train for a race, as though that race was the most important event in my life... I never once thought about why. I had a goal and I worked towards that goal. Two, three times a day... There wasn't even enough time for my workout clothes to dry, for the wounds on my palms to scab over... When you line up on the starting line, you feel as though you're about to experience the moment that will change your life forever. That moment shines when you cross the finish line first... But it's so brief that you don't even have the time to rejoice. You row back to the pontoon with your medal, you change out of your wet clothes, you toss your medal into your travel bag, and that's all. Then the whole cycle starts all over again. Well, yes, then there's the greetings, the articles in the newspapers, being met at the airport... Three or four days of glory and then you go right back to training again. Only, this time you work harder. And that's because from that day onwards the other rowers who you beat are going to train even harder to beat you next time. When did I fall into this regimen? At first, I got into rowing just to get stronger... Am I really such a fighter? How did that happen? Mama was never a fighter. She was just the opposite. Maybe there was a time when she was brave... Maybe when she travelled to Vilnius with me in her arms to search for Father. But her courage ended there. Those first encounters with the KGB took it all away from her... She became weaker and weaker after each time... Then, she grew paranoid. She was afraid of everything, but especially of men with briefcases. All that anxiety turned into an incurable illness. No, I did not inherit courage from my mother... Perhaps I have my father's character? He was in the military. Or perhaps I simply became accustomed to a regular routine? Or maybe all this is simply because I don't know how to do anything else. I don't regret anything. Well, unless I regret that God didn't give me nerves of steel. I would never like to feel that terrible fear that I felt before a race ever again. Then, you can't even talk... Your hands and legs grow weak just thinking about the race... Not many athletes have strong nerves. Everyone is nervous at the starting line. But there are some exceptions. Too bad that I never ended up among them. I must have taken on my fear from my mother. Our home was always full of stress. She would cower at the sound of the slightest footstep, tremble when anyone knocked on the door. She became mistrustful and private... Sofija took a deep breath. *Perhaps all those medals have led me to my father. I would never have made it to Canada if it hadn't been for rowing. I never wanted to admit it to myself, but every*

time I went abroad, I had a tiny hope that I'd see my father. How foolish…
I was so naïve… Why didn't he ever try to find me? I'll find out soon. In a
few days, I'll meet him and I'll ask him everything. I hope I won't be disap-
pointed. I hope that I may still find him. No, I will find him, truly I will…

"Good day, Sofija," a voice behind her spoke in Lithuanian. It was
the Latvian coach, Rolands Sprogis. The Lithuanians and Latvians often
greeted each other in their native tongue. Unfortunately, after the greeting they would switch to Russian because that was the language that they
knew the best and the language they all spoke. "Is this your first time in
Canada?"

"Yes, my first."

"It's a shame they didn't take any Lithuanians on the team."

"Don't worry, we'll show them yet. In a year we'll get out position
back," Sofija said and smiled. "Come and sit next to me. We'll have a
chat. My neighbour won't mind. He went to the back of the plane to sit
with his friends."

Rolands Sprogis, the Latvian coach, was a friend since back in her
rowing days. All the athletes loved him. He cared for them like a second
father. The athletes he coached have been on the Soviet team since 1965.

"At least three adults from your team will travel to Nottingham."

"Maybe even four? Ramoškienė, Butkus, Kaminskaitė, Čikotas…
How about your juniors?"

"I'm bringing my eight."

"I know! Good for them! I heard that they had a good season."

"We won every race. In the Soviet Championship my junior team
won against the second senior team! Their boat flew! It's such a shame
they dismantled my team…"

"Dismantled?"

"Yes, I mean, they removed three. They switched them out with their own. Now my crew is not the same. The boat doesn't glide. Their strokes are different. They lean to the side. The boys are upset. I don't know how this will work out… They didn't have enough time to find their rhythm together. Can you imagine what it means to change the bow and the third seat in an eight? Both on the left side. Whoever we seat there, we won't regain our balance."

"Why? Were they were trying to make the team, 'stronger'?" Sofija asked with a wane smile.

Rolands pressed his lips together tightly and wound his fingers together. Sofija turned around and gazed into his eyes.

"You don't want to talk about it? I understand… I went through many qualification and trial races myself. In 1970 I won everything, but they left me as a standby. You can't win with them."

"There's nothing to tell… We were less than a month away from leaving… It was our last training camp in Birštonas. They came and told me: Vilnis Priede, Andris Priede and Andris Stigis are not travelling anywhere. Their documents are "not in order.""

"Undesirables?"

"The two cousins are from a family of Siberian deportees. The third one forgot to mention that he had relatives in the West."

"Maybe he didn't want to? Before you could hope they wouldn't find out. These days, they find out everything, trust me," Sofija said and nodded knowingly.

Rolands gave her a look.

"Oh, it's nothing," Sofija said and plastered a fake smile on her face.

I can't tell him about Father. Why tell him a story when I don't know the end myself. Oh, there are times when I feel that I really need to talk to someone about it… I'm always alone with my thoughts… Rolands looks like the kind of man you can trust, one of your own kind. But you can never know… Maybe he also received an "assignment" from the KGB. It's better to keep quiet. Although, I would never take him for an informer. But you never know who might overhear our conversation. They probably have the entire airplane bugged.

"They could have switched them out with some of my own… I have a few more good Latvian rowers. But, no, they jubilantly used the opportunity to shove three Russians on me."

"That's nothing new."

Suddenly Rolands' face went red.

"Oh, I'm sorry, I really didn't mean to insult you."

"Me?" Sofija asked, surprised.

"I have nothing against Russians. There are many good Russian people. I myself have good Russian friends. I'm truly sorry… I really didn't mean it…"

Sofija smiled.

"If you think you've insulted me, please don't worry about it. I'm not Russian."

"Really? I'm sorry, but I thought your surname was Russian."

"I'm a pure Pole, through and through. I was born in Warsaw. They changed my surname to a Russian one later when they issued my passport."

"Oh, that's what happened," Rolands said and sighed. "How did you end up in Lithuania?"

"I was brought there during the war. I was a year old, maybe even younger."

"There are many Poles in Lithuania, aren't there?"

"Yes, our histories are intertwined."

"And how is it they are bringing you to Canada?" he asked directly, not even aware that he could not have asked her a more difficult question.

"Me? I wanted to see where women will race in the Olympics for the first time," Sofija said and laughed, pathetically trying to avoid the question but at the same time making it clear that she was not going to tell him anything more than that.

Rolands' look made her cringe. *He probably thinks that I got in through communist party connections... Or that I'm working for the KGB... Oh, how wrong he is...* Sofija wished she could tell him the truth, but suddenly she felt terrified and broke out in cold sweats. *But it is true. The KGB did ask me to inform for them. But did I agree? No, no, I didn't... They bought me in exchange for the permission to go see my father. They pressured me and I gave in... But that doesn't mean a thing! I refuse to serve them. I'll only pretend to work for them, but I won't really work for them... I will not report a single person. I will not follow anyone. I will not write anything bad about anyone. I won't see what I'm not supposed to see... All I want is to see my father. I will never ask them for permission to travel anywhere ever again. They will never get the opportunity to pressure me again. For this meeting to happen I agreed to pretend to be something that I'm not, that I can never be. I did it all to keep my promise to my dead mother...*

Shivers ran through her body. Until now, everything seemed so far away, so unreachable, and so unreal. And now, the resolution of the greatest secret of her life was only a few days away.

There's no way back... Why did I need to do this? Maybe there is a huge disappointment awaiting me, a loss, an even greater secret... What am I afraid of? I don't owe anything to anyone. This is my life and mine alone. I can simply enjoy Canada and not try to look for my father if that's what I feel like doing. What's the worst that could happen? That I won't find him? That he won't see me? I'll live… I've lived without him for thirty-six years of my life. I don't even know him. He is a complete stranger to me. I don't even know if I'll feel anything when I see him. Shivers ran down her spine once more. *Why am I so afraid that I am trembling? Why? Because my childhood memories might be crushed? Maybe whatever I find out, whatever it is, will destroy all the fantasies I have created in my mind. The memories that I myself have created. After all, they are nothing more than my own imagination. But I will need to live on… How strange it is that the future can alter my past. I never thought about that before…*

CHAPTER TWENTY

AUGUST 6, 1975, MONTREAL, CANADA – DAY ONE

Before they even departed, they had heard over the news that Canada had hit a record heat wave with temperatures at 37.6 Celsius on August 1st. *Racing in that heat will be a disaster,* Sofija thought to herself. *The boys are in for a hard time. I know what it means when the heat zaps all your strength. You feel as though your head is about to explode before you even reach the finish line. During practice runs you've just got to soak your hat in the cold water and put it on your head. That cools you off for a minute or two, but then it dries out again. The oars slide out of your hands from the sweat. You're afraid to lose your oars. In a sweep boat at least you can grab a minute to wipe the sweat from your palm, but in a sculling boat there's no chance. Then all you can do is clutch the oars and just hope they don't slide away.*

Before she ever left on any trip, Sofija always read about the country that she would be visiting, so that she'd know what she ought to see. It was assumed that they would visit Niagara Falls. Everyone said that it was a miracle of nature. They bring all tourists there, including Soviet tourists. That was the entire point of her journey.

Among the sites she wanted to see most was Toronto with its high-rises. This year, on April 2nd the Canadians completed construction of a television tower that was 553 metres tall. That tower stole the record for height from Moscow's Ostankino television tower. They say that you can see this tower from 50 kilometres distance. Then she wanted to see the parks in Ottawa and Quebec. And then, she had to find a sporting goods shop to purchase a ping-pong paddle.

Saint Catherine is not far from Niagara. It would be interesting to go there to see the rowing canal. In the 1970 World Championship two Lithuanians raced there – Benjaminas Nacevičius ir Mindaugas Vaitkus. The eight came in second. I had to retire from rowing in 1970. It's too bad... I pretended as though it didn't matter, but it did. It hurt... Of course, I knew that sooner or later my rowing career would come to an end, but I thought it would end differently... It's too bad that I never asked about Saint Catherine. I wonder if they saw anything besides the rowing canal? Nobody allows athletes to go anywhere. Someone said that the Royal Canadian Henley Regatta takes place there. Just like in August. Only, I wonder on what days? I will need to ask when I get there. I'd like to see that regatta. Or at least the canal.

"I've never flown this far in my life," the rowers were saying to each other, dragging their luggage towards the arrival hall. "My neck hurts."

"My feet don't fit in my shoes."

My feet are also swollen, Sofija thought to herself.

"Oh, I'm so hungry, I wish I could have something to eat, it all smell so good..."

"I want to sleep... I could not fall asleep during the entire flight. There wasn't enough room for my legs."

"I couldn't sleep either... I had too much on my mind... It'll be easier to get accustomed to Canadian time."

"What's the time difference?"

"Eight hours."

Isn't it seven? Sofija thought.

"I think so… It's night back home, but the sun's shining over here."

"Just imagine, how long our day has been? Twenty-four hours plus another eight. That's means our August 5th was thirty-two hours long."

"Yeah, but when we fly back, our day will be eight hours shorter."

By the time we fly home, I will have met Father…

"Welcome to Montreal," a man holding up a sign reading "USSR Delegation" greeted them in Russian. "My name is Steve. I will be your guide during your trip. Let's wait for everyone to gather in one place."

Steve flipped open a notebook.

"I have thirteen people on my list: Dumbadze, Grucova, Tkachuk…"

Sofija listened as he read off the names.

"The athletes and coaches will be on the second bus with Mike," Steve continued. "He's right over there in the blue jacket."

A middle-aged man walking past the group called out in Russian, "Hello Stepan, who are you meeting today?"

"Your name is Stepan?" Sofija asked, turning around, surprised.

"Yes," the man answered awkwardly. "I'm from Ukraine. But here in Canada they call me Steve. You may call me Steve."

"Of course… Steve."

Sofija pronounced his name clearly; however, she wondered if he caught the irony in her tone of voice. Who was this disappointing man who was trying so hard to hide his origins? *Mike over there must be Misha,* she thought.

"I'm also from Ukraine, from Dneprodzerzhinsk, I'm Anatoly," Anatoly Tkachuk said, extending his right hand. He was a former rower, a European champion, and a two-time Olympic medal winner.

"Hello, Anatoly. Soon we will all introduce ourselves. The first thing we need to do is to bring you to your hotel. You can settle in and have some lunch, take a rest. Tomorrow morning, we will travel to the rowing venue and we will show you around Montreal."

"Is the venue far?"

"Let's all go to the bus now. It's right there – across the street. I'll tell you everything as we drive," Steve said and waved over his delegation into a tight circle around him.

With frightened, but curious, glances, they watched the passers-by. They quickly scooped up their cases and travel bags and followed Steve towards the exit, each of them terrified of lagging behind and getting stranded in a country where no one understood their language.

They were all exhausted from their flight and the long formalities at the border. They all wanted to relax in the bus, the sooner the better.

"Stepan, will we be housed together with the athletes?" Nina asked.

"My name is Steve. Call me Steve, or Mr. Steve," he shot back.

"Thank you for your response," Nina muttered quietly.

Sofija cocked her head and gazed at Steve in wonderment. *What would have to happen to me to make me give up on my homeland? Unless my life was in danger? Or the lives of my loved ones? But why would one be so ashamed of one's roots. I don't understand... He is trying to pretend to be a foreigner... It's ridiculous... It's obvious that he works for the Soviet KGB. Otherwise, they would not have sent him to take care of our group. Steve... What a phony...*

Steve ignored Nina's question and took over his role as tour guide:

"In October they will open a new airport in Montreal. This airport, called the Dorval airport, has been in operation since 1941. It's a little out of date. But it's not far from the centre of the city, about fifteen kilometres. The new airport will be fifty kilometres distant. It will take an hour to get there from the city centre. Now, we will travel just twenty minutes.

"I read somewhere that people in Montreal orient themselves directionally according to the mountain," Algis said.

"Mount Royal," Steve said in a voice full of wonder. "The name of the city of Montreal comes from the name of that mountain. The mountain is not so tall that you would see it from here, but tomorrow when we go site seeing in the city, you will see the back of the mountain. It looks like the back of an animal. It's beautiful in autumn when the leaves turn red and yellow. Too bad you won't be here long enough to see the leaves turn colour. Now, getting back to your question... You are exactly correct, Montreal is the only city in the world where the sun sets in the south. Your points of orientation here are the mountain and the river. Mount Royal is considered to be in the north when it is actually in the west. The Saint Lawrence River is considered to be in the south when it is actually in the east. The rowing venue is in the city centre, on Notre Dame island."

"Does that name have anything in common with the Notre-Dame in Paris?" Algis asked.

"Montreal also has its own Notre Dame basilica, and it is more beautiful than the one in Paris. But I will tell you all about it when we visit there tomorrow. The island was constructed from reclaimed land in 1965. They took stone that they dug up when then built the Montreal metro to construct its base."

"When did they build the metro?" the Russian coach Oleg asked.

"In 1966."

"We had a metro in Moscow in 1935!" Anatoly said proudly.

He has lived in Moscow for years and was immensely proud of his adopted city. "I wonder where they put all the earth they dug up when they built the metro in Moscow?"

"They poured fifteen million tons of earth when they built the island. This island was attached to the island of Saint Helen. Together they make up the *Park dez il*, or the Islands Park. They built it especially for the 1967 Expo.

"What language was that?"

"French. *Parc des Îles* means Island Park. You probably heard that Montreal is a French speaking city?" Steve raised his eyebrows and glanced around at his audience. "In the seventeenth century French colonists arrived here. They named this land 'New France" and for two hundred years it was a colony of France."

"So, we need to speak French here?" Sofija asked, surprised. "Does anyone understand English here?"

"Don't worry, you can speak English here, if you know how. Although the British defeated the French in the Seven Years War, the residents over here resisted them. There was nothing left for the British to do but to grant Quebec a special language and cultural status. Montreal is considered one of the most beautiful cities that has retained the French spirit and French architecture. Many people call the Old Town or Montreal a "little version of Paris." You'll see, it is a lot like Paris. Has anyone been to Paris?" Steve winked and gave a self-satisfied smile. "Of course, how would any of your poor souls ever make it to Paris."

"We flew through Paris," one of the men chimed in.

"That was just the airport! That's not Paris!"

What an egomaniac this Steve-Stepan is… I was in Paris… Sofija smiled to herself and turned towards the window. *That was just after I won the European Rowing Championship… And I'd just found out about Father… Everything seemed so close then, just out of reach. And then those eight years flew past so quickly. Now, finally, the chance to see Father has come to me. Paris is beautiful. It's a good thing that Sasha and I managed to see a lot... Oh, and we were in such a jubilant mood after taking first place... Probably that's why those memories are so wonderful... The other girls spent their time in Paris buying shoes. By now, they've worn out those shoes and tossed them away, but I have my memories of wandering the city...*

"Steve is that island, where the rowing canal is, surrounded by a river or a lake?" a man called out from the back of the bus.

"The Saint Lawrence River runs through the city. Both islands are surrounded by the river."

"Then the rowing canal is dug out inside the island? Is it still water or is there a current?" Anatoly asked.

"The canal is cut off from the river. There is no current. They dug it out last year. The construction just ended recently. They built it especially for the Olympics."

"They already completed it! The Olympics is only a year away!" the men called out and burst out laughing. "There might not be enough room for the junior teams to race."

"I was there a few weeks ago myself. Everything is ready. They can hold the Olympics tomorrow if they wish. Here in Canada, men, they do everything yesterday and not tomorrow!" Steve stated with pride.

"We'll see..."

"The junior championship is their way of checking to make sure that everything is in good order for the Olympics. If something goes wrong, they have a year to fix it."

"Will they drive us to the canal, or will we need to walk there?" Nina asked.

Sofija considered that it must be hard for her to walk because of her age.

"They will drive you. There will be a special time set aside for strolling. The program has been scheduled ahead of time and we will all go everywhere together."

No, of course they won't allow us to wander off on our own... They don't have enough KGB agents to follow each one of us around... Unless... everyone in this group is informing for the KGB... It may very well be that every single person in this group has been ordered to follow the others... Sofija glanced at the faces around her. Every single person in the bus one way or another received special permission to travel outside of the Soviet Union. Without a conversation with the KGB there was no way that you would be allowed to leave on a trip like this. Her conscience ate away at her for the "yes" she gave the KGB agent. Yet, her reason was sacred – to see her father... *But I don't think everyone on this trip will follow their orders. Everyone wanted to travel abroad to the West. They all want to shop for nice things, bring goods back home to their loved ones, see another world... Only my reason for coming on this trip is different. Probably... Or maybe someone else is also here to see their relatives? So many people fled to Canada during the war. I wonder...* She ran through the list of people whom she'd met on this trip only yesterday. *No, it wasn't likely...*

"When will we find out the programme schedule," Sofija asked. She wanted to get a hint from Steve if Niagara Falls was on the itinerary.

"This evening after dinner. We'll meet in the hotel lobby and I'll go over tomorrow's schedule."

"What cities will we see on this trip?"

"Don't worry, you'll see all the most important cities in Canada."

Sofija bit her lips. She saw that the guide was wary to not reveal too much valuable information.

I don't believe that we wouldn't go see Niagara Falls. How can we be in Canada and not see such a wonder? That's impossible. Only, when? I must somehow get in touch with my father... I don't know where he is... Maybe he isn't even home? Maybe he's away on a trip? How can I force Steve to reveal our travel plans? I can't ask too many questions. That will make him suspicious.

"I never thought there were so many churches in Canada..."

Sofija tuned in to listen.

"Montreal is also called the city of Saints," Stephen explained. "It's also called the city of a hundred bells. Almost a hundred years ago the famous American writer, Mark Twain, said when he arrived in Montreal: 'This is the first time I've been to a city where you can't throw a brick without breaking a church window.'"

"That's good. Who else would say that except for Mark Twain? Do all the churches operate according to their function?"

"What do you mean?"

"Well, have some of them been converted into cinemas or warehouses," Sofija continued. Horrified, she gasped at her own carelessness. She had just put into words a state secret. *Has the devil taken control of my tongue?* She hastily glanced around her to see if anyone had heard what she'd said.

Steve's eyes bore into her. A chill ran down Sofija's spine. *One hundred percent, he was KGB.*

"Most of the churches operate as churches and are open to tourist. You can see for yourself tomorrow. But you're probably more interested in seeing how Montreal is preparing for the Olympics."

"Of course, but not just that. I've heard that the nature in Canada is amazing and that the parks are impressive."

"That is true. We won't be able to visit all of them, but you will see enough to get a sense of the nature."

Thank God, that means we'll be going to Niagara Falls for sure, Sofija comforted herself. Without realizing what she was doing, she kept opening her handbag to check and make sure her address book with her father's telephone number was still there. The moment she thought of him, she felt weak. There must be a phone in the hotel. As soon as things are clearer, I will call him."

"What parks are we planning to visit?"

"I will tell you everything, don't worry," Steve shot back, annoyed.

Sofija quieted down. This was not the time to ask about Niagara Falls. Steve would immediately get suspicious and report her. Then they'd send her "companions" who wouldn't allow her out of their sight for an instant.

"We have arrived," Steve announced. "Please don't wander off. We need to register all of you at the hotel. Prepare your passports. Lunch is at four at the hotel restaurant on the first floor. Let's check our watches. It's quarter to three right now."

"May we explore the city today?"

"Today you must rest. It has been a long and tiring flight. Besides, you all need to adjust to the local time. You'll be experiencing jetlag. You may fall asleep after lunch and not wake up until midnight. Then you won't be able to sleep until morning. Try to stay awake until nine pm at least. Otherwise, you'll confuse day with night. Besides, after dinner, at eight, I will come and tell you about tomorrow's programme. I will wait for all of you in the hotel lobby at the reception desk."

"What's the weather like here?" Nina asked, "how shall we dress to go see the canal?"

"Sorry, give me a minute to calculate," Steve said, scratching his head. "This April we switched from Fahrenheit to Celsius and it's difficult to adjust. Montreal in August is usually hot and humid. At night, the temperature drops to fifty-four, and during the day it goes up to seventy-five Fahrenheit. Sometimes it can even reach ninety. How shall I convert that? I suppose in Celsius that would be between twelve and thirty-four degrees. The coldest it has been, I think, has been fifty-seven. Take away thirty according to Fahrenheit and that comes to thirty-eight Celsius.

"We read that you have record heat this year."

"This August has been extremely hot. There were a few days, I think August 1st, were we hit a record for heat for this time of year. That was a hundred degrees Fahrenheit. That makes it thirty-seven Celsius. Tomorrow and the day after tomorrow will be cooler, around ninety. At night it will be around twelve to fifteen degrees. It's probably the same for you back home?"

"We all have different temperatures back home," Nina said and laughed. "For us in Georgia, your heat wave is a joke. But in the Baltic States they haven't even experience a high of thirty degrees, isn't that right Sofija?"

"I can promise you Georgian air from Friday on. The prognosis is thirty-seven degrees. But it's humid here, so the temperature seems hotter during the day and colder at night. On Sunday and Monday, we had a lot of rain, but there's no forecast for rain in the upcoming days. Take your sweaters and jackets with you when we go out because it is cool in the evening."

Steve gave a slight bow and led the group off the bus and towards the hotel lobby.

Two women and eleven men, all of them carrying their luggage, trailed after him towards the large glass hotel doors.

CHAPTER TWENTY-ONE

AUGUST 7, 1975, MONTREAL, CANADA – DAY TWO

The bus passengers drove across an impressive metal bridge to an island in the middle of the river. For a moment, they felt as though they had found themselves in a calm oasis. A street hugging the shoreline wended its way towards a majestic bubble.

"What's that enormous bubble?" the passengers asked, curious, pressing their faces up against the bus windows on the right side.

The bubble was impressive. It reflected the sun's light, emanating a profound brightness.

"That's the American pavilion. It was built for the Expo."

"Will we have the chance to walk around it?" Algis asked.

He was beginning to single himself out among the others for his curiosity and need to explore absolutely everything.

"Naturally, we'll take a look at the canal and then we will walk through the Expo, that is, while you still have the energy. The distances are long here," Steve stated pompously. "It's not the same as it was during the Expo. After the exhibition ended, there were fewer people. The condition of the structure deteriorated, and fewer spaces remained open to visitors."

"Is the Soviet pavilion on this island as well?"

"No, it was on the other island. We will go there as well today. It stood directly across from the American pavilion. But it is no longer there. After the Expo was over, they dismantled it and brought it back to Moscow," Steve said, pulling a photograph of the structure out of his folder and holding it up for everyone to see.

"That's correct," Anatoly said, "it stands at the VDNCH now."

"It looks like our Sports Hall in Vilnius!" Sofija blurted out in surprise. "I wonder who copied whom?"

"Don't for a minute consider that we copied from you," Anatoly said in an ironic tone. "When did they build your Sports Hall?"

"They started construction in 1965," Sofija said, avoiding a confrontation, "and completed the structure in 1971."

"There, so you see, ours was built in 1967! Your Sports Hall wasn't even built then yet!"

"But the architectural plans were drawn up, and they had to be approved by Moscow… As far as I know the curved roof structure was recognized as the invention of our architects… So much for that," Sofija said, waving her hand, "what's the difference anyway… Only, I don't understand why they had to take apart such a large building and transport it across the ocean. Wouldn't it have been easier simply to build a new one in Moscow?"

The men gaped at her, shocked that this woman could ask such a bold question.

"Why leave something that good behind for the capitalists!" Steve shouted out merrily, and then scanned the group for a reaction with his beady eyes.

Not a single one of them responded. It was obvious that Steve's comment was a provocation and any one of them who answered back could be written up in the KGB report. They all squirmed in their seats and pretended that they had not heard him.

The bus turned towards a narrow bridge that led to another island where there was a rowing canal.

"I saw a documentary film about the Expo," Anatoly shared. "They showed our pavilion. They said that the Soviet pavilion was the most beautiful and the most interesting of them all. Everyone was amazed by it – even the Americans. They showed people running to get inside the Soviet pavilion. Is that how it was for real?"

"Was it a Soviet film or a foreign film?" Steve asked, raising his eyebrows.

"It was ours, Soviet."

"The Soviet pavilion was impressive! It was constructed out of metal and glass and let in a lot of light. The architecture was modern, I'd even say, western," Steve explained, satisfied with his own explanation. "The exposition was interesting. Especially about space. No one will ever meet us in the arena of space exploration! All the countries were competing each other to show the best they had."

Sofija bit her lip just so she would not burst out laughing. *How many people believe this propaganda?... I saw that film as well. Of course, everyone "was dying" to see the majestic sculpture of Lenin and the grotesque hammer and sickle in the doorway. It's easy to film people running and then say that they are all running to get inside the Soviet pavilion. It's a shame they didn't show us the other country's pavilions. I don't believe that they were all cold and soulless.*

"There aren't many Expo buildings left on this island then?" Someone asked.

The bus drove through the other island. The passengers scanned the area, searching for more Expo buildings. However, it was clear that the island had been transformed to accommodate sporting events. There was a row of pontoons and milling around them young men wearing team shirts from several different countries.

"Not many. Before they could dig out this canal, they had to knock down a few pavilions. As far as I remember, they took down pavilions built by Germany, India, Mexico, and one more country... Hum... Yes, that's right, Thailand."

As Steve promised, the rowing canal was prepared for the competition. From that moment onwards, the canal with its 2.2-kilometre length, 110 metre width, and 2.5 metre depth became the largest manmade canal in all North American. To accommodate the youth championship, they built a starting pontoon 500 metres beyond the opening of the canal, so that the juniors could race a 1.5-kilometre distance.

Inside the rowing venue there were the grandstands, a finish tower, boat racks, a changing room, and two rowing tanks, one for rowing and the other for canoes and kayaks. There was also a cafeteria.

"Ten months ago, none of this was here," Steve explained, pulling from his folder an old newspaper clipping with a photograph of the Expo Park territory from an aerial perspective. "This is what the island looked like seven years ago. I brought this photo today specially to show you. See, the pavilions are spread out over the two islands. Between them ran a single gauge train. On the Notre Dame Island – where we are right now – there were more canals. Boats travelled around them. Trains ran between the islands, on the islands, and even inside the pavilions. The tracks were raised above the buildings. It looked like an amusement park."

Everything had been prepared for the World Junior Rowing Championship.

"Not bad!" the passengers commented in awe. "Is the Olympic Village also complete?"

"The plan is that it won't be just a village, but an entire Olympic Park with the main Olympic buildings – the stadium, velodrome, swimming pools, and Olympic village," Steve bragged. "To be honest," he confided, "I'm not so sure they will manage to build all that in a year. It's been moving very slowly. There are a lot of scandals over construction."

"What kinds of scandals?"

"There's something wrong with the financing... The stadium construction is complex and expensive. No one seems to take into consideration that the northern winters here are harsh and it's difficult to work outside in winter."

"Oh, but you said that here in Canada they did everything yesterday, not tomorrow," the coach from Saratov called out from the back of the bus.

"This is another case," Steve said uncomfortably.

"We saw the cranes as we drove past, and they weren't moving. Isn't it working hours? Or are they taking a break?"

"Unfortunately... This is a problem with capitalism. The workers are on strike since May. They've fallen behind schedule."

"What are they striking about?"

"Who knows... Maybe the working conditions or maybe about pay. Oh look, we have arrived. Here the rowing Olympic events may as well start tomorrow," Steve said, waving towards the grandstands.

They disembarked from the bus and followed Steve.

Athletes were moving about the rowing course. Most of them must have arrived much earlier, perhaps a week or two early. It takes time to adapt to differences in time zone and climate, and for this reason many of the teams worked a training camp into their schedule.

Everything felt new and fresh, but it was all organized intelligently.

The canal embankments were reinforced with rubble excavated from where there was now water. It was the same rubble brought in during the construction of the subway. At the left end of the course there were two blocks of boathouses – six in each building. The octagonal finish tower was supposed to ensure impeccable visibility in all directions. Trails on both sides of the canal could be used for cycling or walking to the starting line. On a big scoreboard on the other bank of the course, the results of the competition would soon be displayed. The grandstands built on this side closer to the finish were covered and those further away were open. But perhaps the most impressive view of the course was from the grandstands on the other side, where the legacy of Expo 1967 was evident. Now, eight years later, well ahead of its time, the area was impeccable. The bubble of the American pavilion, though located on the other island, St. Helena, looked as though it had landed on top of the covered grandstands. Perhaps most stunning site of all was the magnificent view of the French pavilion at the thousand-metre? mark.

Beside the boathouses they spotted the familial blue wool tracksuits with the letters CCCP sewn onto the front. Most likely the Soviet junior team had already arrived for training. They apparently had rigged their boats yesterday. Now they were carrying their oars and either heading to the pontoon or the boathouse.

The canal is quite open, Sofija thought, *there is no protection from the wind. They could get waves. It is a lot like Bosbaan. Even there it was less open.*

"The canal is wide open, like in Bosbaan," Anatoly said, as though he'd read Sofija's mind and spoke her thoughts out loud. In 1964 he won the gold in Amsterdam in a coxed four. "If the wind hits them from the side, they'll have poor conditions."

"And if it's a head wind! Watch out! There doesn't seem to be anywhere to hide from the wind, not unless near the grandstands. It's wide open," the coach from Saratov chimed in.

"A head wind is death to me… I lost a few times – painfully – because of a head wind," Sofija said and sighed.

She'd never be able to forget Amsterdam in 1966 and 1968 in Grünau… She could never erase the humiliation from her mind.

"Of course, it's difficult for someone as petite as you to row against the wind," Anatoly said and nodded.

"It'll be hard on the junior team as well. They're not used to suffering for long just yet."

"Let's just hope the race will be downwind."

"Perhaps we can take a walk around this area?" Algis interrupted. "Your group might be more interested in checking the conditions here, but some of us would like to explore the Expo."

"Good, I'll go with you. We'll be back in an hour," Steve said, nodding and scanning their faces.

Probably Steve decided that it was less of a risk to leave the five rowers on their own rather than to allow a group of eight to wander off by themselves.

One after another, members of the group stood up and walked down the grandstands steps. Four men remained behind with Sofija, an Estonian and three Russians.

What an interesting group, Sofija mused. *Five rowers and eight functionaries. And Steve. They could care less about rowing. And they could care less about Canada. They probably just want to sell off their caviar as fast as they can and storm the shops.*

"I'll stay with you," Nina said, turning back towards them. "It's hard for me to walk a long distance."

"The women will race in the Olympics here in a year," Sofija said and sighed.

"What a shame that it happened too late for you," Anatoly said.

"There's nothing to regret, unless I should regret that I was born too soon," Sofija said and laughed. "Of course, I'm a little jealous of the women who will have the honour of competing in the Olympics. It must be an amazing feeling to make it into the Olympics. What a shame that they only added women's rowing now. Four years ago, I would have had a chance."

"When were you born?"

"1939. I'm thirty-six."

"I see... I heard that in the West they row until an older age. They throw us out on our thirtieth birthday."

"That's right, they just throw you out and you're finished. Rather, more accurately, they unseat you out of the boat," Sofija said. She smiled sadly. "It doesn't even matter what shape you're in and what you've accomplished."

"The eight looks good. Only the first and the third seat aren't working out," Anatoly said, waving his hands to indicate the Soviet men's eight rowing past. "The sixth isn't hitting the rhythm either."

"They're new on the crew," Sofija said. "They added them only a month ago, maybe less, at the last training camp."

"They shouldn't break up crews like that. It takes years for an eight to find their rhythm together. What a strange decision. Look how the boat is leaning to the left."

Sofija nodded, but held back from telling them what Coach Rolands had shared with her. No one ever spoke of such things. *If they really want to know the reason why, they can find out for themselves. There's no reason for me to stick my nose into it.*

"The question is… Why did they switch them out," Anatoly continued, "probably because their documents were not "in order?" I saw this team in Moscow during the Spartakiad. It's a crime to break up a crew like that! They flew, simply flew! I've been following that team for a while now. Let's see how they do here."

"What have you heard about our trip itinerary?" Sofija asked, surprising herself with her own boldness.

She simply could not stop thinking about her father and the possibility of meeting him. That thought was causing her anxiety to grow even greater. She wanted to discern if there was any chance that she could see her father in Niagara Falls.

"I don't know," the coach for Saratov answered. "What? Do I care? Wherever they take me, I'll be happy to go. Do you have something you particularly are dreaming of seeing?"

Sofija shot him a wide smile.

"All my life I've dreamed of seeing Niagara Falls."

"But isn't Niagara in America?" the coach said, surprised.

"You can see the Niagara Falls from the American side," the Estonian coach chimed in, "but they say it's more beautiful from the Canadian side."

"Oh, then we absolutely must go see it! This might be our only chance in our lives to see the Niagara Falls from the Canadian side. Who knows if we will ever make it to America in our lives. We must see Niagara this time," the coach from Saratov exclaimed.

Sofija was surprised by his emotional response.

Good. Everyone wants to visit the Niagara Falls. That means we will see it...

A wave of anxiety coursed through Sofija's body. *I always thought that the anxiety attacks would stop when I was no longer racing,* she thought. *I feel the same way I do as before a race. Take a deep breath... And another... And another...*

Sofija stood there breathing deeply, but quietly, so that the others would not notice.

Calm down, she self-soothed. *This is not a race. There is a way. If I don't decide to meet him, then it is not a big deal. I will say to myself that it's good enough to visit Canada. Everything is so interesting here. Ridiculous... I know that I'll never forgive myself if I don't get to see Father... Everything will be fine. You don't need to rush things... When we arrive in Toronto... We are going to Toronto?... In Toronto I will craft a plan to get to Father... Now, I simply need to relax and enjoy the trip... I am on the other side of the world, on another continent... I must take it all in and enjoy everything I see around me... I will never have the chance to come here again, after all...*

Sofija raised her trusty camera to her eyes and began studying the rowing course through the view finder. The long steel bridge that stretched across the entire island framed the landscape. Behind it, there were the boathouses – small and squat. They appeared small, but they housed all the teams' boats and twenty-eight spare boats, just in case. The athletes and their families rested in the grandstands.

How many parents come to see the races! Only our athletes must always travel everywhere alone. As though we were in the military. I could not even imagine anyone's parents being able to travel together with the team. Not unless they were high-ranking KGB agents. And then... You won't get into a trip like this that easily... But even back home, in Trakai, do any parents ever come to watch their sons or daughters race? It's not done. Mama never got to see a single one of my races... Not even in Vilnius... Why? She never even gave it a thought... It is completely unacceptable in the Soviet Union for parents to watch their children race. You return home a week later and tell them about the results, and that's it. You return home from being away at training camp a month and you say, "Hi, everything's fine" and that's the end of your conversation. You're afraid, and ashamed, that your friends might call you a Mama's girl or Mama's boy. Why do we have such cold relationships with our parents? Who taught us to bury our emotions like that? The war? School? The government? Fear? Fear... We always live in fear... We're afraid of our teachers.... We're afraid of the KGB... We're afraid of the militia... We're afraid of our elders... We're afraid of shopkeepers... We're afraid of our friends' opinions of us... We're afraid to make a mistake... Afraid to lose... Afraid to stand out from the others... Afraid to be different... Afraid to live differently than everyone else... Afraid to be someone different from the masses...

From the left, a couple around her age walked into the scene she was observing through her viewfinder. They were cheerfully chatting with a young rower dressed in an American team tracksuit. The mother reach over and pushed back her son's dark hair from time to time. His father threw his arm around his shoulder... The young man was enthusiastically telling them something, probably talking about an experience he'd had. Perhaps he was sharing his dreams?

I never had a father, Sofija thought sadly. *All I have are his letters. Letters from a stranger. My father never threw his arm across my shoulders and asked me about my dreams. He never even asked me anything about myself in his letters... He just wrote about inconsequential things... Soon that may change... I cannot return to my childhood, but I can find my real father...*

Anxiety overcame her more and more often, triggered by the slightest thought about meeting her father. But the worst was the not knowing. *How? When? Will I make it in time? Will I find him?* The lump formed in her throat, tingled in her hands, made her weak in the knees. *It's just like before the start of a race. I probably was this anxious back in 1968 in Grünau when we knew before we even started that we couldn't win. The head wind was so strong that the only thing that could have prevented us from falling behind would be our competitor's boat capsizing or breaking. But that rarely happened in a race at that level. What could save me now? Pull yourself together! It can't get any worse. The very worst that could happen is that I wouldn't see my father. That would be the end of the world! Enough! Time to start enjoying this trip...*

"Shall we walk over to see the Expo?" Sofija said, turning towards the men. She pulled on her red plaid jacket. The weather had cooled down to twenty degrees. "We can talk about coaching along the way. Look, there they are our coaches, walking towards us along the shoreline."

CHAPTER TWENTY-TWO

AUGUST 8, 1975, MONTREAL, CANADA – DAY THREE

Today I must let Father know that I am in Canada. Oh, what if it turns out he is not that far away from here. Maybe he's in Montreal?

It was four in the morning. Sofija was restless and could not sleep. In Lithuania it was mid-afternoon. It was difficult to adjust to the time difference. By six in the evening, she felt drowsy.

There are payphones in the lobby. All I need to do is to make a phone call when no one from the group is around to see me. That would arouse too much suspicion. They'll know that I'm not calling Lithuania. Perhaps I should sneak out and make a phone call during breakfast, while they're all eating? Races start today. We'll be leaving early for the rowing venue. Are there any telephones at the canal? I didn't notice... I could call him before we got on the bus. But what if he's still sleeping? I don't know anything about him. Poor Mama.... She died without ever seeing him. Oh, what did she know? What was she hiding from me? I still remember her burning papers in the stove. What was written on those papers? What was she trying to destroy? What was she hiding? Maybe I'll find the answers on this trip. It makes me sad to remember how she died. She couldn't even recognize me anymore. She didn't understand anything... She simply lay there trembling with fear... She'd jump at the slightest footstep, startle from the slightest glance... If she can see me now, she will lead me to Father. If she wants me to find him.

Mamusia... I'd do anything for you. If only I could shake off the guilt, I feel over the way we lived... I know, I know, I'm not to blame for it, but I cannot shake my feelings of guilt. It would be good to get some sleep... But how? If only Tatyana Mikhailovna was here... She'd pour me a glass of red wine, like back then in Vichy... Sofija chuckled, remembering. *That really helped them. It was my anxiety that was keeping me awake then, now it is the time difference. Maybe the bar is open downstairs. Oh no, there's no need to throw my money away on drinks. I need to have enough to buy the ping-pong paddle for the KGB agent. What a thought... Ugh...*

Sofija quietly rose from her bed and on tippy toes, to not wake Nina, and walked over to the window. From their seventh-floor hotel room window she could see a panorama of Montreal, still lit up in the darkness. She could see the lovely Old Town, which so similar to Paris. Far beyond the Old Town she saw the framework of the Olympic Stadium. They didn't let them out to walk around and explore the area. They simply drove past it. Steve said, "No use wasting time walking around a construction site."

The enormous territory was filled with construction vehicles, tractors, building materials. The ground was torn up by tractor treads. The framework of the stadium was interesting. It looked like the skeleton of a dead animal. However, in a year the Olympic opening ceremony would take place there. Rowers never participate in the opening ceremony. They race the following day. Beyond the half-built stadium, she spotted two large concrete buildings that looked like pyramids rising into the sky. Steve told them that would be the Olympic Village. The Velodrome was almost complete. The form was clearly visible, and it had a roof already.

Back home it would take five years to construct all that. Here, it took eleven months. The Olympics are in July? It's hard to believe that all those buildings will be constructed by then, but then again, this isn't the Soviet Union. Oh, I wish I could see the Olympics! Of course, I know I won't. At least I'm seeing them now. I'll tell Genovaitė about everything I saw. She'll probably race in the Olympics. Not me... I was born too soon...

Sofija sat down on the windowsill and pressed her head to the glass. *It was just like this that time the KGB called me in for questioning. I couldn't sleep then either. I came home on the train from Jelgava. I lied to Mama that I needed a doctor's certificate... I was shaking as I spoke those lies. That was the last time in my life that I couldn't sleep all night. That was awful... Facing the unknown is awful... I couldn't control my anxiety at all.* She remembered how she felt weak in the morning, not having slept all night. Her legs and arms were tingling. There was a lump in her throat, and she couldn't say a word or even swallow a gulp of tea. That was the day she learned that her father was alive. Eight years have passed since that day. And now here she was, in her father's adopted country.

Why does Father live here? Why not in Poland? Why, come to think of it, why not in Lithuania? How did he travel all the way to Canada? It's so far away from Europe. This isn't a day trip, or even a week's journey... He journeyed from Smolensk to Niagara Falls... That's thousands of kilometres. The distance from Smolensk to the nearest boat was about two thousand kilometres... Then there was the journey across the Atlantic Ocean... That would have taken a few weeks. And the war was on! What was he thinking about as he crossed the ocean? In those days, there were no airplanes that flew across the ocean, only ships. Was he thinking of me? Of Mama?

Sofija imagined the handsome man with the dark hair in the military uniform with three stars on his epaulettes. She imagined him seated on the deck of an enormous ship, wrapped in a ragged wartime jacket. She imagined him pulling from his pocket a small photograph of Mama and her, and then wiping the tears from his eyes with a handkerchief, just like the one Mama had. She imagined him caressing the photograph and pressing it to his lips. *Jak ja was kocham! Oh how much I love you!*

What changed in his life that caused him to lose thirty years? What was he doing during those thirty years? Did he ever think of Mama and me and try to imagine our lives? Perhaps he wanted to go back? Maybe he wanted to bring us to Canada to live with him? What would have stopped him? Of course, the KGB and the Iron Curtain…

Sofija sat on the windowsill quietly waiting for dawn. She wanted to take a shower, but she was afraid that the sound of the water would wake Nina. *Thirty years have passed, and I'm still frightened of my neighbours… I'm still carrying that fear from when the horrid Golosovs would scream and Mama and me if we dared turn on the water in the bathroom. Even when I lived in the training camps with the other girls, I'd only turn on the water in the shower to the slightest trickle, so that I could wash myself quickly and not make too much noise and annoy the others. They often teased me, "Sofija, did you fall asleep in there?"*

"Are you having a hard time sleeping?" Nina asked when she woke up at six and saw Sofija sitting on the windowsill.

"It's jetlag. I woke at four and could not fall back asleep. I should have gone out for a walk."

"I don't seem to have a problem with jetlag. When I was your age, though, I had trouble with insomnia."

Nina was twenty years older. She was fifty-six.

"I decided I'm not going to worry about it. I'll simply have more time to see everything in Canada."

"There's only so much you can see through the window."

"That's true… Only the city at night. Montreal is beautiful at night.

There are so many colours and lights!"

"All cities are beautiful in the dark. Do you know why?"

Sofija gazed at her older companion with curiosity in her eyes.

"Because you can't see all the trash and chaos," Nina said and laughed.

"Probably... But maybe also because we always dream about visiting a place that is more beautiful than where we are."

"That's also true. All cities are more or less alike. Your first city is interesting, but after that they all seem similar."

"That's why I prefer seeing the nature in different countries," Sofija said brightly, using the opportunity to her advantage. "I'd like to see some provincial parks in Canada. I heard that the nature is beautiful and quite varied."

"The only difference between cities are the people and the culture," Nina continued, as though she hadn't heard what Sofija had said. "Just go out into the street, the market, the cafes, and observe the local people, their traditions, how they behave, how they talk, and you will get to know much more about the local culture than visiting touristic sites. Tour guides have memorized a country's history, but they will never give you a sense of the spirit of a city or a country. Especially our tour guide, Steve," Nina said and laughed boisterously.

"I agree Nina Yakovlevna, but ever since I was in school, I dreamed of seeing Niagara Falls. I can't wait until they bring us there."

"Niagara Falls ought to be impressive, but I won't be able to keep you company there. I have difficulty walking long distances, and in such places the distances are great. You take some photos and show me later, will you?" Nina said and laughed.

"Very well," Sofija said and smiled politely. *I hope that Nina's the only one who is not interesting in visiting Niagara Falls. There's no way the men*

would want to pass up such an opportunity. Unless... Not unless they prom-
ised their wives to bring back plenty of goods and will ask to be brought to a
shopping centre rather than to Niagara Falls...

"If the weather is like it was yesterday, we can walk, but if the temperature goes up to thirty, like Steve said it would, then that's too hot for
me, even though I am a true Georgian.

If it gets hot, I will find a place in the shade to rest. But, if they do take
us somewhere else in Canada, it will only be next week, after the races are
over. That's what Steve said..."

"Yes, of course," Sofija said, a little relieved that Nina was still unsure.
"To be honest, I'm here to watch the World Junior Championship. This
is my first time at a World Championship. For us, the men get to race the
world, but we women may only race in Europe."

"But why? That's not fair," Nina said indignantly.

"I don't know... Those are the rules of our sport. Perhaps rowing is
considered a man's sport."

"But women also row?"

"Of course, they row."

"How long?"

"Almost as long as men have been rowing. Only, in some countries
women don't get the opportunity to row. In America the women's rowing
clubs are far inferior to ours."

"How's that? They have separate clubs for men and for women?"

"That's right."

"Well, I wouldn't put up with that type of discrimination. Discus
throwing doesn't seem very feminine, but we have our own women's
team. We don't have that level of male chauvinism."

"You may compete in the Olympics, but we may only compete starting next year. Women's rowing will be held for the very first time in the Montreal Olympics."

"That's too bad... With your racing results, do you think you would have been selected to compete?"

"Yes. Only six years ago I was still a member of the Soviet team. And how about you, Nina Yakovlevna, how was it for you participating in the Helsinki Olympics? When did they first allow women's track and field in the Olympics?"

"Since 1928."

"That's an old tradition then."

"That might seem old to you, but at the time I was nine," Nina said and laughed. "In 1928 there were only five sports allowed for women, but discus throw was one of them."

"It must be an amazing feeling to compete in the Olympics?"

"For every athlete it's your greatest dream. When your dream comes true, you feel special. The Olympics are not just a competition, they are an enormous celebration. Just the opening ceremonies are a spectacle you'd never want to miss. Oh, the feeling of marching through the arena with the best athletes in the world... I wish that experience for every athlete."

"It's too bad, but rowers never have that experience."

"Why not?" Nina asked, surprised.

"They always race on the first day, so they need to rest and save their energy."

"That's a shame. The opening ceremony is a beautiful experience. Everyone is in a good mood and relaxed."

"The rowers don't get to participate in the closing ceremonies either. They take them home after their final race, halfway through the

Olympics."

"Wow! That is so unfair. Why may all the other athletes participate in the closing ceremonies, but the Soviet team must leave after their final race?! It's not only the rowers. The others leave right after their competition as well. Aren't we as good as them? What are they so afraid of? Or are they saving money? Or are they afraid we'll see too much of the capitalist world? They're probably afraid we'll try to run away to the West," Nina said sarcastically then burst out laughing.

Sofija shrugged. She was not so sure if she should continue this conversation or not. *Who knows? Maybe Nina was placed in the room together with her to provoke her and compromise her? Why is she on this trip? As a decorated retired athlete? Or as an agent for the Communist Party? Because she accomplished that much in track and field? It's so awful that we can't just relax and be open with each other. But I can't let my guard down. She seems like a decent and honest woman, but just like the rest of us, she'll file her report when she gets back.*

"You know," Nina continued, "when I stood on the pedestal, I wanted the entire world to know I was Georgian. Our nation has not produced many Olympians. But everyone thought I was a Russian."

Sofija bit her lip nervously. She was tempted to take the bait but didn't want to get into a conversation about their ethnicities.

"I'm sorry, I have nothing against Russians," Nina said, reading Sofija's silence as injured feelings.

"I'm not Russian, Nina Yakovlevna, I'm Polish. Many people think I'm Russian because of my surname. I was even born in Warsaw."

"Is that so! You are a real foreigner then?" Nina said and smiled warmly. "I was born in Odessa, but my father was Georgian."

"Nonetheless, it must be an amazing feeling to receive a medal in the

Olympics, stand on the pedestal, as tens of thousands of people applaud you," Sofija said, turning the topic away from a dangerous direction.

"It only lasts for a short time. And you can only enjoy it if you manage to focus on the moment and not worry about 'if only I'd come in first' or 'what if I came in third, then what?' Such a moment you hold onto your entire life. If you miss it, you'll eat yourself alive the rest of your life because you know that you can never get it back. You're only on that pedestal for five minutes. At most, twenty. That's all. Then it's history. You've been an athlete a long time and so you know how short lived the glory is, don't you?"

"Yes... Only I understood that much later..."

"For some reason, the pain of losing does not subside for an awfully long time. Everybody else forgets about it, but you keep on eating away at yourself. You feel as though everyone was pointing fingers at you, making fun of you, writing you off, or even worse, feeling sorry for you. Many great athletes have condemned themselves to such negative emotions."

"How about you, Nina?"

"Me? It's the nature of competing in sports that you always want to perform better and better. I did everything I could the best that I could. I don't torment myself over anything anymore. That's what I teach my team as well. Don't hold onto regrets. Let them go and work harder. Know that if you won this time, everyone else is going to work harder to beat you next time. Isn't that so?"

"That's true," Sofija said and nodded, although her thoughts were wandering somewhere to the west.

"Was it difficult for you to stop competing, Sofija?"

Sofija took a deep breath.

"In that moment, when I made the decision, it was not difficult. At the time, I was emotional, I felt hurt, and my pride was injured. But it was hard the next day. I felt as though my life had fallen apart. Ever since I was sixteen, a young adult, I went to sleep every night knowing exactly what I would be doing the next day when I woke up. The first morning that I woke up without my usual routine, I felt awful. I didn't know where to go, what to do with myself. I felt as though nobody needed me anymore. I felt as though everyone had turned their backs on me. That feeling stayed with me for a while."

"That's probably how all athletes feel. It hurts until you see that you can still compete, but through coaching."

I must go and call Father now. When everyone sits down to eat breakfast, I can sneak out to the payphone.

From early morning until late at night, Sofija could not shake the thought that she must make that phone call. She surreptitiously tore the page with her father's phone number from her address book and slipped it into her pocket.

"Shall we go have breakfast?" Sofija asked Nina. Just like yesterday, she had to wait for her older companion to get ready.

"You go ahead. I'll catch up. I still need ten minutes."

Sofija took the lift down to the lobby. She slowly turned towards the reception desk, eyeing the payphone to the side of the lobby.

Perhaps I should try now? Oh, but I don't know who is downstairs already, who might walk past as I place the call. Let me go and see if they're all in the restaurant already. What if Nina comes down earlier than she said she would? No, this isn't a good time... It isn't safe... There's no saying how long we will talk. I can't just hang up on him...

Sofija's heart was pounding with anxiety as she entered the restaurant where the scent of coffee and croissants overwhelmed her.

It smells like Vichy. Like Paris. Like when we won the European Rowing Championship… The scent was even stronger in Paris. Probably because we were the champions… Sofija inhaled the scent of sweet croissants and coffee. *This is the scent of Paris. You'll never find this scent anywhere back home.*

She glanced around the large hotel restaurant. No one from their group had come down yet. *I'm the only one who rushed down here… I'm really hungry after not sleeping all night… I'll have something to eat and then I'll go and make my phone call…*

Sofija placed two croissants in her plate, poured herself a cup of coffee, and seated herself in a corner so that she could observe the entire restaurant. *Nina said that we must observe people. That is how we may learn about other cultures… I wonder how many of the people here are locals? Probably those over there who are eating their croissants and conversing in French.*

Or maybe they're from France? I'm eating the same breakfast as them… Because I'd like to taste the local food… Or perhaps they are the ones who are the most relaxed and smile the most? No, it's difficult to get a sense of the local culture in a hotel restaurant. All the same, it is interesting to be here.

Sleepy athletes began to gather in the restaurant. They filled their plates to the maximum capacity and sat down to enjoy French cuisine. The anxiety of the upcoming race may have dried out their mouths and put butterflies in their stomachs, but their Soviet eyes had never seen so much free food. Therefore, they piled their plates high with the free food, even though there was no way they could possibly eat it all. Probably, they'll end up shoving half of it into their pockets.

The coaches always encouraged athletes to eat well before a race, otherwise, you won't be able to pull. But all that good food might just end up floating on the Notre Dame canal after the finish when their nerves give out. Sofija observed the young rowers and saw how nervous they were. Some of them chewed half asleep while others were far too talkative and enthusiastic. Those were the minority. Only a few seemed calm and focused. The ones who were yawning, she knew, were already burned out.

Maybe they have insomnia like me? It's the worst for the single. I think his name is Sergey... You're all alone out there. You've got to handle your fear on your own, and you also celebrate on your own... I'd like to give him some advice, but I don't want to interfere with another coach's crew. Every coach has their own method of pepping up the team before the race. It's always easier in a crew, both physically and psychologically. Even if someone gets a stroke wrong, the others will compensate for it. In a single it's all on you...

The Latvians sat off to the side on their own. They stood out from the others because of their language and their demeanour.

Rolands is an excellent coach for them. I can see that from a distance. He's always respectful and friendly to his team. He never humiliates them or talks to them in a mean way. On the Soviet team it's the norm to poke fun at an athlete and humiliate them. Like in the army. Humiliation, insults, all that is supposed to get an athlete angry and force them to work harder... It doesn't always work. To be honest, I've never seen any rower respond positively to that method. All that humiliation leads to hurt that they carry around with them the rest of their lives. How don't the coaches understand that an athlete may leave the sport, but they'll take the hurt with them? I must go to the payphone now. Oh, there's Nina. I better slip past her before she sees me.

Sofija slid towards the door, glancing around her to make sure no one saw her. Then, she crept into the lobby. She pulled the few coins she'd saved up to make the call out of her pocket and pulled out the scrap of paper. A man stood at the payphone, talking loudly into the receiver, gesticulating with his hands, from time to time emitting loud boisterous laughter. Sofija slowly walked past and went over to the souvenir counter.

Oh, I rushed through breakfast and now I have no idea how long that man will be on the phone...

Sofija pretended to be examining the souvenirs while listening to the man's conversation in English. He seemed to be talking about golf. She thought he might be narrating a game, move by move, to a golf partner.

It's probably not worth waiting around. He doesn't look like he's about to hang up soon... Perhaps I should stand beside him to give him the message that I need the phone? Oh, perhaps I should just go back and join Nina, so she wouldn't get suspicious. I'll call at lunch time. I still have time.

Just at that moment, Steve appeared in the lobby doorway. Sofija froze. *That agent will get suspicious.* She quickly took a big step towards the souvenir shop window and acted as though she was interested in buying something.

"Good morning, Sofija Ignatyevna!" Steve called out, noticing her immediately. With his round red face and shiny eyes, he looked ill. She took a few steps towards him and could smell the alcohol on him.

"Are you selecting your souvenirs? Don't buy anything here. The prices are always higher in the hotels. I'll show you some really good souvenir shops. There are plenty in every town. This is just Montreal you'll still be traveling to many places. Save your money."

"You're right, I won't buy anything yet. I'd like to bring back a postcard from every place we visit."

"But you have a camera. Wouldn't you rather take your own photos?"

"Yes, that's right, but my photos are black and white," Sofija said and smiled.

"You don't have colour photography in the Soviet Union?"

"No, not yet."

"I see… You know, I have an acquaintance who mails himself a post-card from every city he visits. That way he never forgets what he's seen. Isn't that a smart idea?"

"What a wonderful idea! And it's so simple!" Sofija said, cocking her head back in wonder. "Especially, when you have no one else to write to but yourself."

"I'll need to try it one day," Steve continued. "I always tell myself I will, but then I don't find the time, or I simply forget and only remember when I get home."

Easy for you to talk, Stepan, when you live here. Our postcards from the West will land directly in the hands of the KGB.

"I'll try it as well. Where will I have the opportunity to purchase my next postcard?" Sofija asked, trying to get the trip schedule out of Steve. Meanwhile, she kept an eye on the phone, trying to judge how much longer the golfer would occupy it.

"We'll be in Montreal until Monday, until the races end. Take the time to walk around the Old Town, climb Mount Royal. On Monday we're going to Quebec. There you may buy some pretty postcards and souvenirs. You'll take some good photos there too, even if they are black and white."

"Will we? spend only a day there?"

"Yes, one day is plenty. After that we will travel to Ottawa…"

Sofija was relieved that Steve was finally naming the cities on their travel route.

"On Wednesday we will fly to Vancouver. We'll spend three days there. After that, we're going to Toronto."

"How long will we stay in Toronto?"

"Two days, well, actually, a day and a half. Then we return to Montreal. What do you think?" Steve asked, squinting, carefully studying Sofija's expression.

"I heard that Niagara Falls are not far from Toronto. We'll probably go there as well? I've dreamt of seeing Niagara Falls ever since I was in school. I've read so much about it." Sofija said all this while struggling to conceal her disappointment.

Why was Steve so quiet? Why has his demeanour changed?

"Have you had breakfast, Sofija Ignatyevna? Or were you just going now?" Steve said, turning towards the restaurant.

"I did," Sofija said, "but I'd love another cup of coffee."

Just a minute ago, she wanted nothing more than to get rid of him, but now she found herself following him. The unfinished conversation tempted her to keep talking with him.

He knows everything about me. He knows that my father lives in Niagara Falls... Of course, he knows! What a fool I've been! It's one hundred percent certain that he knows every single detail about every single one of us.

Just at that moment, the golfer finally hung up the phone.

I've lost my chance. Now I'll have to come here during lunch. The most important thing right now is to find out what Steve is thinking about my question. Or I could look for a payphone in the Old Town... Maybe I will manage to slip away unnoticed on my own.

CHAPTER TWENTY-THREE

AUGUST 9, 1975, MONTREAL, CANADA – DAY FOUR

The previous day Sofija had no success making a phone call to her father. In the morning, Steve interrupted her. During the day, she attended the race. In the evening, she could not get away from the group. In the evening, the phone was occupied again.

Sofija did not experience jetlag that night; however, she awoke at six-thirty with only one thought in her mind: *I must call Father…*

I must get up. It's only six thirty. I still have time. Today is Saturday. We will be in Toronto in a week. Today I will call Father. I must. If I can't call during breakfast, then I'll call at lunch, or in the evening…

It was becoming more and more difficult for Sofija to manage her emotions. Whenever she thought of meeting her father, a lump rose in her throat and her body grew weak. Then, came the realization that it wasn't other people who were getting in the way of Sofija calling her father. She was using her own fear as an excuse. Every single time an obstacle arose that prevented her from making that phone call, Sofija would sigh with relief, knowing that she could put off for a little longer the act of picking up the phone, dialling the number, waiting for someone to answer.

Since when have I become such a procrastinator? Since then when I must make my own decisions? When I was an athlete, everyone else made every single decision for me. My life was organized around a strict schedule – I knew the exact time I need to wake up, to train, when to race, when to sleep… How is it that I'm incapable of managing my own life? Nonsense. I am perfectly capable. I'll get up, get ready, and go downstairs and make that call. Sofija began to tremble, and a lump formed in her throat. *I must call him. Who else will tell Father that I am in Canada? The only reason that I am here is to meet him. He won't call me to ask: Is there any chance that you might be in Canada right now? Why am I so afraid? Is it because I am afraid of what will happen? Is it because I don't know what will happen and how this will end? Most likely… I don't want to change anything in my life… I don't want to find out something now that would change my life…*

The second day of the race dawned sunny and warm. A southwestern wind rose. That meant that the race would take place with the wind blowing crosswise towards the finish line. The teams assigned to the fifth and sixth lanes will get the largest waves, but also the best wind.

I feel our team members' anxiety, Sofija thought to herself as she could barely force down her croissant at breakfast. *The fear of racing is that ingrained in me… That fear creeps up on you a few days before the race and from then on it just grows… Then the morning of the race dawns and you know there is nowhere to run… Outside your window the world hasn't collapsed, there is no natural disaster taking place, the race will not be cancelled… You must pull yourself, find the strength for warm-ups, even when your feet are giving out from under you and for some reason you cannot stop yawning. You'll have to gather yourself and not look at your competitors, even as you feel their eyes on you. You'll want to sneak a look to establish that something has happened to your rivals to make them weaker than you today, less able to compete, easier to beat… You must carry your boat to the pontoon at exactly the right time… Be prepared to race at the starting line at exactly the right time... You must be careful not to be late with your first stroke but also not to make a false start... And then, you must suffer... Whether you like it or not, the moment will come when your body refuses to move, when your body will scream out in pain, but you must keep on rowing... You must not slow down to accommodate your pain, but do just the opposite, speed up... That's because if you allow yourself even a second to catch your breath, to slow down your pace, you probably won't be able to get back into the correct rhythm...*

Sometimes the body works without us being aware of it. Like back then, in 1969 in Klagenfurt. Everyone watching from the shore gave up on our quad just before the finish line – they assumed the Romanian crew would take first – and just then, suddenly, I picked up the stroke rate and we won by a bow ball.

I don't remember any of it... My soul had probably already left my body... My arms and legs were working automatically if I really was rowing? The rowing body is odd – you have no awareness of what you're doing, but you don't stop rowing until you hear the gong... And then you vomit over the side of the boat...

I must go and telephone Father... I am going now... Ugh... My legs gave out again... I'm not racing, what is this? Why am I so afraid? During a race there is no road back, but in this instance, I do have the choice to simply give up searching for Father. If I wish, I may change my plans. But if I do, will I regret it later? Oh, yes, I will, and how... Sofija took two deep breaths, placed her coffee cup down on the saucer, wiped the crumps off the tablecloth, sprinkled them onto the saucer. She looked around for boastful Steve and for the few members of their group who'd fumbled their assignment by admitting that they were spying on the others. *Oh, I didn't bring the paper with his phone number... By the time I go back to my room to get it, we'll be boarding the bus… Am I making excuses again? No, today I'll call him for sure… There are pay phones at the Expo, I saw them. All I must do is find a moment to break away from the group. When will the most interesting race take place? The eight? Oh, I want to see the Latvians race… Perhaps the fours? Most likely the best time to break away is at the start of the races, before the functionaries get bored…*

CHAPTER TWENTY-FOUR

AUGUST 10, 1975, MONTREAL, CANADA – DAY FIVE

"Hello?"

An older man's voice came through the telephone receiver. Sofija broke out in a sweat. Yesterday she had covered on foot the entire Expo territory on Saint Helen Island. She observed the payphones, secretly read the instructions, picked up and replaced the telephone receiver, hid from the other members of the group and anyone she heard speaking Russian. She chose her words carefully, counted her coins precisely, and placed them neatly inside her purse. During the peak of the excitement, during the semi-finals, when their entire delegation was seated together with Steve, she slipped out to the payphone beside the cashier's desk and the entrance into the American bubble. She finally found within herself the courage to pick up the receiver, drop in the coins, and to dial the number, which she had now memorized by heart. She waited as the phone rang fifteen times. Nobody answered. Probably, no one was home. She actually felt a wave of relief pour over her. But only for a short time. There was almost no time left now and she became anxious that all her efforts, that this trip, had been all for nothing.

I simply cannot put this call off any longer, she had told herself, *I must call.*

Now she was back at the payphone once again. This time it was easier to pick up the receiver. Still, her mouth was dry, and her legs buckled under her.

"Hello, I'm listening," the older man said on the other end of the call.

"*Dzień dobry*," Sofija said hello in Polish.

"*Cześć, Vanda, czy to ty?*" Hello, Vanda, is that you? The voice inquired in Polish.

"May I speak to Ignacy Gruca," Sofija asked in Polish.

"I am Ignacy Gruca. With whom am I speaking?"

Sofija froze. She couldn't gather her thoughts to reply. She'd rehearsed this conversation over and over again in her mind, even before she left on this trip, and now she could not utter a single word. She dreamed of this conversation for years, ever since she received Father's first letter. She felt a pain in her eyes, her lips trembled, and she simply could not utter a single word. Her heart was beating wildly. Sofija gripped the receiver tightly, leaned her forehead into the phone booth glass and gazed at her reflection as tears streamed down her face. She tried her best not to sob. She could not understand what it was inside of her that had caused all this uncontrollable emotion. It was not that sense of missing her father, nor was it tears of joy. It was more like a deep feeling of hurt and self-pity. She froze for a few moments, but it seemed as though she'd been silent for ages and that the man on the other end of the receiver would soon hang up on her.

"*Tato, to jest Sofia...*" Daddy, it's me, Sofija.

For a long time, there was silence on the other end of the receiver.

"Hello? It's Sofija, hello?" she repeated.

She seemed to have lost the connection. *Oh, of all things... Perhaps the phone is malfunctioning...* Sofija banged the side of the phone a few times, like she would back in Vilnius, in the Soviet Union, where everything broke down and malfunctioned.

"Yes, yes, I can hear you," the man said, "Sofija? It's you?"

"Yes, it's me, Sofija…"

"Where are you calling from? You sound as though you were right next door."

"I am in Montreal, Daddy." She felt strange saying that word, "Daddy." She had never called anyone by that name in her life. She'd heard children playing out in the yard calling their parents, Daddy, but never her… "I'm in Canada."

"Really? When did you arrive? Will you be here for a while?" Her father's questions sounded odd to her, just like his letters were odd.

"I will be here one more week. I came to the World Junior Rowing Championship."

"Are you rowing or watching?"

"No, no, I haven't competed for a few years now. I'm too old. I came to watch…" *And to see you…* she thought to herself but did not dare say out loud.

"How's the weather in Montreal?"

"In Montreal? It's warm, sunny. Not very hot at all. Nice. Most importantly, it's not raining."

"It's hot here for us, around thirty degrees, so I spend my time at home."

"I see," Sofija said and slid a ten-cent coin with the face of the queen on one side and a sailboat on the other into the slot. Her palms were sweating.

"It's too bad that Montreal is so far from my home. I don't drive anymore…"

"Next Friday I will be in Toronto."

"Could you come to Niagara Falls?"

"I'll try, but that is only if they bring us to Niagara."

"I'm usually at home, but sometimes I go out for a walk. Call me if you come to Niagara. Do you have my address?"

"I do. I'll call you before I come."

"That's good, do call."

"Goodbye for now, Daddy."

"*Do zobaczenia!* See you later." Father hung up the phone.

Sofija's hands were shaking, and her legs were weak. She stood in the telephone booth and could not move. *I did it... I finally called him... And we spoke about nothing... About the weather... I imagined that our conversation would have been completely different. Father's voice did not sound the way I imagined... Why was our conversation so short? Everything's confused in my head... No matter, I'll call again. Next time, it won't be as hard...*

Sofija hung up the receiver, glanced around her to make sure no one had seen her, and walked back to the bridge that led to the spectators' grandstands on Notre Dame Island. She was overwhelmed with grief. Tears welled up in her eyes. *That man is a complete stranger to me. I thought that when I heard his first words, I would feel warmth and love, but I felt nothing. He was just some man who spoke Polish with me... Perhaps he was shocked as well. That call must have been a complete surprise to him. He probably didn't know what to say. He is probably also regretting that our conversation was so brief. Of course, this was all a shock to him, and he was lost. Maybe he was crying as well? Perhaps that is why he didn't know what to say? I must see him... Now I really must... I will not leave Canada until I have seen my father!*

There was a fuss in the grandstands. Fans were waving team flags, but mostly parents. Coaches were encouraging their teams onward with loud enthusiastic shouts.

"Where were you, Sofija? We missed you?" Nina asked with a concerned look on her face.

"I was sitting way over there," Sofija said, waving her hand to indicate a group of spectators. "I met a coach I knew when I was young," she lied.

"One of ours?"

"No, a German from the DDR," she responded evasively. They had never been friendly with any coaches or members of the DDR team, but if she'd told Nina she spoke with someone from West Germany that would have been unacceptable. Steve would be onto her right away.

"I don't understand what's going on, you'll have to explain it all to me," Nina said, using the programme booklet as a fan, although it wasn't all that hot.

"Of course, what would you like to know?"

"Nothing makes sense," Nina said and laughed. "What's the difference between those boats? How many metres will they race?"

"Usually, men row two kilometres and women row one. The distance is shorter for the juniors, a kilometre and a half. And the boats," Sofija surveyed the course, "see, over there. That's a four. A four means that each rower has one oar, one on the right and the others have one on the left."

The Polish four rowed past the spectators to the starting line. Sofija sighed and watcher her country's rowers with sadness in her eyes. *I never raced for my own country. Oh, and I could have watched as the Polish flag was raised, and I could have listened to my homeland's national anthem. Many times... I wonder if I would have felt differently. I would have spoken Polish, and everyone would have understood me... I wish Mama had more courage during the repatriation.*[24] *I wish she would have returned to Warsaw with me. It was simply bad luck that during the first repatriation I came down with the measles, and then during the second there was a problem with her patronym. Her father's name was Karl, and instead of Karlovna, someone made a mistake and writing in Cyrillic confused the letters "p" and "l" and her patronym became Karpovna.*

Sofija closed her eyes and remembered how whenever she watched the red flag with the hammer and sickle rise, in her imagination she'd "stick" a piece of white cloud on top of it and imagined the white-red Polish flag, and that she was hearing the Polish national anthem. Anytime she was required to wear the red team shirt, she would add a white cap and imagine to herself that she was wearing the white and red Polish uniform.

"Hey, Sofija, can you hear me? Or did you fall asleep?" Nina asked in a loud voice, leaning over to peer into her face.

"Oh, I'm so sorry, Nina Yakovlevna, I was daydreaming. Were you asking me something?"

"I asked who is that little person sitting at the end of the boat without an oar?"

"Oh, that's the cox. That's a four with a cox."

"Oh yes, I heard you had one of those! He's so small though."

"That's right. The cox must be small so that the rowers wouldn't need

24   Repatriation is the legal process of granting permission under international law for people who are citizens of another country to return to their home countries. According to official statistics, during 1944 – 1947 a repatriation of Polish citizens out of Lithuania to Poland took place in which 171,000 (actually 180,000 – 190,000) individuals returned to Poland. According to a March 25, 1957 agreement between the Polish government and the USSR 48,000 people were granted permission to leave Lithuania and repatriate to Poland (of that number, over 40,000 were ethnic Poles).

to carry too much weight."

"Couldn't they just seat a child in the boat? Wouldn't that be easier?"

"Unfortunately," Sofija said and laughed, "the weight is regulated. The cox cannot be lighter than the rules allow."

"How much should the cox weigh?"

"For a female team, forty-five kilos, for a men's team, fifty, I believe."

"What if he weighs more?"

"Then he doesn't get to eat and must run laps until he loses the weight," Sofija said and laughed again. "Of course, only before a race. The weight isn't an issue during training. In fact, sometimes having a heavy cox is a good thing – it gives you an extra workout."

"Do they weight them before the race? Like they do boxers?"

"Yes, they weigh them, just before the start of a race. If they're too light, they add a sandbag into the boat. But, if they don't find that sandbag at the end of the race, that boat is disqualified."

"Yes, but I'm looking around now and not all the boats have a little guy onboard."

"Not all do. For men, there's a coxed pair, a coxed four, and an eight. For women there's a quadruple scull, a four and an eight."

"What did you row?"

"Mostly the quadruple scull, that's with a cox. Although, I got my start in a single."

"Does that cox get in your way? Such extra weight to carry…"

"In that sense, yes, you are carrying extra kilos, but on the other hand, you don't need to steer, and you don't need to turn around to see where you're going. Also, a good cox is like having another coach in the boat. During a race, when you need it most, the cox will shout encouragement, inspire you, tells you when to pick up your pace. That's a good cox… But there are all sorts… You know, there's an interesting story about a certain cox. During the Olympics in Paris in 1924 the cox on the Dutch coxed pair was far too heavy and they knew they would barely make it to the final. They saw that there was no way they could win carrying that weight. So, they switched him out for a boy from the audience. They showed the boy how to steer and they won the gold. They took a photo with that boy. The boy bid them farewell and disappeared into the crowd. Nobody knew his name, or surname, or where he was from. They searched for him through newspapers, ads, but could never find him. I saw the photograph. That boy became an unknown Olympic champion."

"What a story! So, they didn't weight them before a race back then?"

"No, I don't think they did in those years. Only, I'm curious what language that boy called the commands in. The cox leads the team the entire distance."

"You better be a loudmouth…"

"Oh yes, they scream their lungs out. If they didn't, the person in the bow seat wouldn't hear them."

"Well, maybe only in the back. The one in the front sits opposite the cox, or doesn't he?"

"No," Sofija said and smiled. The first seat is the rower who crosses the finish line first. Across from the cox sits the fourth or the eighth, the last rower."

"Oh, I see, it's all reversed!"

"We are the only sport that crosses the finish line backwards."

"We finish in a circle," Nina said and laughed.

I wonder if Father knows anything about rowing? It would be strange if he were not interested in rowing. I did write to him that I'm a rower. But rowing is the type of sport that you can't really understand unless you see it for yourself. Just like with Nina. Although she is an athlete, an Olympian, a coach, she cannot possible be an expert in all branches of sport. I wonder if they have a rowing club over there in Niagara Falls? At least in Saint Catherine's they must have a club, after all, the Henley regatta takes place there. And the World Championship. I must ask Father. Sofija felt a shiver go down her spine. *In a few days, I will see Father. I've been waiting for this moment my entire life… It's a strange feeling – I am filled with anticipation, but at the same times it's all happening too fast… I don't feel prepared. I'm afraid…*

Suddenly, her thoughts and her anxiety were replaced with interest in watching the final races. The young men's teams took their positions at the starting line. Although there were many different uniforms out on the water – German, British, American, Italian, etc. – they all looked the same in terms of anxiety, fear, and concentration. The fear of the start seemed to radiate away from the young men out on the water and infect anyone on the grandstands who had ever raced. The athletes took their warm-up strokes, bit their lips, and nervously repositioned themselves on their seats, glancing over at the other boats, then back at the back of the head of the rower in from of them. They did their best not to respond to the shouts of their fans or their families. The most important event of their lives thus far was about to begin in half an hour.

They've got it harder than I do right now, Sofija consoled herself. *They will have to suffer through the entire distance, and those who lose, they'll have to work through their disappointment. It's difficult for young people to manage their feelings. They imagine that this race is a matter of life and death. They imagine that winning will be the most important thing that ever will happen to them. At the same time, they imagine that losing will destroy everything. There is so much more that they will need to experience until they understand that life doesn't end with rowing...* There were times when Sofija reminisced on her first races in the single, when for the first time she felt on her body what an incredibly challenging sport rowing was. But by evening, all that suffering would be over, and they will have a wonderful time together until the time comes to go home. *But for me, all the difficulty lay ahead...* Again, she felt pain in her legs. *What difficulty? The unknown? Perhaps it won't be terrible, but great joy? I must stop thinking about it. I will see father somehow. In three or four, or five, days' time I will see him. During that time, I will forget that I am on the other end of the earth. I must stay present and enjoy every minute. Right now, it seems as though Canada can be reached so easily, but who knows, when I go home, if such an opportunity will ever present itself again...*

CHAPTER TWENTY-FIVE

AUGUST 11, 1975, MONTREAL, CANADA – DAY SIX

The Soviet Rowing Team was packing its bags. Out of the seventeen athletes who competed only one – the singles rower Sergey – was not taking a medal home. The Soviet team managers wrote in the team ledger that two first place wins, two second place, and a third place were positive results. However, the fact that they did not race a coxless four against the Germans left a hole in the ledger. The most important victories were team standings.

The Latvian crew was not pleased that they took third. They struggled along the entire distance falling to the left. This hastily slapped together team bore no resemblance to the crew that simply flew and won everything that season for their age group. They also won in the senior Soviet Championship. Replacing three team members for political reasons just before the World Championship destroyed their dream of taking the gold. The next year, they would all transition onto the senior team. Then, they would need to fight it out in the trials until some of them fell away, and only the strongest and the most patient remained. The senior Soviet team would never again have a men's eight like they did when *Žalgiris* was at the top of its game. The authorities simply do not allow such teams to exist. They claim that they are "strengthening" the team by adding ethnic Russians, but in reality, they weakened the teams and frustrated the team members. They "strengthened" the Lithuanian and Latvian teams until the athletes were exhausted and gave up.

The rowers will never have the opportunity to see Canada again. They will only see Montreal. And only today. Tomorrow morning, they will board an early morning Aeroflot flight that will take them home. All they will have seen of Canada would have been as much as they managed to see from their bus windows in the morning driving to the canal and returning in the evenings. Yesterday, after the races, the young men were granted the privilege of taking a short walk around the city. They were given permission to purchase a small souvenir and to window shop standing outside the famous *Phantasmogoria* music store. They took the opportunity to carefully chose the one record they would buy with the meagre allowance they were given when the shop opened on Monday. When they returned home, they could tell their friends about what they saw in Canada, brag about the music the youth listened to in the West, show off in front of the girls, or sell their one record for ten times more than they paid for it. They might buy a *Led Zeppelin* or *Yes* concert poster and hang it up beside their bed. Or they could buy the brilliant red and blue David Bowie poster from his last concert. Those who had been advised by older friends will have secretly brought caviar with them, which they would sell in the hotel restaurant or at some bar in the Old Town. With the money they earned they would buy a pair of bell bottoms, and then they would be really cool.

Today, the coaches would also be secretly carrying bottles of vodka and caviar in their bags. They will sneak around to the back doors of the Old Town restaurants and hope to make a sale. They will speak to the locals in Russian and use hand gestures to convey that they are willing to let their goods go at any price. They'll be very sneaky and careful, so that the functionaries don't see what they're up too, although they themselves have agreed to inform. AT the same time, the functionaries will be playing the very same game. They all know that they are all up to the same thing, but they'll walk around in fear, avoiding each other, always glancing over their shoulders. If somebody caught them in the act, that person could report them, and they'd never travel abroad again… The coaches were interested in buying themselves some nice clothing, buying things for their children and relatives, and bringing back gifts for their friends. When anyone returned from a trip to the West, everyone in their circle expected that they would receive a gift from them. Nobody cared if you won or lost, and nobody cared about seeing your trip photo album.

The delegation wanted to spend trade their "hard currency" as fast they could for Canadian dollars. They still had time, but they wanted to complete the deal quickly, so they could begin shopping. Steve didn't let the group out of his sight for a minute. He knew all the addresses of places where the Soviet tourists could sell their goods, where they could communicate in Russian, because there were plenty of immigrants from Russia and Ukraine in Canada. They played games with Steve. One would try to get his attention, so that another could slip away for a few minutes to secure a deal on a side street. Once the deal was made, the most important site to visit was the shopping mall.

"Sofija, where's your camera?" Steve asked surprised when they came out to the bus carrying their cases and climbed inside. "That's unusual," he muttered.

"Oh my God! I forgot it in my room!" Sofija jumped out of her seat and pushed her way to the exit. "Please, wait, I'll be right back."

Sofija ran back into the hotel. She felt in her pocket and realized that in her distraction she hadn't returned the hotel room key either.

Rolands was standing at the lift.

"Hello, where are you rushing off to?"

"I forgot my camera in my room. In twenty minutes, we're leaving for Quebec."

As they stepped into the lift, a middle-aged couple hurried into the lift after them. Sofija and Rolands continued their conversation in their common language, Russian.

"You're so lucky! This is all we've seen of Canada."

"How are your boys doing? Are they taking their loss alright?"

"My boys? They ran out into town. I should have let them out before the race. That might have helped. I get the feeling that they burned out."

"It's been a long season... What do you expect?"

"They didn't have enough time with the new team members to find their rhythm as a crew. It's tragic. They leaned to the left the entire distance. I would have won first place with my own team. Did you see the Germans? They weren't a miracle team, but you could tell that they've been rowing together for a long time, just like my boys."

"I'm sorry, I know what it feels like."

"Are you traveling?" Rolands asked, changing the subject.

"Yes, to Quebec. Tomorrow we will visit Ottawa. Then Vancouver and Toronto."

"That's quite a trip! I'm jealous. You'll see a lot. As for us, they're packing us up and sending us home tomorrow... Have a good trip, Sofija!" Rolands said and exited the lift on the third floor. She watched his back disappear down the hall as the lift doors slid shut.

"Russians," the woman whispered to her husband.

Sofija's cheeks burned red. "I'm not Russian," she spat out in English.

"My apologies," the woman said, flustered. "Where are you from?"

"I'm from Lithuania, but I am Polish."

"*Bardzo przepraszam. Jesteśmy także Polakami*," her husband said in Polish. "Very sorry. We are also Poles, but we've been living in Canada for a long time now."

The doors slid open on Sofija's floor. She nodded at the couple and stepped out. "Wait a minute," the man said and stepped out after her. "We had no intention of insulting you."

His wife followed him out of the lift.

"*Nic takiego, nie skrzywdziłem cię,*" she said in Polish, "don't worry, I'm not insulted."

She glanced around the hallway to make sure no one from the group would spot her chatting with these westerners. Then she remembered that they were all on the bus, and that none of them understood Polish.

"What brings you to Canada?" the man asked, changing the subject. "Do you need advice or help?"

"No, thank you," she said.

They all were terrorized into mistrusting the locals and God Forbid, accepting any help that they offered.

"I'm here on a touristic trip. We came for the World Junior Rowing Championship."

"Will you stay in Montreal or do you have plans to visit other parts of Canada?"

"We are going to Quebec, Ottawa, and Toronto."

"What city are you from?"

"I was born in Warsaw, but I live in Vilnius."

"Oh, Wilna? We have our own Wilna here! It's not far from us, maybe ten kilometres away. We live in Baris Bay, Ontario, near the Kamaniskeg Lake."

"There's a town called Wilna?"

"More like a village, but yes. It's the oldest Polish settlement in Canada. It's over a hundred years old. They have the oldest Polish parish in Canada. If you pass by the area, you must stop and see it. The nature and landscape look a lot like Poland; that's why Polish people settled there first."

"There are mostly Kashubas there," the woman added.

"Kashubas?"

"People from the Baltic Sea coast, from Gdansk," she explained.

"We travel to Wilna every year on Labour Day. That's a long holiday weekend. At the parish of the Virgin Mary, they serve a chicken dinner. Will you still be here in September?" the man asked.

"We'll be here one more week and then we're heading home," Sofija said, glancing at her watch.

"What a pity. We'd love to invite you over for a visit. What's your name?"

Sofija did not answer.

"My name is Ignacy, and this is my wife, Maria."

"My father's name is also Ignacy," Sofija blurted out, suddenly feeling a strange sense of connection with these random strangers. "He lives in Niagara Falls."

"How did it happen that you live in the Soviet Union and your father lives in Canada?"

"He escaped during the war and could not turn back."

"Was he an officer by any chance?"

"You guessed right. He was."

"Then that was the only way he could escape execution by the Russians."

Sofija gazed intently at Ignacy.

"I mean in Russia," the man explained, seeing that Sofija did not quite follow him. "Smolensk. The Russians executed all the Polish officers in Smolensk."

A cold sweat ran down her back.

"I don't understand?" she said, pretending she didn't know the history, although she had a vague notion of it.

"Well, they took them all into the forest near Smolensk and shot them all. Twenty thousand Polish officers... Some managed to escape."

"It wasn't the Germans who shot them?"

"How could it have been the Germans if the execution took place in 1940."

"They taught us a different history in school..."

"I'm not surprised. The Russians will never admit their crimes. They shift all the blame onto others, so they may hide their crimes. As far as I know, here in Canada there are a few officers who managed to survive the killings in Smolensk."

Suddenly, Sofija was terrified. She didn't know who these people were. They could be spies or informers sent to trap her.

"Do you visit your father often," Ignacy said, sensing how uncomfortable Sofija felt.

"It will be my first time... I've never met him..."

Sofija wished she could tell this man everything, but she chose her words carefully and glanced around to make sure no one had followed them.

The couple looked at each other, confused.

"You want to say that you will see your father for the first time?'

"I really hope that it works out... I'm sorry, but I'm in a hurry. My bus is waiting for me outside. We're leaving for Quebec."

"Yes, or course, we're sorry to hold you up. Will we see you in the evening?"

"I don't think so. We're not coming back here. *Do widzenia...* Good-bye."

Sofija hurried to her hotel room and with her hands shaking, unlocked the door. She snatched up her camera from the desk, noted the time on the clock, and rushed back to the lift.

She felt so confused that she could no longer focus on the pleasures of the day trip or about her father. She simply wanted to sit down, shut her eyes, and calm down. Sofija took a few deep breaths. She composed herself, so that no one on the bus would suspect anything, and then stepped out of the lift, returned the hotel room key, and headed for the bus.

The morning was misty, but the temperature had risen to twenty-five.

CHAPTER TWENTY-SIX

AUGUST 15, 1975, TORONTO, CANADA – DAY TEN

The five-hour flight from Vancouver to Toronto on the Air Canada Boeing 747 was coming to an end. The passengers stretched in their seats while the stewardesses strode up and down the aisles, bringing drinks to passengers and collecting trays with trash. They were ever pleasant and smiled at the passengers, even though their lipstick had smeared, and their uniforms reeked of second hand cigarette smoke.

All Sofija's impressions of Quebec and Ottawa were now mere memories. On the rolls of film packed away in her luggage there were photographs documenting a walking tour of beautiful Quebec City, breathtaking Vancouver, the Lynn Canyon park with its hanging bridge, and its Peace Arch with one leg in America. She was impressed with the blueberry plantation but disconcerted by the local Lithuanian émigrés who somehow found them and offered to show them around. Then, she had the photos she shot secretly of a demonstration taking place outside of the Soviet Embassy.

Once she returned home, she would develop her photographs in her bathroom under the dim red light. She'd anxiously await the emerging images and hope that she set her focus and aperture correctly.

But she was saving her last roll of film for the most important part of the trip… She didn't mind that she wouldn't have film to shoot images of Toronto – a postcard will have to do. The most important part of the trip was yet to come, meeting Father.

There's not much time left now… Sofija trembled. *Either today or tomorrow…*

The varied and intense schedule tired them out, but nobody wanted to go home just yet. The contrast was simply too great. They were overwhelmed by the size of the cities, how well maintained and attractive the urban landscapes were, the beauty of the nature, but most of all, they were amazed by the warmth, kindness, and joyfulness of the local Canadians.

Seeing this completely different world did not make them happy. It was quite the opposite. They were all overcome with grief that neither they, nor their loved ones, would ever live in such a land. They could not possibly engage in such a conversation among themselves. Nor could they discuss how their tins of caviar and bottles of vodka, which they converted into jeans, shoes, cassette players, would never make them happy because then they would have to admit that back home these material goods were valued more than anything else.

Sofija already knew what would be written about in the report. First, that grey-haired old man from Tbilisi was going to write her up. He asked her and the other Balts, the Latvian, the Estonian, and the other Lithuanian, to write out their surnames for him because they "were difficult" for him to remember. What did he need that information for unless to note it in his report to the KGB? He should need to pay for following his own people. On top of all that, he himself brought a a one-kilogram tin of caviar and asked Sofija to help him sell them.

She'll write that Steve is a spy. Perhaps even a spy for a foreign country? Or she'll write that Steve is engaged in anti-Soviet activities. In Quebec, when she and Algis were sitting on a bench exchanging small talk, she noticed a strange device hooked onto the back of the bench. It was not a radio, but more than likely a listening device. Before they sat down, Steve must have casually attached it onto the back of the bench while strolling past them. To detract their attention, he pointed to the Château Frontenac Hotel and said a few words about it. That's what Sofija will write: *The guide was spying on Soviet citizens in the Soviet delegation. He was recording their conversations. Oh, that would be rich,* thought Sofija, *one Soviet informer reporting on another Soviet informer.*

Through the airplane windows they tried to discern how much of the Toronto tower had been completed. It was the tallest television tower in the world. Then, they tried to spy the Niagara Falls on the other side of the enormous lake. However, the plane was approaching Toronto from the northwest and therefore only the pilots had the best view of the tower.

"Will we visit the television tower, Stepan?" Anatoly asked.

He'd left his seat and was leaning over Steve.

"We don't need to drive over to see it. The tower is enormous, and you can see it from anywhere in Toronto. However, if you like, you may walk there on foot. It's in the city centre."

"What will we see? What's on the itinerary?" Sofija asked, jumping in on the opportunity to illicit information.

"We will visit the zoo, the Edwards Gardens, the Toronto Botanical Gardens, the Saint Lawrence Market…"

"When will we go to Niagara Falls?" Sofija blurted out. She simply could no longer control herself. There was no point in putting off this question any longer.

"Niagara Falls is not in our itinerary," Steve replied coolly.

Sofija felt weak.

"Why not? How can we miss out on Niagara Falls? It's right here? It's not far away at all. How can we visit Canada and not see Niagara Falls? How is that possible?" Sofija insisted.

"It's not included in the programme," Steve said, his eyes boring into Sofija's, mocking her.

He knows everything, Sofija concluded. She was drenched in sweat. *He really and truly does know about my father. He is doing everything to make sure that I do not meet with my father. He was probably informed about everything before we even landed in Canada. He was instructed not to take us to Niagara Falls, to not allow any opportunity for us to make contact with locals. What will I do now? No, no, no, that can't be.*

Sofija turned towards Nina, who was seated beside her.

"Nina, don't you want to see Niagara Falls? How about you Anatoly?" she asked, turning towards the left where the men were seated.

Nina shrugged. "I've got nothing against the idea. My only issue is that I cannot walk far."

"I don't understand! How can we travel all this way to Canada and not see Niagara Falls? That's a crime. How is it that I'm the only one in this group who wishes to see Niagara Falls?"

"Why don't we just go ourselves," one of the men seated behind her said. "How many kilometres is it to Niagara Falls?"

"A hundred kilometres," Sofija shot back. "That's an hour's drive. Steve!"

"It's not on the programme."

"There were many things that were not on the programme, but we saw them anyway. What's the problem here? Why can't we go to Niagara Falls?" Sofija insisted.

"We don't have enough time."

"Then perhaps we should skip the zoo? In Moscow we have the same animals in the zoo. What's the difference? Besides, what's so interesting about staring at animals in cages when those animals aren't even native to Canada. Perhaps that would be interesting for children, but we're adults. We're not on a school trip!" Sofija was almost shouting now.

The others shrugged. Sofija was frantic. She did not expect that the group would be quite this apathetic. *All they care about is shopping.*

Steve, the KGB agent, sat there with an impassive hard look on his face. She had to change his mind using another tactic. Steve's face was red, as always. He was obviously hung over and could not be bothered.

Sofija was burning up. She had to compose herself, otherwise the whole trip would be ruined and she'd never reach her goal. Her arms and legs felt numb. The moment she realized that her dream of seeing her father would not materialize, she was sick to her stomach.

Stay calm... Think... Calmly... I must talk with every person in the group – eye to eye – each one of them separately... Or maybe I should just speak the truth? Oh, just so I wouldn't ruin everything... Oh, it just can't all end like this...

"Maybe it's not necessary for the entire group to travel to Niagara? Maybe not everyone wants to go? Those of us who do can buy our own tickets and take the bus."

"I ask that you don't disorganize the trip," Steve said in a flat voice that revealed his boredom. He yawned loudly and closed his eyes to nap before the plane landed.

"Nina, please take my side," she whispered to her companion, "I know he'll listen to you."

Nina turned and stared intently at Sofija. For the first time, her female intuition kicked in. "Do you have some business you need to take care of there?" she whispered back.

Sofija bit her lip and nodded a few times. Her eyes brimmed with tears.

"I see," Nina said and patted Sofija's hand. "We must convince the men. I also don't want to go to the zoo and see how they torture animals by keeping them in cages."

"Algis," Sofija whispered to the other Lithuanian from between the seats, "wouldn't you like to see Niagara Falls?"

"Hum?" Algis was dazed, he'd just woken up.

"Drive to see Niagara Falls," Sofija repeated.

"Of course, I do. Why do you ask?"

"Steve said Niagara Falls are not in the programme."

"Why not?"

"I don't know. All I know is that we're not going to Niagara Falls. I don't think we'll ever have a chance to see a miracle like Niagara Falls again in our lives."

"I thought that we were flying to Toronto so that we could visit Niagara Falls?"

"Steve said no. He said we're flying to Toronto to visit the zoo."

"That's nonsense. We can visit the zoo back home."

"Exactly!"

"Steve?" Algis said, standing up from his seat and towering over Steve, who was slumped back in his seat. "Is it true that we won't be visiting Niagara Falls?"

"What is wrong with all of you!" Steve shot back, annoyed, "No! We're not going to Niagara Falls!"

"Why not?" Algis demanded.

"Because we're not!" Steve shouted back. "It's not in the itinerary!"

"And if we ask very nicely?" Algis said, using his diplomatic negotiation skills.

Steve ignored him.

"Maybe I should buy him a bottle?" Sofija whispered to Algis.

"A bottle? Hum, I don't think one will be enough," Algis said and laughed. "It looks like he finishes off two every night."

"We'll buy him two then," Sofija said to her newly found collaborator.

"There's no reason to throw good money after bad," Algis said. "We'll get him to change his mind."

Silently, Sofija began to count how many dollars she had, setting aside enough for the ping-pong paddle and souvenirs. She never checked to see how much alcohol cost in the shops here. She still needed a little to buy bottled water and a cup of coffee each morning. *Maybe someone in the group still has some vodka left? But I couldn't ask them outright... Everyone pretends as though they're not selling contraband... Besides, everyone takes note of each other's sales... No, that wouldn't work, even if someone did have a few bottles left. Steve himself would write them up for selling contraband...*

"Anatoly, how about you? Would you like to see Niagara Falls?" Algis asked the man seated beside him.

"Why not? Of course, I do. I didn't get a chance to see the Niagara Falls in 1970 when the championship took place in Saint Catherine. I don't think I'll ever have another chance. Probably never."

Just then the plane's wheels connected with the tarmac. They all rushed to turn their watches three hours ahead.

"We just lost three hours of our lives," Nina said and sighed.

"We used them up when we flew in the other direction," Sofija said and smiled, although she truly did feel as though she'd lost three precious hours that could have been spent getting to know her father.

The clocks showed a quarter after five.

There's no time to drive to Niagara Falls today, Sofija thought, *maybe tomorrow. Today we must convince Steve. Algis probably convinced Anatoly. Then, Anatoly will get the other men to agree. They respect him.*

The airplane slowly rolled to the tall square airport building and stopped with its nose just barely touching the glass wall. A long corridor rolled towards them. She'd never seen something that modern in the USSR. In Canada you exited directly out of the plane into the terminal. You didn't need to climb down the stairs or walk outdoors. Soon a baggage cart arrived beside the airplane and handlers began unloading their luggage.

I've got to exit the plane before the others and run to the airport shop and buy Steve a bottle, Sofija thought, working out her plan how she was going to bribe Steve. *Oh, but the shops are only in the terminal area beyond the baggage claim, and we've all got to collect our baggage together… I'll need to be very fast… Or I should ask someone to hold up Steve…. I don't know the airport, and I don't know where the shops are… I'll pretend that I need to use the toilet… Then everyone will have no choice but to wait for me. How much can a bottle cost? Will ten dollars be enough? Ten dollars is the price I must pay to see my father… Ten dollars to get out of spending the day in the zoo…*

The Soviet delegation strode down the long corridors towards the baggage claim area. Enormous posters of Niagara Falls on the walls on both sides of them seemed to be inviting them to visit. More precisely, the posters of Niagara Falls were advertisements for L&M cigarettes.

"Steve, so are we going to travel to Niagara Falls or not?" Algis asked again.

"What is going on what all of you? Niagara, Niagara, Niagara… I was instructed that I must not take you there."

"Who told you that?"

"Your trip organizers."

"So, then perhaps we can change our itinerary. We're all adults. Nobody is interested in spending the day in the zoo. This is our once in a lifetime chance to see Niagara Falls," Algis continued.

Sofija listened with one ear while scanning the airport for a shop that sold alcohol. It was obvious that Steve would not be swayed by words alone.

"Davai, Stepan, poedem! Nevže tak važko zminiti programu?" Anatoly switched to Ukrainian, saying 'Hey Stepan, how hard is it to change the itinerary?'"

"Could you please pick up my case for me? It's brown, plaid," Sofija said to Algis, deciding that she'd better hurry up and buy that bottle for Steve.

"I remember, fine, but what happened?" Algis asked.

"Nothing. I've really got to use the toilet."

"Don't worry, I'll pick it up for you. Let's meet at the door."

"I may be back in time."

Sofija hurried off down the corridor to search for a shop. She'd only gone around twenty metres when she smelled the aroma of freshly brewed coffee. That was a good sign. And it was. Beside the café she found a small souvenir and delicacy shop. A row of bottles was lined up, but she didn't recognize any of them. She'd only seen such bottles in the advertisements here in Canada.

Which one should I buy? Oh, I know nothing about expensive drinks… Sofija's eyes scanned the shelves… *Maybe Walker's Canadian Club? Eight dollars, that's fine... What kind of a drink is this? It'll be fine...*

Sofija nervously swayed from side to side as she waited her turn in the queue. It never fails. She was in a hurry, but the four people in front of her took their time, chatting with the cashier, carefully selecting a multitude of candies, chewing gum, drinks.

Hurry, hurry, hurry, oh, why did this always happen to me... As she stood there waiting, she felt as though her last opportunity to get to see her father were slipping away. Every few seconds, she glanced at her wristwatch, as though she could slow down time. She was amazed by the cashier, who was smiling pleasantly... *In all my life, neither in Lithuania nor in the rest of the Soviet Union, have I ever seen such a patient, smiling cashier. But all the shopkeepers I've seen so far had been like this, kind and helpful... In the Soviet Union, the shopkeepers considered themselves superior. That was because they hid the special imported goods under the counter and saved them for their own people. The queues were always long, but they didn't care, they slowed down their work on purpose just to tantalize people and feel important. You felt small, unimportant, and frightened in front of those Soviet women who ran the shops. If the slightest thing annoyed them, they'd raise their voice and shout at you. They especially shouted at children. 'What do you want?' they'd shout. 'What are you doing here? Take what you need and get out!' But, if they saw a Soviet functionary or someone that they needed something from, then they were as sweet as sugar...*

"Yes, what would you like?" the shopkeeper asked pleasantly, interrupting Sofija's thoughts.

"Canadian Club," Sofija said, pointing to the bottle. She handed over her ten-dollar bill, took the change. The shopkeeper placed the bottle into a colourful shopping bag and handed it to Sofija.

She hurried back to re-join the group.

She strode into the wide corridor and saw the group approaching with their luggage. In his left hand, Algis was carrying her case. Sofija instinctively hid around the corner. *After they pass by me, I'll join the group from behind, so it'll look as though I'm catching up with them...*

* * *

"The trip to the hotel will take half an hour," Steve announced as the bus doors closed behind him. "The distance to the centre is twenty kilometres. This evening is a free evening. You may stroll around the city. Breakfast is served at eight tomorrow. We meet in the lobby at nine."

How shall I give him the bottle? In front of everyone? Or alone, eye to eye? If I hand it to him in front of everyone it'll look like a gift from all of us to thank him for "taking such good care of us." Shall I give it to him now? Or in the hotel? There's no more time to work it out. I've got to take action now. Whatever happens, happens...

Sofija waited for the appropriate moment, when Steve wasn't talking with anyone and when the entire group was seated. Her heart pounded against her chest. How many times had she been in this awkward position in her life? When she had to "thank" someone.

I hate this... I always feel embarrassed and don't know where to begin... What if he doesn't take the bottle? Then what? He'll take it... He won't refuse a bottle... He's a drunk.... Soon... soon... Sofija calmed herself down so that she would not lose her voice.

"Um, Steve?" she said shyly.

Steve was rummaging around in his briefcase and ignored her. "Steve!" she repeated in a loud voice.

He turned around but continued to shuffle his papers.

Sofija stood up, gazed at all her fellow travellers, and in a voice trembling with emotion began her speech:

"Because this is our final stop in Canada, in the name of our entire group, I'd like to thank Steve for this amazing trip."

She extended her hand with the bottle wrapped inside the colourful shopping bag and shook his hand. Steve's face transformed immediately. He stood up to receive his bottle. His face no longer wore that look of boredom but shined with self-satisfaction.

"Thank you also for taking us to Niagara Falls tomorrow," Sofija added.

All the men in the group stood up and began to clap. They all wore looks of surprise on their faces.

"*Maladec*, well done, Sofija. Thank you for thinking of this kind gesture. Women are always more understanding than we men," one of the men from the group called out from the back of the bus.

"We'll pay you back," Nina whispered in Sofija's ear, "I'll take up a collection."

"Don't worry about it," Sofija said and smiled.

Steve did not look pleased at all.

"I already told you that Niagara Falls is not on the itinerary," he growled.

"So, let's add it!" Algis said, shrugging his shoulders. "How hard can it be? What difference does it make where we go?"

"There's nothing special to see there. One waterfall is just like another. You've all seen waterfalls."

"We haven't seen a waterfall," Algis said and shook his head. "Honestly, I'm telling you the truth, I've never seen a waterfall in my life, except on television."

Sofija bit her lip. *There's no time to lose. I must speak out the truth. Maybe people will understand and support me.*

The men at the back of the bus were soon engrossed in their own conversations. Sofija looked around her – Algis, Nina, maybe a few others would hear her.

"I must go to Niagara Falls, Steve," Sofija said in a loud and determined voice. She gathered all her courage and fought back the lump in her throat, hoping that if she spoke the truth, the KGB agent might be swayed.

"What happened?" Nina asked, gazing up at Sofija.

Sofija fought back her tears.

"My father lives in the town of Niagara Falls. I've never seen him, not even once, in my entire life. He ended up here during the war. I grew up alone with my mother."

"Oh, my goodness," Nina gasped, shocked at Sofija's revelation.

"I only learned that my father was still alive recently. All I want is to see him," Sofija said, lifting her chin to fight gravity, so her tears would not stream down her face.

"Steve, this is remarkable," Nina blurted out, "Steve, we must go to Niagara Falls!"

Nina's cheeks reddened with emotion. She continued, "There cannot be any discussion about this. It's understood that we must take Sofija to Niagara Falls. I will make a personal phone call to the Sports Committee if that's what it takes to change the itinerary."

The last thing Steve expected was for Sofija to openly admit her reason for wanting to travel to Niagara Falls. He nervously passed the bag with the bottle from hand to hand and blinked in confusion.

"Steve, you don't need to come, we can go there on our own," Algis said. "This is no longer about a whim, this is serious, this is about family."

"I won't create any problems for anyone, I promise," Sofija explained, seeing that she had the support of her friends. "All I want is to see my father for one time in my life…"

"Okay, okay, just wait a minute," Steve said, suddenly lifting his right hand.

Everyone quieted down.

"If all of you vote to go to Niagara Falls tomorrow, then we'll go. Hey, you in the back, did you hear me?"

The men in the back of the bus looked up and focused on Steve.

"Who votes that we go to Niagara Falls tomorrow?"

"Raise your hands! Do you hear me!" Nina called out across the bus.

"One, two, three, four… Okay, that's enough, the vote is unanimous," Steve said and sighed. He gripped the bottle in his hands.

"What did we just vote for?" Someone in the back asked.

"We're going to see Niagara Falls tomorrow!" Anatoly announced happily.

"Tomorrow, as I said before, breakfast is served at eight. We leave at nine. Don't be late. There are crowds of people at the Falls on Saturdays."

Dzięki Bogu… Thank God, Sofija thought to herself in Polish.

Suddenly all the fear that she had been feeling fell away and she felt incredibly tired. She wanted to laugh and cry all at the same time. Her throat was constricted, and she felt a pain in her chest. However, as always, Sofija knew precisely how to reign in her emotions, so that no one around her suspect a thing about what she was feeling inside.

As they drove through Toronto, the men gathered on the right side of the bus to gaze at the incredibly tall television tower. Steve secretly opened his bottle of Canadian Club and without removing it from its bag, tossed the brown liquid down his throat.

Then, he scratched his head, sighed loudly, and collapsed back into his seat. He beat out the tempo to the song playing on the radio with his left hand as his cheeks grew redder.

I really got on his nerves... It's nothing though... He'll get over it... Now, there's no road back... All will be well... Just as soon as we arrive at the hotel, I will call Father... Sofija still felt the burden of the stress she'd carried with her throughout the entire trip, and in the six months beforehand. *After tomorrow, that stress will go away... Tomorrow I will meet Father... Finally...*

CHAPTER TWENTY-SEVEN

AUGUST 16, 1975, TORONTO, CANADA – DAY ELEVEN

At two in morning Sofija found herself once again standing at the hotel window unable to fall asleep. She tossed and turned in her bed for a good three hours, then finally gave up on sleep, and now stood gazing out the hotel room window in the direction of her father's home.

It's seventy kilometres across the lake. The very last seventy kilometres... It has been such a long journey, and now everything seems so close... She watched as an airplane, signal lights blinking, made its descent into the airport.

Somewhere out there my father is sleeping... Or perhaps he cannot sleep either? When I called him yesterday evening, he seemed upset... He must be upset... How else could he feel right now?

Sofija closed her eyes and tried to imagine herself in her father's place. In the morning, he would see his daughter for the first time... A daughter who he had not seen for thirty-six years... *He only saw me as an infant. When officers and soldiers were mobilized in Poland in 1939, I was only four months old and two days... Then, on September 1st, the war began.*

What does a four-month-old baby look like? A tiny infant... Could I even smile at that age? Could I even see who was speaking with me? Probably... I remember when I went to see Genovaitė's baby... She was around three months old then... That's only one month less than when my father last laid eyes on me... One month less than when I was left fatherless... I must ask Genovaitė how she felt when she had to leave her baby with her mother and return to her training routine... She went back to rowing when her daughter was around a year old... I could see that it was hard for her... Often, she was teary-eyed... But she's the mother... What does a father feel? Can a man have the same bond with a child as a woman? How much time must pass before a father forgets about his children? A year? Two? Ten? What feeling is left after thirty-six years have passed?

Sofija stood with her eyes closed, imagining Lithuania, far, far away, engulfed in mist, tiny Lithuania, tiny Vilnius, and in a tiny flat, her tiny self as a baby... Viewed from a distance, she could fit her entire life into the palm of her hand... Sofija closed her fist and squeezed it tight. It seemed to her that she was clutching onto the last strands that tied her to her roots, that after tomorrow may either become a metal chain or erode to the thinness of a spider web and then disappear.

Sofija dressed quietly, picked up her shoes, and carefully, on tippy toes, so as not to wake Nina, slipped out the door and into the corridor. She wished to go outside and take a walk under the starry summer night-time sky and release her anxiety to the stars. In her red plaid jacket pocket, she patted her address book that contained her father's phone number.

He was surprised. Very much so. But was he glad? He is so reserved that it's hard to tell... I probably inherited his personality. I may be tearing myself up inside, but no one can tell from the outside. Ever since I was a small child, I was forced to be quiet and never show anyone what I was thinking or feeling. Everyone around me takes me for a cold and strict person... Oh, if only they knew the inner battles that waged inside of me... No one ever taught me how to express my feelings... I had to conduct myself as though I had no feelings... Mama always hid her feelings from me... How she must have felt? Mama...

She waited for Father every day, every day for thirty-three years... She died never having the opportunity to see him again...

Once she'd slid through the door and softly shut it behind her, Sofija slipped on her shoes. She walked softly towards the stairwell. She decided not to use the lift because it would wake people up with its noise. This anxiety over not making a sound had followed her entire life back from the days when she and her mother lived on Pervaža Street, when they did not dare to even move because one creak of the floorboards would set off curses and slurs from the flat's occupants on the other side of the wall.

How will I slip past the reception desk? What will I tell them? She thought and froze. Then she remembered that she is in Canada, in the free world, and that she didn't need to report to anyone where she was going and what she was doing. *Poor me,* she reflected, *I've lived my entire life in fear... What a waste...*

The lobby was full. People were coming back from the bars, intoxicated, reeking of cigarette smoke. Others were carrying suitcases. Apparently, they were the hotel's new arrivals. She pushed the glass doors open and exited onto the street. The weather had cooled. She spotted an outdoor thermometer that read sixteen degrees. The wind had died down. It was a Friday night, and the streets were filled with automobiles. It didn't matter that it was late, and not that warm, nonetheless, groups of young people were out partying together. The city lights of Toronto were lit up. With its new tower that looked like a brightly lit spaceship in the sky, Toronto seemed indescribably beautiful to her.

The feeling here is so free... You may dress however you like, style your hair as you wish, kiss anyone anywhere and anytime you wish to, you may listen to the music you like, sing out loud if you feel like it... No one persecutes you for simply being your own person... No one throws you out of school for having your own personality...

Sofija sat down on a bench in the small square across the street from the hotel and gazed up at the stars. *Oh, there are so many... I hope it's a clear day tomorrow... Although, what difference does it make? I will see Father one way or another – whether it rains or snows. The most important thing is not to forget my address book in the hotel room with his address.*

She pulled the address book out of her jacket pocket and opened it to the page with Father's address. It was as though she wanted to convince herself that the address was still there, that it had not magically evaporated.

Orchard Avenue 6584, Niagara Falls, Ontario, Canada...

She knew his address by heart.

She turned the pages of her address book to the very last one where she had tucked her father's photograph – the very same photograph she would gaze at as a little girl and count the stars on his epaulettes. *One star, two stars, three stars...* She'd taken the photograph with her so that she could recognize him more easily.

"Why does Father have stars on his shoulders?" she would ask Mama.

"Every star represents a good deed that he did for his country, for Poland," Mama would answer.

"One star, two stars, three stars, four stars, five stars, six stars... Mama, that means Father did six good deeds for Poland, doesn't it?"

"Most likely..."

"What if he did more good deeds for Poland? Then those extra stars would not fit on his shoulders. What would he do then?"

"Then they would give him one very big star on each shoulder."

"Oooh, what's this?"

"These are his medals. He received them for doing good work for

Poland."

"Why are there only four?"

Mama smiled at that question.

"When I grow up, I will earn a hundred medals!"

That made Mama smile even more.

A hundred medals... Sofija smiled to herself. *Funny how childish dreams had a way of coming true... Perhaps I was not imagining my rowing medals back then... Perhaps I was thinking of the crosses Father had earned, but it was pretty much the same thing...*

She gazed up at the sky where an abundance of stars was shining in the August night. Somewhere in the distance, lightening flashed. *I wonder if Mama can see me now? Would Mama approve of my journey to see Father? Does Mama wish for me to meet Father, or to forget him? We never talked about it... But I saw how she cried all the time, how tormented she was... She was tormented with thoughts about everything that she had lost, all her dashed expectations... She cried all the time, thinking that I didn't see her tears... I saw her tears and I pretended that I didn't see them... I never asked her how she felt... Why? Why didn't I ever ask her why she was crying? Perhaps that was all she needed – one question from me, one indication that she was not alone in this world, that I was there for her. Now I may never ask her, and I will never know... I will never receive any answers from her, from our relatives, from our family... Which is better – to know or not to know? I am sorry now that I didn't ask Mama for answers... Now I am sorry... But maybe it was better that way? Perhaps it is better to live in the present moment and not to root around too deeply into the past? Yes... But that only works when you're young, when you're racing into your future, while you dream and believe that the world is your oyster... Then, time catches up with you and life no longer seems so perfect. Then you ask yourself: Who am I? Why am I like this? Why is my life like this? What are my roots? Then, you find no rest from those questions. That's when you start searching for answers. But by then, it's too late, by then all the answers to your questions have been taken by your elders to the grave...*

Sofija stood up from the bench and wondered where she ought to go. The noisy street dissipated any thought of sleep. She knew her thoughts would not allow her to fall asleep, not tonight. *Shall I join the crowd and walk along the street? Go to a bar? I wouldn't dare...*

She returned to the hotel and leaned up against the wall under an awning. She watched as a rain cloud emerged in the night sky. Then she heard the clap of thunder right over her head. Sofija jumped. Still, despite the oncoming rain, it was good to stand outside, to feel the danger of the approaching lightning storm, to feel as though she were a part of nature, just like she did back home in Lithuania.

No matter where you are, nature behaves the same... Nature acts according to its own laws and it unpredictable... All you need to know is how to read nature's signs... And what about a human being? He is unpredictable and difficult to understand... He would like to be as free as nature, but at the same time he is dependent... He loves and he hurts others without obeying any laws of nature...

She turned and gazed at the hotel lobby through the plate glass window. She spotted the payphone. Sofija could still feel the weight of the receiver in her hands when she called her father for the second time.

What will he look like? Has he changed a lot? Or does he still look the way he does in the photograph? Will I recognize him? Of course, he must have changed... Over thirty-six years have passed since that photograph was taken. I must recognize him. No other older men could possibly live with him at the address I have in my book?

Sofija glanced at the clock in the hotel lobby.

In seven or eight hours, I will see him... Perhaps I ought to try to go to sleep... Tatyana Mikhailovna's method might help... Is the bar still open? Oh, but I didn't bring any money with me... So much for that... It was a silly idea anyway... I'll go back to bed and somehow, I'll fall asleep...

Drops of rain began to fall intermittently. The wind picked up and scattered newspapers left out on the park benches. The wind picked up the trash out on the streets.

Sofija entered the revolving door and exited into the lobby. Before she realized what she was doing, her legs carried her towards the hotel bar. Inside music was playing, people were sitting in groups chatting, swapping stories, and laughing. The air was heavy with cigarette smoke. She walked up to the bar.

"How late are you open?" she asked the bartender in English.

"Until three. We close in half an hour," the bartender said, glancing over at the clock on the wall behind him. "What would you like?"

"I'll be right back... I need to go get my wallet," Sofija said and turned to leave.

"Wait! What would you like? You can come back and pay tomorrow?" the bartender said with a flourish of his hand.

"I'd like a Canadian Club," Sofija said, shocked at how those words had tumbled out of her mouth. On the wall hung a poster with a photograph of a bottle of that whiskey and a jet-skier with the Toronto Tower in the background.

Oh no, what have I done? Sofija fretted. *I've never tasted hard liquor in my life. The advertisement must have had an effect on me... And Steve's bottle... But maybe it'll help me fall asleep? I'll taste what it is that I bought for Steve... If a litre cost eight dollars, then a glass will probably cost around a dollar…*

"Here you go, your whiskey," the bartender said, setting a wide glass filled with ice and an amber-coloured liquid down in front of her. "Where are you from?"

Sofija wrapped her hand around the cold glass and smiled. "I'm from Poland," she said.

"Really? I know Poland. My co-worker is from Poland. Tomas?! Come over here," he said, waving towards a young man around thirty serving drinks at the other end of the bar. "I've got someone here from your country! She's from Poland!"

The young man came over immediately and addressed Sofija in Polish: "Hello, I'm Tomas, are you really from Poland?"

"*Dobry wieczór*, good evening," Sofija said in Polish. "Yes, I was born in Poland."

"My parents are from Warsaw. They came here before the war."

"How about you? Have you lived your entire life here?"

"Yes, I have. I was born in Canada."

"But you speak Polish perfectly!"

"My parents taught me Polish. They didn't want me to forget my roots."

"Are their many Poles in Toronto?"

"Yes, many. Also, a lot of them live in the cities surrounding Toronto, in Hamilton, Saint Catherine, Niagara Falls…"

Sofija felt a chill run down her spine.

"Do you know any Poles in Niagara Falls?"

"I don't, personally, but my friend's relative live there. Will you be in Toronto for long? We have a big Polish community here. Tomorrow we have Polish mass in the morning. Let me write down the address for you.

It's at Saint Casimir's Church near the lake and High Park."

Tomas looked around him for a scrap of paper to write on.

"I'm so sorry, but tomorrow – more accurately today – is our last day in Canada."

Sofija took a sip of the whiskey. *Oh, this tastes disgusting!*

"Do you have plans? Mass is only one hour long."

"Tomorrow morning our group is traveling to Niagara Falls," she said.

Sofija glanced at the whiskey remaining at the bottom of the glass and pushed it away. She stood up to leave, afraid of revealing too much to this friendly young man. "How much do I owe you for the whiskey. Your colleague said that I could come back and pay you tomorrow."

"You don't owe a penny," Tomas said and smiled, "it's on me."

"*Dziękuję, Tomasz,* thank you, Tomas. I'm sorry, but I can't finish it."

"Don't worry about it! It was lovely meeting you! I rarely meet a real Pole from my homeland."

"Thank you, it was a pleasure speaking with you," Sofija said, then got up from her barstool and hurried towards the exit.

Her hand still felt cold from the ice-cold glass, but warmth and peace flowed through her body. Every single time she had a moment chatting with a local Canadian, she felt warmth, intimacy, and friendliness from the encounter. She felt like a child again at the Church of Saint Peter and Paul in Vilnius.

At least now I will fall asleep… she told herself.

CHAPTER TWENTY-EIGHT

AUGUST 16, 1975, NIAGARA FALLS, CANADA – DAY TWELVE

The bus rolled along the shoreline of Lake Ontario. Sofija pressed her hand to her brow to shade the bright morning light as she gazed across Lake Ontario trying to image what her father was doing just then on the other side of the lake. She imagined him dressing in his white collared shirt, knotting his tie, combing back his dark, or perhaps grey, hair. Sofija imagined her father pacing across the room. She imagined him seated at his kitchen table reading the morning paper.

Or, perhaps, he was standing at the window, gazing outside, waiting for her to arrive…

Maybe Father couldn't sleep last night either?

Last night she ironed her white blouse with narrow red plaid decoration and pretty blue flowers. It was the best blouse she owned. She stood before the mirror for a long time, brushing her short dark curly hair. She wanted to look her best for this stranger. She did not understand why? Perhaps so that he would see what a fine daughter he lost when he left her and her mother behind and never returned. That morning she reminded herself that this father of hers was no more than a stranger and that she had no tie to him, and yet, she did everything in her power to make him proud. She wished that he would praise her for all the competitions she'd won… That he'd never seen her win… He'd never been there beside her, but she wanted him to somehow feel that he contributed to all those wins, all those medals. Sofija reflected back on how when she received her father's first letter, she knew that the only way that she would ever have the chance to see him would be through sports, through rowing, through winning. That's what it would take to open up the gates of the Iron Curtain.

It has taken hundreds of medals… Hundreds of races… Hundreds of the hardest kilometres of my life to reach my father…

"Here to the left," Steve's voice broke through her thoughts, "is one of the oldest rowing clubs in Canada, the Argonaut Club."

All of them rose from their seats to catch a glimpse of the club boathouse.

"They row in Lake Ontario?" one of the men said, surprised. "There must be a lot of waves out there."

"Most likely, I wouldn't know," Steve responded. "I'm not a rower; in fact, I'm not interested in rowing at all. I was told that this club opened in 1872."

As the bus rowed passed the boathouse, the men studied the building intently. Once they'd driven beyond it, they returned to their seats.

"What are those gates over there, Stepan?" Anatoly asked. After two weeks on the road together, he still could not force himself to call his countryman by an English name.

On the left side of the road, they saw a white arc with columns in a semi-circle around it.

"These are the gates to the beach and the public swimming pool. This is where the city comes to swim. And over here, take a look, we are passing by a statue of Sir Casimir Gzhovsky, one of the most famous Canadian engineers of the last century.

Sofija jumped in her seat. "The name sounds Polish," she said.

"Yes, that's right, he was of Polish heritage. His father was from Poland. The park over there is named after him. He made a significant contribution to the engineering of railway tracks and bridges. Also, he was the first director of the Niagara Park commission. Now, take a look further in the distance – there's a monument to Queen Elizabeth. That statue stood near the entrance to the highway, but only this year, when the lanes were expanded, the monument was transferred into the Sir Casimir Gzhovsky Park. Slow down," Steve directed the bus driver, "look, over there you can see the busts of King George the Sixth and Queen Elizabeth. Then down below, on the pedestal, a lion protects them. Some people call this the Lion's Monument."

Stepan is inspired today... That litre of whiskey must have put him in a good mood... Sofija mused to herself, smiled, and delved back into her own reflections.

"Now we will be driving away from the lake and onto the Queen Elizabeth Way," Steve continued. "This is the first highway in North America that connected several cities. It was built in 1937. The construction was copied from the *German Autobahn*. The highway runs in two separate directions and has multi-storey intersections. This road had the longest illuminated stretch in the world at the time. The highway is one hundred and thirty-nine kilometres long and ends at the border with America – on the Peace Bridge.

That's already beyond Niagara Falls and my father's home... Sofija began to tremble with fear and anticipation over the upcoming reunion.

"Just before Burlington, we will approach Lake Ontario again and cross the bay. Then we will see Toronto from the other side of the lake. This highway will take us to our destination – the city of Niagara Falls and the famous waterfall. The huge Niagara Falls on the Niagara River is known around the world. The name, translated from the native Indian word "Onguiaahra," means Water Thunder.

He talking as though it were his idea to drive to Niagara Falls today, Sofija thought, amused. *What a hypocrite.*

"There are actually three waterfalls in the area: The American Waterfall, the Bridal Veil's Falls, and Horseshoe Falls. The Horseshoe Falls are the largest and ninety percent of the water passes through this waterfall. You will see how powerful that is! It is truly amazing!"

Sofija trembled. *When I see those waterfalls, I will have already met Father.* She felt needles in her stomach. *There's only one hour left. This is like one training session.*

A sign flashed past that read: *Niagara Falls 48.*

That's miles... In kilometres that would be around eighty... Sofija comforted herself with these thoughts. She still did not feel ready to meet her father. And now, she'd dragged the entire delegation into her personal drama... *I wonder which one will report me to the KGB? I really could care less... They can never allow me out on a trip to the West ever again for all I care. After I've seen Father, I have no reason to travel anyway... Once I've met Father, I can go back and live my life quietly in Vilnius... Are they going to throw me out of my job? Why would they? I have no intention of defecting... Many people in Lithuania have relatives in the West. So what? They let me out many times and every single time I came back... Even after I knew I had a father in Canada, I still went back to the Soviet Union. They always let me out to race...*

Sofija glanced at her fellow passengers. They were all more interested in gazing out the windows and discussing the multi-storied highway overpasses than listening to anything Steve had to say.

Because of me, they all would have lost out on the opportunity to see Niagara Falls. It's a good thing that I figured out in time that it was because of me that Niagara Falls was not added to the itinerary.

Sofija felt pins and needles all over her body. Her heart pounded against her chest. She was having difficulty breathing. Sofija closed her eyes and tried to stop herself from thinking about anything at all.

Before the start of a race, it was different. It was awful, but it was different. Then, I knew what was coming up. I'd have no energy during warm-ups, I'd be overcome with apathy at the starting pontoon, during the first twenty strokes I wouldn't believe it was really happening, then my legs and arms would feel intense pain, I'd become short of breath and my ears would ring, then the pain would shoot through my entire body, then the pain would disappear completely, and the end gong would ring in my ears. Later, I would remember all the terrible pain when I felt that I could not move, when my head was splitting. But by then, it would all be over... But now... I'm not facing any physical pain, but the fear is much stronger...

The weather had cleared since the rain last night and the temperature was getting warmer by the hour.

"Would anybody like to take a ride up in the observation tower?" Steve asked and scanned the bus. "The weather is clear, so you will see a great distance. The lift takes you up and you can see everything from a bird's eye view. Of course, it costs extra. If anyone is interested, I'll ask about the prices. There are a few observation towers. The Panasonic Hotel is located in one of the observation towers."

Isn't that the observation tower Father wrote about in his letter? Sofija remembered. *I think that he wrote that he participated in the design of the tower... Oh, I don't remember exactly... All my anxiety has washed my mind blank. I'll have to ask...*

"You won't see much driving on the highway," Steve warned. "This is an industrial region. The view gets better when we approach the lake again."

How much longer? I don't see a single sign... Sofija craned her neck to search for signs. Then she glanced at her watch. *Maybe half an hour... Maybe less... Just like the warm-ups before a race... When only that much time is left, you push off from the pontoon...* Her palms were sweaty, and a lump was lodged in the back of her throat. She took five deep breaths in and out.

"Are you anxious," Nina asked, turning around to peer into Sofija's face.

"Yes... It feels just like before a race," Sofija said, her voice trembling. She hoped that no one would notice that she felt anxious, but she was almost glad that Nina had shown some concern.

"It's understandable... Everything will be fine, don't worry," Nina said and patted Sofija's hand.

"I know," Sofija whispered as she fought back the urge to cry.

"It'll all be fine, you'll see," Nina repeated, comforting her.

The highway approached the lake from the left side. On the right, she could see the bay. They passed fruit trees heavy with ripe fruit.

"Oh, I'd like to take a bit out of one of Anatoly's tasty apples," a coach sitting behind them said.

"Alright, alright, enough," Anatoly shot back. "What was I supposed to do, throw them away?"

The others had not stopped teasing him about his apples the entire trip.

"Oh no, much better to eat the whole bag of apples than toss them away!" the coach quipped.

The group had formed friendships over their two weeks together and now felt comfortable teasing one another. Only ten days ago, when they'd landed, they all stood with clenched teeth and watched as Anatoly ate his way through an entire carry-on bag stuffed with Ukrainian apples as the Afro-American border control guard stood by patiently waiting for him to finish. They were all amazed that after he'd been told he could not bring the apples into the country with him, he rectified the problem by consuming them all, one after the other.

"I did offer you an apple! Why didn't you take it? We would have finished them off faster if you had helped me. I offered everyone apples!" Anatoly shouted out in his defense.

"We've arrived at Saint Catherine," Steve announced. "It's fifteen minutes longer from here to Niagara Falls."

"This is where the rowing championship took place in 1970," Sofija said.

She remembered how much she wanted to see the Royal Henley course, but now it didn't matter, not unless they could make a quick stop there after Niagara Falls.

"Really?" Steve was surprised. "Were you here, Sofija Ingatyevna?"

"No, I wasn't. Women have only been able to compete in the World Championship since last year. When I was rowing, we only had the European Rowing Championship. And even that took place separately from the men's championship."

"Such discrimination!" Nina called out angrily.

"Our World Championships used to take place every four years," Anatoly joined in, "between the Olympics. Only this year, we had two in row. From now on, they will take place once a year. But the Saint Catherine competition was a disaster for the Soviet team. We only won a silver and a bronze. It was a failure. In our days, all the teams brought back the prize."

"When were your times?" Nina turned around in her seat to ask.

"1964 and 1965."

"Are you referring to the European Rowing Championship?" Sofija asked.

"That's right... but also the World Championship – in 1966 four crews won medals. In 1962 only the coxless four didn't win a medal. Oh, look!" Anatoly shouted as the bus rolled over the bridge, "there's the rowing course!"

Steve turned towards the window not quite sure what Anatoly was pointing at. He leaned over to the driver and asked in English, "What's that?"

"It's the rowing course," he said, indicating the water with his head.

"Yes, that's the rowing course," Steve confirmed.

Sofija then asked the driver in English, "Is that the Henley course? Where the World Championship took place?"

"Yes, that's the very one. The Royal Canadian Henley Regatta takes place here. It just ended a few weeks ago. Five years ago, they held the World Championship here."

"That's the starting line?"

"Yes, and there at the end is the finish line. Do you see? Pity, but we cannot make a stop on the bridge. There's a rowing club on the island."

"What's he saying?" Anatoly asked impatiently.

"He confirmed that this is the rowing course, and that the club is on the island."

"Can we make a stop there after Niagara Falls, Stepan?" Anatoly asked.

"That depends on the time," Steve answered.

Sofija grew anxious. Road sign after road sign confirmed that Niagara Falls were getting closer. Then she saw a sign that read: *Niagara Falls 6.*

Six miles! That's only ten kilometres. Ten minutes and we'd arrive. Ten minutes was the length of a break between races… Some boats start their race, then you line up and you wait for ten minutes… The fear back then was just like the fear now… There's nothing that I can do to stop this anymore… I have no choice but to take whatever comes my way…

The road led them out of the town, over another bridge across a river, and then into open fields.

Now anxiety grabbed her by her throat. Sofija was overcome with the irrational fear that her legs will give out and she won't be able to climb out of the bus. Her legs were numb. She inhaled deeply, closed her eyes, and breathed out. She began to count, just as she counted strokes during training, one, two, three…

"What's the exact address?" the bus driver asked in English, interrupting her thoughts.

Sofija hurriedly extended her arm and held up her address book for the driver to see with the page open to her father's address: Orchard Avenue 6584, Niagara Falls, Ontario, Canada.

"I see. That's close to the falls, just a few blocks away."

"Really?" Sofija gasped.

"Steve," the bus driver called out, careful not to take his eyes off the road, "Shall I let all of you out at the falls and bring the lady to this address?

"That's a great idea," Sofija said happily, "why waste everyone's time because of me."

"Oh no! Absolutely not!" Steve commanded. "We will all go to that address together and then we will all depart for the falls together. I don't expect the lady will take up too much of our precious time."

Oh, Steve got me back…

"What did he say?" Nina asked.

"The driver said that he can drop all of you at the falls and then take me to my father's address. But Steve doesn't agree with that plan."

"Hey!" Nina shouted, "Stepan! Why can't we let Sofija out on her own and the rest of us go see Niagara Falls?"

"Listen! I've already made plenty of concessions for you! I changed the entire itinerary for you, and you're still trying to boss me around! Now I'm telling you what my orders are. We all must stick together at all times. That's how it'll be! I ask you not to bring this up again!" Steve was shouting, losing control, his face burning red in colour. "We will give the lady fifteen minutes, and then all of us together, like one nice big friendly group, will go visit Niagara Falls. Agreed?"

"What?" a man from the back of the bus called out when he picked up the word, "Niagara." He obviously hadn't heard most of what Steve had said, but he called back, "We agree! We agree!"

Sofija could no longer utter a single word. She sat hunched over, squeezing her address book in her hand and clutching her camera.

A sign flashed past that read: *The Falls. Follow 420.*

We are close… She took a deep breath. She began to wonder about her father: *How did he get here? And why here? Is it because there's a Polish community here? Or because he was offered work? This is the other end of the earth from Europe…*

The highway signs capped with the Queen's crown continued. Route 420 dipped and curved through many overpasses and underpasses, finally taking them into the town of Niagara Falls. They could see at least three observation towers in the distance.

"We have arrived in the town of Niagara Falls," Steve commented. "Tourism came to this town at the beginning of the nineteenth century. It's only natural that towns grow up around wonders of nature like the falls."

Sofija gazed back and forth along both sides of the street. *What does my father do with his days here and why is he here?* She wondered. *The town is pretty, the houses are cosy and neat, but is that reason enough to forget your home? To leave your family?*

The bus driver navigated the two-lane roads slowly and carefully, looking for the correct turn. Sofija spotted a sign that read: *Drummond Road*.

"People live well here," Nina said and sighed. "The houses look like gingerbread houses. Do you think each house belongs to only one family? Oh, and they take such good care of the yards, they are all so pretty! I haven't seen a single piece of trash on the street yet."

The bus turned left, onto a narrow road, called *Dixon*.

In front of them, a little to the left, they saw an observation tower that looked like a disc.

"That's Skylon Tower," Steve announced. "It's the tallest bower beside Niagara. It was built in 1964."

Sofija wished they would all stop talking. She needed to assemble in her head the words that she would speak to her father. She had thought it over so many times, but now it had all evaporated. Her panic was growing, and she felt as though she could barely form a single word or thought.

"Oh, I'm sorry," the driver suddenly said in English, "I passed it. Now I've got to turn around."

He rolled the bus into a driveway, backed out, and returned in the opposite direction. Twenty-three metres down the road he turned left where the words *Orchard Avenue* were written on a signpost. The driver scanned the numbers on the houses, searching for 6584.

"Six five six eight... Six five seven six... Yes, there it is, six, five, eight, four."

The bus passed a wooden telephone post and pulled onto a paved driveway. The driver parked the bus, careful that the end did not poke out too far into the street, obstructing other drivers. Every single passenger on the bus gazed at the house with the numbers 6584 written on its front wall.

The red brick building with white shutters and a white porch was just like all the other houses up and down the street. The grass in front of the house was neatly trimmed. Pink and yellow rose bushes grew on both sides of the porch. Red roses and vines wound around the columns on either side of the front door. The driver opened the door. Clutching just her camera, Sofija rose from her seat. She looked at the stairs that led out of the bus. Her legs wobbled under her, but somehow, she managed to climb down those few steps.

"Everything will be fine," Nina whispered to her, grabbed onto her hand, and gave it a firm squeeze.

Clutching onto the door for support, Sofija stepped down onto the soft grass. The curious passengers pressed their noses to the glass watching her.

"You may either sit and wait in the bus or get out and take a walk. This won't take longer than fifteen minutes," Steve said. Then he climbed out of the bus behind Sofija.

Sofija stood and gazed at the house but could not force herself to take a single step forward. Her cheeks burned red. Her teeth hurt because she was clenching them so tightly.

A short, elderly man, dressed in a white dress shirt and a dark blue pinstriped suit, stepped outside, and made his way carefully down the porch stairs to where Sofija stood in front of the bus.

"*Tata...* Daddy", she said in Polish.

Sofija stood and watched as the man slowly walked towards her. He wore his hair slicked back, exactly as in the photograph, only his hair had thinned and greyed. The dimple was there in his chin. His gaze was the same, although his eyes were sunken in. He smiled just the slightest, or rather, he carried with him an immense sense of calm... But there was not a single star on his shoulders... All that time she had imagined her father wearing his military uniform.... Sofija felt as though they'd stood there facing each other for eternity. She knew that she must take a step forwards, but her legs failed to obey her. She stood, barely breathing, half deaf from the insistent ringing in her ears and the banging of her heart against her chest.

"*Dzień dobry*," he said in greeting, good day. With a reserved smile, he took a step towards Sofija.

"*Dzień dobry, tata*," Sofija replied, although she could barely hear her own voice.

Father extended his right hand to Sofija and said, "Welcome to my home."

Sofija took hold of his hand and in his palm, she could feel his masculine warmth. Although he was no longer young, his grip was strong. With their touch, Sofija seemed to come alive. Heat rose to her pale face. The lump that had formed in her throat melted away. She gazed at this stranger and felt absolutely nothing. He was simply an elderly man standing in front of her and nothing more. He seemed to be in better shape than men of his age in Lithuania, she noted. He stood straighter and was more relaxed. He did not seem exhausted by life, like his contemporaries in Lithuania. He seemed happy. And yet, he was a complete stranger to her. She always imagined that she would cry when she met him, that uncontrolled tears would stream down her face, but her eyes remained dry.

"Shall we step inside?" Father said politely and indicated the stairs.

Sofija took a step forwards and couldn't understand what was upsetting her now. She stepped inside and Steve followed close on her heels behind her. *What's he doing here?* She thought angrily. *Of course, he's going to listen in on our conversation.*

The windows of the veranda were covered with straw blinds, blocking out the light and providing shade. The entrance into the house was dark. Only a few footsteps inside the house revealed a large living room, filled with light from the back yard. Two women and a man stood up from the sofa in the living room where they had apparently been waiting for her arrival.

"Sofija, may I introduce my wife, Ana. Ana, this is Sofija."

Wife?

An older woman with blond hair, dressed in an elegant suit and matching white shoes stood up to greet Sofija. It was difficult for Sofija to determine her age because women aged differently in the West than they did in the Soviet Union. Back in the Soviet Union after a woman turned fifty, she became an old woman with a scarf tied under her chin.

"*Dzień dobry.* I'm Ana," the woman said in a sweet voice.

Sofija took a step closer and saw that she was covering her head with a blond wig.

"I'm Sofija, *Dzień dobry.*"

"And this is my daughter, Vanda," Ana said, taking a woman who looked to be around fifty by the elbow and introducing her. "Although," she added, "many people think Vanda's my sister," she added and chortled. "What? Aren't I telling the truth?" Ana said, turning towards her husband, who looked taken aback.

"*Dzień dobry,* Sofija," Vanda said warmly and hugged Sofija.

Sofija felt a sharp pain in her eyes as she fought back tears. Such a warm hug was what she had expected to receive from her father.

"It's a pleasure to meet you, Vanda," she said, pushing her head back so that she wouldn't blink and release the tears that she knew would stream down her face. She pushed out her bottom lip and blew upwards to dry out her tears. "We are sisters then?"

"No, no, I'm Ana's daughter. They do not have children together. Father has only you. This has been a miracle for me. I never in my life imagined that Father has another family... That he has a daughter... He never said a single word about it."

"This is Vanda's husband, Jurek," Ana broke in. "Come, Jurek, why are you standing there like that?"

"Hello, I'm Jurek, Vanda's husband," Jurek said. He was a grey-haired man around sixty who was slightly similar to Father. Like Father, he also wore his hair slicked back. He was also not very tall, like Father. Only, he was friendlier and wore a broad smile on his face. They all spoke Polish amongst themselves.

Suddenly, Ana noticed Steve standing behind Sofija, fidgeting nervously.

"Hello, I'm Ana. Who are you?" she asked in English.

"Hi, I'm Steve, the tour guide. I hope you don't mind that I'm here."

"Are you a local?"

"Yes, I live in Ottawa."

"Clearly, it's obvious from a glance that you're not from the Soviet Union," Ana said and laughed cynically.

"Perhaps we should go out into the garden," Father said, pretending that he had not heard the dig Ana had directed towards Sofija. He opened the door to the backyard.

"You're not very far from the falls here?" Sofija said, stepping out into the well-kept backyard filled with manicured shrubbery and flowers.

"That's right. We're only three blocks away," Father said. "See, over there, on the right. That's the tower that I wrote about in my letter. Our company worked on the project. I had a hand in that as well."

"Interesting. I'll have to go and take a look," Sofija said.

"I worked on it before I retired. It was built in 1961."

"Stand here, Sofija, I'd like to take your photograph," Vanda said, leading Sofija into the middle of the yard. Like Sofija, she also had her camera ready.

"Be careful to make sure both towers fit in the frame," Father said.

Vanda smiled and nodded.

"Now, stand here with your Father. Daddy, stand beside Sofija. Turn towards the maple."

"Could you please take a photograph with my camera?" Sofija asked.

Sofija set up the focus, the diaphragm, the aperture, and handed her camera to Vanda. She nervously placed her right hand on her father's forearm.

Sofija could see that her father could not take his eyes off her and that he was examining her every feature, but she pretended not to notice. She gazed into the camera lens. An uncomfortable shyness and fear of making eye contact stopped her from gazing directly at her father and reading what was hiding in his gaze. She just prayed for the uncomfortable moment to end more quickly.

"I also want a photograph together with Sofija!" Ana called out, hurrying into the yard, abandoning Steve in the doorway, and gripping onto Father's right arm. "Vanda, take our photo just like this! Good, now I want one alone with Sofija. Go away, Ignacy, just me and Sofija now."

Ana hugged Sofija across her waist and smiled broadly. Sofija hooked her left hand onto the waistline of her jeans. That was her habit when she didn't know where to place her hands. She did not want to put her arms around Ana...

"Mama's ring," Father said, noticing the ring with Sofija's mother's family coat of arms on her finger.

Sofija gazed down at the ring.

"Yes, I always have Mama's ring with me. I will be buried wearing this ring," she said, looking directly into Father's eyes, as though wanting to say that she would never betray Mama.

Father smiled sheepishly.

"So many years passed..."

"Thirty-six years, *Tata*, I am thirty-six."

"I know. I haven't forgotten... I never forgot the both of you... From the very beginning I wrote letters home to Warsaw, but..."

"You have a nice home here," Steve broke into their intimate conversation. It was obvious that he was following every word that passed between Father and daughter. Because Steve spoke Ukrainian, he could understand them. Polish and Ukrainian were similar languages. "Do you hear Niagara Falls from here?"

"We're used to it, so we don't hear the falls. But people who visit only seldom say that the falls are as loud as the crashing waves of the ocean."

Father seemed to know exactly who Steve was and what he was doing there in his backyard.

"Jurek, could you please offer Mr. Steve a drink? Ana, could you brew some tea, or perhaps you'd like something a little stronger?"

"Thank you," Steve responded in English, "but we must be leaving now. The entire bus is waiting."

"We'll make this fast, Steve," Ana said and gripped Steve's arm. "Don't tell me you'd pass up the opportunity to have a drink with us? Come inside."

"Well, we can have one, but only if we all drink together," Steve said, determined not to leave Sofija alone with her father.

However, Ana's guess was right that Steve would not say no to a drink, even at ten in the morning.

"Fine, we're coming too," Father said and walked very slowly, trying to gain at least a minute alone to talk with his daughter.

"We must be going soon, *Tata*..."

Sofija realized that dragging out the time would not work. But she didn't know what to talk about in the minutes they had left together. She had so much to ask and to tell him, but now all her words escaped her. She simply did not know where to start and the time had already come to say goodbye.

"How did you end up here, *Tata*?"

"During the war... We ran together with a few other officers out of Russia... Only a few of us survived... Someday I will tell you the entire story... When you come and visit me next time, without him," he waved his hand towards Steve's back.

"There may not be another opportunity," Sofija said.

"Are you afraid I'll die soon?" Father joked. "I'm only eighty-three!"

"Sofija Ignatyevna, we must be leaving now," Steve said from where he stood in the doorway.

"I'm coming," she answered.

Sofija and her father stepped inside the living room. Ana had arranged six shot glasses filled with dark red liquor on the coffee table.

"I just can't get over this," Vanda whispered into Sofija's ear so that her mother would not hear. "Jurek and I only heard the news yesterday. I simply don't understand how Father could have hid the fact that he had a wife and a daughter for so many years? We didn't have the slightest suspicion... I don't feel good about this..."

"Have they been married for long?" Sofija asked.

"This year makes it twenty-nine years. Please forgive my mother. She's a little strange. Sometimes I'm embarrassed by her, but what can I do, she's the only mother I have."

"Thank you for the drink. It's time for us to leave now," Steve said abruptly after tossing back his drink.

Steve shook Father's hand, then Jurek's, then signalled with his eyes to Sofija that she must follow him out through the veranda.

"It's too bad that we must be leaving already," Sofija said, following Steve.

"I'll walk you to your bus," Father said and followed Sofija and Steve out the door.

"I'm also coming, wait!" Ana called out after them.

They all walked outside together.

Members of the delegation were stretching their legs, strolling around the yard, only a few remained seated in the bus. There was nothing to occupy them out on the street – no shops, nothing interesting to take up their time, only residential homes. They were clearly bored and impatient. When they saw Steve emerge out of the house, they all rushed inside the bus, eager to go and see one of the natural wonders of the world.

"Stop, I'd like to take a photo of all of you beside the roses," Vanda said, lifting her camera to her eye.

Again, Ana hugged Sofija around the waist.

"Take a photo of me and Sofija, then with Father."

What an odd woman... How could Father have exchanged Mama for this strange hyperactive Ana?

"*Do widzenia, tato,*" Goodbye, Daddy, Sofija said, stretching out her hand towards Father, hoping that this time he would hug her.

"*Do zobaczenia, Sofia,*" Until next time, Sofija, Father said, holding her hand in his. He continued to examine her every feature and glance, but did not reveal his own emotions, not even for a moment. "I will send you an invitation to come visit me. Next time you come we will have more time to talk."

"That's good, Father. Goodbye..."

CHAPTER TWENTY-NINE

AUGUST 16, 1975, NIAGARA FALLS

Sofia stood on the cliffs of Niagara Falls, leaning up against the metal fence, gazing at the emerald water, sparkling, and bubbling, cascading downwards, and forming a sea green-coloured mist beneath her feet.

That's all...

Her heart was empty, and cold. At first, she thought, *No, that can't be all, I must return to my Father's home to speak out our hearts! Nothing has turned out the way that I had expected!* However, standing and gazing at the never-ending flow of water, feeling the cool mist wash over her, had the effect of cooling down her emotions as well.

I can't change what happened in the past. I came here alone, and I will leave alone... I don't feel anything for that man, absolutely nothing... I feel neither love nor hatred... Absolutely nothing... Not even the slightest hint of an emotion for him... He is simply a stranger who never played any role in my life and never will... He was nothing more than a man in a photograph with stars on his epaulettes... If Mama were alive, it would all be different... I'm relieved, though, that she didn't see him living this way... Thank goodness that I don't need to return to her back home with this news... After all, I only came on this trip for her... This was all about her...

Without realizing it, Sofija lifted her gaze up into the sunny blue sky. Mist from the falls splashed onto her face and slid down her cheeks like tears.

That's all...

Her head was no longer ringing. The thundering noise of Niagara Falls drowned out all the other noise. She wanted to stand there like that until everything returned inside of her to how it once was.

Nothing is permanent in life... Life simply flows, forever moving forwards, like the Niagara Falls... I cannot stop the flow of life... I can try to fix the past, to go back and rearrange events, but it will never work, it's pointless... Just like you cannot force the flowing water of the falls to move in reverse... It's impossible to relive a day that has already finished... Even this day, which has only just begun... Most likely, tomorrow I will regret how I lived today, but this moment will have already passed and there will be nothing that I can do to bring it back... This day will be relegated to history, my personal history... Now, this is all simply my life, and mine alone... My life will be a little different from now on, and I will be different... And that is because I now know more than I'd like to know, and now I'll need to learn to live with that...

All around her tourists were snapping photos of Niagara Falls. Children ran around, joyously enjoying their outing, but Sofija could care less. All she heard was the sound of the roaring water, drowning out all her other thoughts. She felt good gazing at the majestic waterfall and putting into perspective that all of humanity's problems are short lived and inconsequential in the face of the power of nature.

How much this water must have witnessed... Happy people, and unhappy ones... Newlywed couples and lonely singles... Courageous people and suicides... Happy children and abandoned children... How many people have gazed at these waters who have now moved on and are in heaven... And still, the water never ceases to fall... Everything passes in life, just like these waters...

The grandeur of Niagara Falls mesmerized Sofija so that she felt as though she were lost in a dream. She no longer wished to go anywhere. All she wanted to do was to stand and gaze out at the amazing verdant water and its white froth. She felt as though her heart would burst...

And that's all...

EPILOGUE

Sofija returned to visit her father in Niagara Falls in 1977, two years after their first meeting. Ana did everything in her power to prevent father and daughter from meeting again. It was only after the threat of legal action, which would have revealed his bigamy, did she back down. Then, Ana agreed to a three-month invitation for Sofija to come to Canada, granting her the permission to exit the Soviet Union.

During that second visit, Sofija's father and his friend, a doctor who lived in the neighbourhood, narrated the story of how the two of them, along with a few dozen other Polish men, who were incarcerated in a Soviet concentration camp for Polish officers, managed to escape and complete a long and arduous journey through Iran to England, and from there to Canada. Unfortunately, Ana repeatedly interfered in their conversations and prevented them from getting close. The only person in the family who supported Sofija emotionally was Vanda, Ana's daughter. Vanda took on a strong feeling of guilt and responsibility for what had happened to Sofija and promised her that she would gift her half of her house, so that Sofija could emigrate out of the Soviet Union and become a permanent resident of Canada. However, a strange turn of events occurred. Vanda died of a heart attack on her birthday. She died in Sofija's arms.

After spending three months in Canada, Sofija returned to Lithuania and for many years worked as a women's rowing coach. When the Soviet Union collapsed in 1991, Sofija's old rowing friends invited her to work for a few years as a coach in Lübeck, Germany. In 1997, she returned to live in Vilnius. It was not the city that she was born in, but it was the place where she felt at home.

Sofija's father, Ignacy Gruca, died in 1982. He was buried in the Niagara Falls cemetery.

Sofija's friend, Genovaitė Šidagytė-Ramoškienė, together with Leonora Kaminskaitė, became the first Lithuanian women to row in the Olympics. In the 1976 Olympics in Montreal, they won a bronze medal in the women's double sculls. However, in the USSR Athletic Team Ledger this Olympic win was recorded as a loss because the expectation was that they would win a gold medal. Four Lithuanian rowers participated in the Montreal Olympics. Besides the women's double Vytautas Butkus and Antanas Čikotas rowed in the Montreal Olympics. Butkus won a silver medal for the quadruple scull and Čikotas took seventh place rowing on the Soviet eight.

1954

1967

For more photos of this story, visit www.rimakaraliene.lt.

SOFIJA GRUCOVA

Sofija Grucova (Gruca) born May 1, 1939 in Warsaw, Poland.

Master of Sports of the USSR (1963), Accomplished Master of Sports (1970), Lithuanian Soviet Socialist Republic Accomplished Coach (1985).

First coach – Jonas Pavilionis.

Ten-time Lithuanian Soviet Socialist Republic Rowing Champion (1857-1966) rowing in a single, on a quadruple scull, and a double scull.

Four-time USSR champion (1967-1970), vice-champion (1965), winner of a bronze medal (1963).

Two-time European champion: 1967 Vichy, France and 1969 Klagenfurt, D.D.R.

Silver medal winner in Amsterdam (1966) and bronze medal winner in Grünau, D.D.R (1968).

ACKNOWLEGMENTS

So that this remarkable story could become a book, I am first of all grateful to my parents, Gita and Povilas Liutkaitis, who introduced me into the amazing world of rowing. Thanks to them, in my life I have been surrounded by people who are immersed in the world of rowing. I did not have the opportunity in life to thank my father, so I now send all my thanks to him to where he is now. I know that he is watching me, just as he always watched me race from the shoreline.

I am deeply indebted to my coach, Sofija Grucova, for not only opening up her heart and sharing with me the story of her youth, which she'd kept hidden for years, but also for giving me permission to write her story and to share it with others.

I would like to thank my parents' rowing friends, who shared with me stories they may not have even shared with their own children. My thanks and gratitude to: Janina Aleksandravičienė, Gita Jagelavičienė, Leokadija Semaško-Macharinskaja, Gaila Majauskienė, Aldona Medzevičienė, Jūratė Narvydienė, Ala Perevoruchova, Genovaitė Ramoškienė, Rita Rudaitienė, Irena Vaitkevičienė, Antanas Bagdonavičius.

I received sincere help from the former American Women's Team, Philadelphia Girls Rowing Club members Sophie Socha, Anita Sacco and Janice Saudargas. I am grateful to them for writing back to me and sharing their memories of the 1967 Vichy European Rowing

Championship.

I am especially thankful to Nikolay Botashev, who gave me permission to use a photograph by his father, the famous sports photographer, Mtsitslav Botashev.

I am eternally grateful to my husband, Aivaras, for his support, patience, encouragement to not give up writing, for keeping my secrets, and for our time together researching this story, traveling to foreign lands to learn more about the people and places documented in this book.

I thank my entire family for all your unconditional support and the freedom to be myself.

CONTENTS

Rima Karalienė
Rowing to Niagara Falls
Irklais iki Niagaros krioklių
A Biographical Novel

Cover Design Tadas Šaučiulis

ISBN 9798745703690

Printed in Great Britain
by Amazon